The Reminiscences

of

Admiral David Lamar McDonald

U.S Navy (Retired)

November 1976
U.S. Naval Institute
Annapolis, Maryland

Preface

This volume contains the transcript of six taped interviews with Admiral David Lamar McDonald, USN (Ret.). They were obtained for the Oral History collection of the U. S. Naval Institute. Interviews were held in several places (the Naval Institute in Annapolis and the Naval History Center in Washington, D.C.) during a period ranging from Nov. 8, 1974 to June 1, 1976.

Admiral McDonald read the transcript and has made some corrections and additions to the text.

This MS should prove of value to historians. Admiral McDonald served as Chief of Naval Operations from August 1, 1963 to August 1, 1967 - a most difficult period and one of increasing involvement of U. S. forces in South-East Asia. His colorful career includes a number of strategic assignments prior to his duty as CNO. He served as Flight Training Officer on the wartime staff of Naval Air Operational Training Command, Jacksonville (1942-44); as Deputy Assistant Chief of Staff at SHAPE headquarters in Paris (1957-60) and as Commander of the Sixth Fleet (1961-1963).

The characteristic vigor and forthrightness of the Admiral are apparent throughout the narrative and give zest to the whole. Interspersed are bits of personal philosophy.

A comprehensive index has been added to enhance the usefulness of the material.

John T. Mason, Jr.
Director of Oral History
U. S. Naval Institute
November, 1976.

DECLARATION OF TRUST

The undersigned does hereby appoint and designate as his (her) Trustee herein, the Secretary-Treasurer and Publisher of the United States Naval Institute to perform and discharge the following duties, powers, and privileges in connection with the possession and use of a certain taped interview between the undersigned and the Oral History Department of the United States Naval Institute.

1. Classification of Transcript.

(X)a. If classified OPEN, the transcript(s) may be read or the recording(s) audited by the qualified personnel upon presentation of proper credentials, as determined by the Secretary-Treasurer of the U.S. Naval Institute.

( )b. If classified PERMISSION REQUIRED TO CITE OR QUOTE, the user will be required to obtain permission in writing from the interviewee prior to quoting or citing from either the transcript(s) or the recording(s).

( )c. If classified PERMISSION REQUIRED, permission must be obtained in writing from the interviewee before the transcribed interview(s) can be examined or the tape recording(s) audited.

( )d. If classified CLOSED, the transcribed interview(s) and the tape recording(s) will be sealed until a time specified by the interviewee. This may be until the death of the interviewee or for any specified number of years.

2. It is expressly understood that in giving this authorization, I am in no way precluded from placing such restrictions as I may desire upon use of the interview at any time during my lifetime, nor does this authorization in any way affect my rights to the copyright of my literary expressions that may be contained in the interview.

Witness my hand and seal this 10th day of August 1976.

I hereby accept and consent to the foregoing Declaration of Trust and the powers therein conferred upon me as Trustee:

Interview No. 1. with Admiral David Lamar McDonald, U.S. Navy
(Retired)

Place: In the Board Room of the U.S. Naval Institute

Date: Friday afternoon, 8 November 1974

Subject: Biography

By: John T. Mason, Jr.

Q: Well, Admiral, it's great to meet you at last. I've looked forward to this series for quite a long time. You've had a fascinating career and now we're going to have the record of that career for the use of historians of the future.

Would you begin, Sir, by telling me just a little bit about your background? First, when you were born and something about your family background, as a prelude to what you're going to say.

Adm. M.: If you don't mind I'd like to point out at the very beginning of our conversations that never in my life have I kept either a diary or notes and since things that we're going to talk about will have occurred from between 8 and some 50 years ago there may be some discrepancies but I'll try to be as factual as possible.

I was born on the 12th of September 1906 in a small town in northeast Georgia. My father was a country preacher; a preacher of the Christian Church, sometimes called Disciples of Christ. He was reared on a farm and went to school at Transylvania in Kentucky. Returning to the area in which he was born, he married my mother, whose father was the owner of a good-sized farm and was a tax-collector, tax-assessor type on the side. My mother was ten years younger than my father.

Their ages were about twenty and thirty at the time of their marriage.

Although my father was a country preacher, we never lived in the country but we lived in small towns and he would preach at the Christian Church in the little towns either one or two Sundays a month, and then he would go to some churches of the same denomination in the country for the other two or three Sundays.

Q: Making the circuit!

Adm. M.: Making the circuit. Usually each summer he would return to the Kentucky area where he went to school and conduct what they called a revival meeting. Sometimes my mother would go with him and sometimes she wouldn't. I had a sister five years younger than I was and we would usually stay with our grandparents if my mother went with him.

Q: Did he support his family entirely from church work, or did he have some other business as well?

Adm. M.: He supported his family from church work, plus a little farm work. My mother's father had about five or seven acres of land behind his house, and my father and I, with the help of a Negro man, used to raise cotton on that to augment his income. But he never got much in cash.

But you didn't need it then because the members of his churches would often provide us with a great deal of food from their farms.

Q: What sort of education did you aspire to?

Adm. M.: They said when I was a small boy I wanted to be a preacher, but from about ten or twelve on I wanted to be a lawyer. I worked hard my last two years in high school - making money to be used for college. Let me start by saying that from the time I was eight years old until I went to prep school I swept out a dentist's office every night. When I was about 14 this dentist obtained for me what he called a laundry concession since we had no laundry in the town. I would collect the laundry on Monday and put it on the train that afternoon. It would come back Saturday and I would deliver it, and I got 25 cents on every dollar.

At about the same time this dentist obtained for me the only pressing establishment in town, which was in the back of the barber's shop, where they had three shower baths. The farmers would come in and take a shower and I'd press their clothes!

Q: That's a unique business.

McDonald #1 - 4

Adm. M.: I think one of the most interesting parts of my young boyhood was that from the time I was twelve, or thirteen, until I left for prep school at the age of seventeen my father had a Ford automobile which he never learned to drive. So I drove him to all these country churches for Saturday night meetings, for Sunday church in the morning, Sunday church at night, prayer meetings during the week, weddings, funerals, etc.

Q: You were the chauffeur.

Adm. M.: I saw quite a few interesting things and I think maybe I got to learn a lot about people then.

Q: I bet you did. You say you went to prep school. What was this in preparation for? A law career, or what?

Adm. M.: Three or four months before I finished high school, the man who owned one of the two banks in our town called me into his office one day and asked me where I was going to college. I told him I didn't know but I wanted to be a lawyer and hadn't quite made up my mind where I was going to school. He said:

"Well, you know my two boys, (They're older than you are) I wanted them to go to West Point but neither of them wanted to go and since I've known you from the time you were three or four years old, I think you might like the life of a military man."

After considerable discussion, he pointed out to me that one could go to West Point, and, if you didn't like it, you could get out upon graduation after having received an excellent basic education. In order to get there all you really had to do was get an appointment from some congressman or some senator. I told him I didn't know any congressmen or any senators but he then said that just about twenty-five miles away in Gainesville, Georgia, was a congressman named Tom Bell who'd been in Congress for twenty-nine years, and he said:

"If you will get in that little Ford and drive up there and tell him who your mother's father is, you can have anything you want."

I didn't know it then but it turned out that apparently my mother's father had been instrumental in getting this man in Congress the first time. So I went up to see Mr. Bell and I did get an appointment to West Point. However, it turned out that I was two months and twelve days too young. Mr. Bell then told me that one could enter the Naval Academy one year younger and asked me if I'd ever considered going to the Naval Academy. Well, I didn't really know anything about that.

Q: You'd never seen an ocean, I assume?

Adm. M.: No, I'd never seen salt water. Of course, as quick as I got an appointment to West Point, every prep school in that part of the country found out about it and descended upon us and tried to convince me and my parents that any young man going to the Naval Academy or West Point from a little Georgia high school didn't last but a few months.

In further discussion with the Congressman he said to me:

"I think maybe I could get you a waiver at West Point or we could go the Naval Academy route. But why don't you go on to prep school for a year and then make a choice? Do you have any money to go?" he asked.

And I did have. As I told you earlier I had worked and I had some money of my own. He said:

"Why don't you go to prep school and this fall, while you're there, you investigate both Academies and when I come home Christmas let me know which academy you want to go to."

This really sounds funny but it's a true story. I discovered during the fall that the cadets at West Point - in the summertime - went up the Hudson and drilled and the midshipmen went to Europe. So I said I wanted to go to the Naval Academy because I wanted to go to Europe. Honestly that's the real reason I selected the Naval Academy.

Q: How did your parents react to this?

Adm. M.: Quite all right. My parents were sure I wanted to be a lawyer; but here was an opportunity to get a good basic education, have a military career if I should so elect, or, if I didn't, I could get out and then pursue a legal or any other career. They really left it pretty much up to me.

Mr. Bell gave me an appointment to the Naval Academy. Fortunately perhaps, I didn't have to take an examination, no substantiating exams, nothing at all. All I did was come to Annapolis and sign my name on the register.

Q: It wasn't under the Civil Service Commission then?

Adm. M.: That I do not know, however, it was easy for me to enter. Odd though it might seem, I came to the Naval Academy in 1924, but I never went to Europe even for the first time until 1955.

Q: You got disappointed?

Adm. M.: I was in one of only two classes, I guess, since 1900 that didn't go to Europe as midshipmen.

Q: Well, you did go to prep school for a while?

Adm. M.: I went to Riverside for a year.

Q: And that was a great help?

Adm. M.: Thinking back upon that year, I don't believe from an academic point of view it really did me much good, but from a military point of view I think I owe a great deal to that year at Riverside. I learned how to be away from home for the first time for any length of time. I think I learned how to get along with others reasonably well. I really learned how to click my heels and say Yes, Sir and, later, Aye, Aye, Sir. I learned how to take care of my room and do things that come a little bit hard to a plebe at the Naval Academy if he's never done then before. I might say that today I have a grandson who passed both the mental and physical exams to enter the Naval Academy this last summer but some of my friends here at the Academy, who really know, thought he should go to prep school for a year since he seemed from his record to be a little immature. That he is going to do and I'm sure that he will benefit as I did.

Q: But you'd ploughed your own way.

Adm. M.: I'd kicked around a little bit, but I do think

McDonald #1 - 9

that that year at prep school helped a great deal. I think if you go back in my record you'll probably find that the highest marks I got at the Naval Academy were in conduct and aptitude, not in academics, and I believe that the things I learned that year in prep school made it possible for me to get good marks in these areas.

Q: It smoothed the way, I can see that. Then it was money well spent?

Adm. M.: Well worthwhile, I must say though that I hadn't changed my mind about my future when I left the Naval Academy. I was going to be a lawyer, not stay in the Navy. I would have gotten out on graduation, but they changed the law. I had to stay for two years.

Q: Even the cruises didn't - ?

Adm. M.: No. After I'd been out of the Naval Academy one year they said "you can get out now." I had a job lined up through a friend of mine and had a resignation written out on the battleship Mississippi in September 1929. Just before putting it in the mail, I received dispatch orders to go to San Diego and take what they called the Eliminative Flight Course. It lasted one month.

I went down there and when I finished that they said, "You passed this successfully. You can go to Pensacola and be an aviator, if you want to."

I then communicated with the man who had obtained the job for me and asked him what I should do, and he said:

"I think you ought to take advantage of this opportunity to learn how to be a flyer and then get out later."

So I went to Pensacola and completed the flight course successfully. Even though subsequent duty in the Fleet was pleasant and interesting I really had no desire to stay in the Navy. By this time I was married and we had one child. In 1935 they ordered me back to Pensacola to be a flight instructor. I think this was probably the most critical time of my life. I don't remember it but my wife does. She said that after I'd been there about six months (I was chief flight instructor in the fighters, in the single-seaters) I came bouncing in the door one afternoon and she said, "What in the world happened to you?" And I said:

"For the first time since I've been in the Navy, I did something worthwhile." She asked me what and I said:

"Well, there's a young student aviator over in Squadron 5, (which was the last training squadron - the one where you took your final exam before becoming an aviator) who wants to do nothing in the world but fly an airplane and he failed his test. I found out what was wrong with him, took him out and gave him some extra instruction and he passed. I don't know who's happier, that boy or me."

McDonald #1 - 11

She says from that day to this I never said one word about getting out of the Navy. I'd been out of the Naval Academy then a bit over seven years.

Q: Indeed, you had. Let's go back to the Naval Academy days for any recollections that have any specific meaning to you while you were there. You received honors in various things.

Adm. M.: One of the great breaks that I received was when I was a plebe one of the first classmen in either the squad or the platoon I was in had gotten into some difficulty on his first class cruise and if he should receive more demerits he would exceed the maximum allowance. So he told me if I would keep him off the report he would keep me off the report. As a result when we'd come to formation I'd take a handkerchief and dust his shoes or knock the dirt off his clothes and what not, and I think that he probably went through the whole year without getting another demerit and I don't think I got one the whole year either.

I didn't do bad things but he did intervene in the little petty things that I might have been put on the report for - and this was very helpful to me because it gave me a good start that I was able to keep up.

McDonald #1 - 12

Q: You indicate by these various illustrations you give that you from the beginning had a concern for other people. I suppose that's an inheritance from your dad?

Adm. M.: Yes. And along these lines let me say that the only distasteful thing about the Naval Academy, at the time and to this day, was what happened to my Naval Academy roommate.

Q: What did happen to him?

Adm. M.: In those days we had just four battalions. The first and third battalions studied Spanish, the second and the fourth studied French, and you seldom mingled with each other. You went to classes with those in your own battalion and sometimes you hardly knew your own classmates in the other battalions. Well, when our senior year started I had four stripes as sub-regimental commander. I lived in the Eighth Company, Fourth Battalion, which was a French battalion. My good friend and classmate, Jimmy James, had four stripes and he was in charge of the First Battalion, a Spanish speaking battalion.

Jimmy was involved in a lot of extracurricular activities - the Naval Academy Log, the Lucky Bag, and various and sundry other things. For some reason or other the powers that be decided that they would switch our jobs. They would give the job of sub-regimental commander to Jimmy and commander of the First Battalion to me. Midshipman stripers didn't rotate during the year like they do now. You got your stripes and you kept them the whole year.

I was called up by the commandant and asked what I thought about this change. I liked no part of it. I said, "This would be very difficult. The midshipmen in the 1st Battalion will say, 'What are they sending him over here for? To straighten this place out?' I don't even know my own classmates over there."

Well, after a few days I was told I was going. "What can I do to make it easier for you?" said the commandant. I said: "Let me take my roommate with me."

He wouldn't do it. I went on over to the First Battalion and he roomed alone. I was moved in with two other people. Not many months before graduation there a midshipman failed to show up for supper formation on Sunday night. My memory might be a little bit hazy on this, but not very. He was in the Second Battalion. When the authorities began to inquire as to this fellow's whereabouts, someone said the last time they saw him he was with (and they mentioned another man who happened to be in the Fourth Battalion). This particular man in the Fourth Battalion sat at the same table with my ex-roommate and succeeded my roommate as manager of the football team. When he wasn't at the table that evening, my roommate left the mess hall early, which he was entitled to do because he was a first classman. He went by the battalion office and saw that this particular man, a second classman, had been marked "A", absent. My roommate picked up a pen and put a line through that "A".

Well, when that was discovered, the authorities began to raise the devil and they called the battalion duty officer and asked who did this. He didn't know. He was told that if he had been on his post of duty no one could have entered the office and if he didn't find out he'd be punished. This was Sunday night.

Monday noon, my roommate went to the commandant and admitted that he did this. He said he did it on the spur of the moment, doing what he thought was helping a friend. During his entire almost four years at the Academy the total number of demerits that my roommate had didn't even equal the total number we were allowed the first year. They put him on report for falsifying official records and kicked him out. I thought it was the dirtiest thing I'd ever heard of in the Navy then, and I think so to this day.

Q: But he voluntarily confessed?

Adm. M.: That's exactly right. He later took the Army flight course, flew the mail from Chicago to Omaha in the great winter of 1935, then resigned his Army Air Corps commission, started flying for American Air Lines in 1935, and had an honorable career, a wonderful record, and flew with them till he had to retire at the age of sixty. At the age of sixty - he lives outside of Palo Alto - he became a professor at Foothill College until he was sixty-six, then they retired him, and he's living in Los Altos Hills now.

Q: He certainly demonstrated a great deal of character in going -

Adm. M.: And his son came here to the Naval Academy and had four stripes himself.

I, of course, registered some objection to the commandant about this. The commandant's answer was that this roommate of mine had a very bad unwritten record, that he, the commandant, knew everything that went on around the Naval Academy, both written and unwritten. I was so mad at the time I asked the commandant if he had anything to do with me getting my four stripes and he said everything. I said:

"Captain, this amazes me because every time Smith (my roommate) has gone over the wall I've either been just in front of him or just behind, and every time he's been drinking I've been drinking with him."

The commandant told me I could leave the office. Within thirty minutes I was called by Commander Deyo, who was the officer in charge of the First Battalion -

Q: Was this Mort Deyo?

Adm. M.: Yes. He called me down and said:

"I think you probably already know why your aptitude mark is going to take an appreciable fall?"

I said, "Yes, Sir."

And I'm probably the only man that was ever given four stripes and kept them during the entire academic year and never received a commandant's letter of commendation. But that commandant didn't think any the less of me than I did of him.

That was the only bitter pill that I ever had to swallow with respect to my four years at the Naval Academy. There were always little upsets, but this was the only thing that I was ever closely associated with that I thought was basically unfair then and I haven't changed my mind to this date.

Q: It still rankles!

McDonald #1 - 17

Adm. M.: That's right.

Q: What about your cruises? Were they pleasant, were they profitable?

Adm. M.: Yes, I think so. Two of our cruises were coal-burning cruises.

Q: This meant you shoveled?

Adm. M.: Yes. On my first cruise I shoveled coal from Annapolis to Seattle, passed the coal from the bunker out to the fireman. On my second cruise I learned how to be a fireman. I was a fireman for a couple of weeks on that cruise.

I enjoyed the cruises very much.

Q: But they weren't glamourous, as you had hoped?

Adm. M.: No, they weren't exactly glamourous but on those trips we did get to meet a lot of very interesting people. I was a small town boy from Georgia and San Francisco was quite a city. As midshipmen we were entertained in a way a little different from perhaps the way the average college men see life. We were encouraged to break out our Emily Post as it were; act like a gentleman, both in appearance and in conduct. Of course, to me, that's one of the great things about the Naval Academy. To put it plainly, boys in the average college aren't taught to place emphasis on conduct or appearance.

Q: Less so now than they were in your time.

Adm. M.: But this is important. For example the average taxpayer doesn't know whether the morale of those in uniform is good or whether they're competent in their particular rates or ratings - the average taxpayer bases his or her opinion of the person in uniform on just two things, what they look like and how they act. And if those in uniform today would place more emphasis on being neat in appearance and circumspect in their conduct, hold their heads high, and throw their shoulders back and be proud of the fact that they are in the service, I think the image of the military would take an appreciable beneficial change.

Recently I've seen people down where I live sitting in officers' clubs, lieutenant commanders and some more senior that I'd be ashamed to introduce as naval officers. This is a fact that we all know. I think that a great deal of emphasis must be placed upon teaching a man to be a gentleman; there's nothing more important in the world

McDonald #1 - 19

regardless of one's line of work.

Q: It's still pretty much in evidence.

Adm. M.: On these midshipmen cruises, when we went into a city the mayor would have a reception or Mrs. Poof and Poof would have a certain number for dinner. Those who accepted went out of their way to be neat and clean and circumspect.

Q: You met the eligible girls in the town, too?

Adm. M.: Yes, but you can meet a lot of fine girls in a lot of places. I think you had more of an incentive, as I said, to be a gentleman. And that, to me - I guess it meant as much to me on the cruises as any of the rest of the things.

Q: That's interesting, indeed. I remember one old-time superintendent of the Academy told me that his purpose, and I think this had generally been the purpose of the Academy, was to train men to be gentlemen and to be leaders.

Adm. M.: That's right.

Q: Those were the two fundamentals that he strove for.

Adm. M.: I guess a man can be a leader without being a gentleman, but you know they go pretty much hand in glove. There's one thing certain, unless you do care for your units and look out for the personnel in them, you aren't a gentleman.

Q: That's one of the facets.

Adm. M.: That's exactly right. There have been people, of course, who in time of battle have inspired their men - even though they were plug-uglies, but that really occurs more in the heat of battle instead of over the long range.

Q: Tell me about your scholastic accomplishments, because when you graduated you had various awards given you.

Adm. M.: My scholastic accomplishments were really very minor, but my aptitude marks brought me up. I would say that I was about an average student. I had difficulty with French because it came hard for me. I think the only thing I failed in one month was English, but that's because I didn't like it. Mathematics and things like that came easy to me. As for honors, I was on the rifle team and I received a medal as the best shot in my class.

Q: You got one in ordnance.

Adm. M.: Well, yes. I don't know what that was for now. I believe it was in practical ordnance and gunnery. Then I got a sword from the DAR for practical seamanship.

Q: Yes, now what -?

Adm. M.: This was really very interesting. We had some - PC boats, they called them, old cutters, that we would go out in. One day, you'd be the helmsman, and then you'd be the signalman, and one day you'd be the officer of the deck, etc. A classmate and I apparently were running sort of neck and neck for this trophy. There was a lieutenant commander - I don't know whether he was in charge of all these boats or not, but he was on this particular boat the day that I was the captain, and he had been on a ship that I was on on a midshipmen's cruise, and we had gotten to know each other. That day as we started to come back in to the dock, he told me:

"Now, don't back down full until you're just absolutely certain you're going to ram that dock."

And that's what I did. I came in and I think everybody was about ready to jump off the boat, then I backed full and just eased right smack up to the dock and the marks I got that day were apparently the ones that enabled me to win the sword.

Q: Did this pertain later in shiphandling? One takes those chances?

Adm. M.: I guess but I never had trouble in the handling of a ship. During the war I was air officer and then exec of the Essex and I had a very fine commanding officer -

Q: Was that Wu Duncan?

Adm. M.: No. It was a fellow named Buddy Weber. Captain Weber was sort of slow-moving like I am. I don't know whether he's lazy like I am or not. Anyway, after he'd been aboard a short while he would nearly always let me handle the ship when we would replenish and refuel. I probably put the Essex alongside more replenishment ships and more oilers during my tour as exec with Captain Weber than he did. I learned a lot and that taught me another thing.

When I was skipper of two ships, believe you me, I very seldom put them alongside myself. I let other people do that. Now, a lot of skippers seem to feel that if a mistake is going to be made they want to make it themselves.

Q: You run a risk, I suppose?

Adm. M.: Yes, but let's be fair. I was on a light cruiser with a captain named Roland Brainerd, who was a very good friend of mine when I was a midshipman. He was executive officer of Bancroft Hall as a commander. I went into the aviation unit on his cruiser for a year in order to stand top watches so I could be promoted to senior lieutenant. He and his wife were at my home one evening and my father-in-law was there. I'll never forget him telling my father-in law:

"Well, Mac and some of these other young fellows probably think I don't trust them when we start out of San Diego because I don't let them take the ship out. But I've been waiting a lot of years to have this opportunity and I just love doing it. It isn't that I don't trust them."

There are people like that, but I was very fortunate in having some very good juniors. One of the comments I made when I retired as CNO was that I felt that I had risen to whatever heights I had acquired by riding on the shoulders of my juniors, and I believe that. Your seniors can give you advice and they might mark your fitness reports, but if you're the kind of fellow that thinks when you get to be the head man you can do it all yourself you're in for trouble. You can do it when you're a JG and a lieutenant, maybe as a lieutenant commander, but as you get more senior you must have help and unless you have confidence in and delegate to your juniors you're going to get in trouble.

Q: Isn't that one of the aspects of leadership, to be able

to delegate?

Adm. M.: Yes, but you know what's real interesting - I think if you'll look over a lot of records you will find that there are certain people who set the world on fire until maybe they become a commander, sometimes, maybe, a captain, and then something happens, and what it was was simply this. As long as they could do it all themselves they did an outstanding job, but when they reached the point where they couldn't do it all themselves and were unwilling to accept any degree of proficiency less perfect than their own they get in trouble.

I don't think you expect your junior to do as well as you can, but if he does it to an acceptable degree, then let him alone and give him a chance to gain experience so that he can subsequently do it as good as you can.

Q: That's a very interesting point you make.

Adm. M.: I've often said maybe it's an advantage to be a little bit lazy, because then you might be more willing to let someone else help.

Q: Maybe lazy is not the right word to use in that case!

Adm. M.: There are people who are too impetuous. And, of course, there are times when you have to be, but basically I really feel it's an officer's business to train others. After all, officers are teachers. The Navy is basically a school until you get in a war. It's nothing in the world but a big training school and, as I told someone the other day,

"I found teaching in that school a very rewarding experience."

He said, "Yes, you would, because you got to the top."

I said:

"No, I'm not talking about rewarding experience because I climbed the promotional pole to the top. I'm talking about the rewarding experience of realizing that I have done something, spent my whole life, doing something for my country that somebody had to do and, concurrently, I was able to mold and guide the lives of hundreds of young men, many of whom are still in the Navy, many of whom are now in the civilian world, successful doctors, lawyers, teachers, pharmacists' mates, electronic - you can name it. And viewed from that point, it's one of the most satisfying careers in the world."

Q: You have a little share in what each and every one of them is accomplishing now?

Adm. M.: We don't often realize this. I live in an unincorporated community about twenty miles out of Jacksonville, and about twelve miles from the Navy base at Mayport, and about thirty-five miles from the Naval Air Station - Jacksonville. I've been in my house about six years. I believe that three-fourths of the journeymen who have come to my house, carpenters, plumbers, the men who take care of the swimming pool, electricians, the painter - I believe that three-fourths of these fellows have been in the Navy and they've told me they learned their trade in the Navy. And it's really interesting because, as you must realize, I've a lot of pictures and paraphernalia around, so much so that I have quite a few pictures in my garage - my garage is paneled and I have a lot of photographs in there, pictures of various kinds. These journeymen will come to check my filter or to check my sprinkler system, and, "Gee, you must have been in the Navy." Then they'll start talking and I find out they were in the Navy and as my wife says, they just won't leave!

It's just too bad that the average tax-paying citizen doesn't realize what a great return he is getting on the money that he invests in the Navy from the vocational training of sailors who get out. They don't have to stay for twenty years and get retirement pay. A lot of them get out in four or six years. Of course, I think this is true of the Navy more than any other of the services, the Air Force next, because in peacetime, you know, the Army spends a lot of time mowing the lawn. They don't have the machinery.

But a Navy ship at sea, you know, is just like an isolated community, and the things these men learn they take back and do them in these towns.

Q: I hope the recruiting officers make adequate use of this point?

Adm. M.: Yes, but not just to get boys in but somehow they ought to be able to get some of that across to the Proxmire and Aspin types; too much emphasis on the fact that moneys expended in the Defense Department are, to a very large degree, half wasted. It isn't true. Of course some is wasted because, as I said earlier, the military is somewhat nonconstructive. But, by golly, you go down where I live - and in a lot of similar places - and see these former bluejackets performing useful and necessary services to their communities.

Q: See these reserves of human beings.

Adm. M.: Just go around and ask these young technical fellows, where did you learn that job, and you'd be amazed, simply amazed, at the number of them who learned it while they were in the Navy. The mayor of Jacksonville said that some of his opponents accused him of starting a second navy

McDonald #1 - 28

down there because he's hired so many retired naval officers to work for the city. But he said: "where else can I get that kind of help for this price," because he says the average civilian with this kind of ability has no outside income that can equate to the retired Navy pay. So the retiree can afford to come in here and work for a lot less. Over-all, he'll be making the same as maybe the civilian would but the city isn't paying him near as much. He says the city is just lucky.

Q: Now, Sir, your basic trade in the Navy was as a flyer. Were you introduced to this at the Academy?

Adm. M.: No.

Q: Did they have aviation summer in your time?

Adm. M.: Yes, but I didn't go to aviation summer. I was with the Navy Rifle Team. There were three or four people in my class who were sent up to Massachusetts with the Navy rifle team to train for the national matches instead of staying for aviation summer.

Q: That was a real diversion!

Adm. M.: So I had no aviation summer. I don't think I'd

McDonald #1 - 29

ever been up in an airplane until I went down to San Diego to solo. I know I hadn't. I went down to San Diego to solo and the first weekend -

Q: This was the time when you were on the battleship?

Adm. M.: Yes, this was in October 1929. I went down to San Diego on a weekend, Friday, preparatory to starting training Monday. However, on Saturday I got into a flying boat and rode up to the Los Angeles area to see a football game at USC. That was the first time I'd been in an airplane.

And when I soloed I wasn't particularly intrigued but I went to Pensacola. It's a funny thing to say - maybe I'm just not an enthusiast, but I thought of Pensacola like I did of the Naval Academy. If I failed at the Naval Academy my pride would be hurt but it wouldn't upset my career. I was going to be a lawyer, anyway. Likewise at Pensacola; if I failed I'd resign and pursue a legal career.

Q: You hadn't lost track of that ambition?

Adm. M.: No. During my training at Pensacola I had difficulty on only one check and I'll never forget what the check pilot said after we landed. He said:

"I'll play you a cool hand of poker to see whether I

give you an up or a down."

I looked at him and I said:

"I don't know how to play poker."

He said, "What have you got to say?"

I said, "If I flew an "up" I want an "up" and if I flew a "down" I want a "down."

And that's just the way I thought of it, other than pride. In other words, I had passed this check or I hadn't, and if I had I didn't need to play poker and if I hadn't I didn't want to have a broken neck. I never had specific burning desires inside of me, to be an aviator, to be CNO or the chairman of the Joint Chiefs or anything like that any time in my life.

Q: A mighty independent streak you demonstrated as a youngster!

Adm. M.: Well, I've said to an awful lot of my juniors who've asked me about their career patterns: "quit worrying about what assigments you should get in order to further your career." Admiral Radford once told me that "the best duty for me was the duty I wanted the most." Now, he said that what he meant was, if you don't want to go to post-graduate school but you think you ought to go there to get it on your record and give you a better chance of being promoted, the chances are you aren't going to do very well when you get there. But if you go to a job that you really want, even if it turns out later that it isn't what you thought it was, you're not going to admit that you made a mistake. You're going to really work like the devil." And I think he's right.

I have known people who were so concerned about what they thought they ought to be doing that they forgot to do what they were supposed to be doing at the time. I know a particular man who I thought was one of the finest captains in the Navy who didn't make Admiral because he was so darned busy trying to figure out what assignment he should try to get next that he didn't devote enought time to the job at hand.

I think one ought to have some goals but basically don't let your ambition, your ultimate ambition, so overwhelm you that you forget to do a good job in what you're supposed to be doing at the moment.

Q: Well, when you graduated you got a battleship assignment?

Adm. M.: Yes, I got a battleship assignment with a group of my classmates, some friends -

Q: This was on the Mississippi?

McDonald #1 - 32

Adm. M.: On the <u>Mississippi</u>. We pooled our numbers and it was a very happy group. I didn't get there till a little bit late. The others finished their aviation summer and got there in late August or something like that and, as I say, I was with the Navy rifle team which didn't break up until about mid-September at Camp Perry, Ohio so I didn't get to my ship until around October.

Q: Would you pursue that rifle business for a while? Did you continue as a member of a Navy rifle team after that time?

Adm. M.: Yes. When I was a plebe there was a 2nd classman who lived on the floor next to us named Duerfeldt, who was quite a rifle shot and he asked me if I didn't want to come out for the rifle team. He inferred that I either come out or get swatted on the behind with a broom, and I elected to go out for the rifle team!

So I started to shoot and then I stayed with it at the Academy for four years. I went with the Navy team then, the summer I finished. Then I came back with that team in late May of 1929 went on up to Camp Perry and did the same thing in 1930. Since then I've hardly shot a gun.

Q: You haven't shot?

Adm. M.: Practically not.

McDonald #1 - 33

Q: Do you belong to the National Rifle Association?

Adm. M.: Yes, I'm an honorary life member. When I was CNO they made me a life member and gave me a Kentucky rifle.

Q: What made you drop it? It was such an achievement.

Adm. M.: I'd just had enough, and rifle-shooting, target-shooting isn't much fun. I wish I'd done a lot of skeet-shooting. I used to go hunting a bit around Pensacola and out in Hawaii, but I haven't done that lately. I play golf, I work in the yard a lot, and I have several jobs. I can't do a lot of things at the same time and do them all well. I like to be pretty good at what I'm doing.

Q: So it's a matter of selection?

Adm. M.: That's right. I like to fish but I haven't had a hook in the water since I retired yet I only have to walk three minutes from my house. But, as I say, I play a lot of golf and I work an awful lot in my yard, which I love to do, and I have these jobs and I write my own letters and keep my own files. I do a lot of reading of current events. I just like to do those things.

Q: Were you fortunate in having a good set of officers on the Mississippi?

Adm. M.: Yes. The first job I had was a junior division officer in the electrical division. My division officer was an old mustang lieutenant, Mr. Becker. I'll never forget one of the first things he told me. He said:

"Ensign McDonald, I think you ought to know that in my opinion the best officer in the Navy is the one who can do the least but still get the most done."

Q: No lost motion!

Adm. M.: In later years I've received two or three bits of advice like that that have stood me in good stead. I once worked for Admiral A. B. Cook. I hadn't been with him very long when he said:

"Young man, I'll very seldom ask for your advice, but when I ask you what you think I want to know what you think and not what you think I'd like you to think."

Another quote I've always remembered came from another admiral I'd known for many years. I saw him during the war not long after he'd made rear admiral and he said to me:

"Mac, it surprised a lot of people when I became a rear admiral, because you know a lot of them think I'm the dumbest rear admiral in the Navy. Maybe I am, but let me tell you, I'm also something else."

I said, "What's that, Admiral?"

He said, "I'm the most polite rear admiral in the Navy. If I'm dumb maybe I can't help it, maybe I was born that way, but even a dumbbell can be polite and don't you ever forget it."

And, by golly, I never have!

But my favorite expression, with which I think I ended every Deputies' Conference in Washington when I was CNO is:

"Always tell the truth and you'll never have to remember what you said."

More people have become tangled up before the Congress by trying to be sort of foot-loose and fancy. You get up there and say something today, just shade it a little bit, and go up there tomorrow and the first thing you know you've really got your foot in your mouth.

Q: You certainly do in this day, with tape-recorders, don't you?

Adm. M.: You don't have to look back very far. You can see right now this whole Watergate mess, it isn't Watergate, it's the unwillingness to come clean.

It's been interesting to me how, as you go along the years, a little thing like Raddy telling me "get the job you want, that's the best job for you, within the realm of reason." These little things that stick in the back of your mind, I think, are really helpful.

But let's get back to the <u>Mississippi</u>. I'd hardly

gotten back from the rifle team in 1929 when they sent me to Coronado to take the eliminative flight course that I spoke of earlier.

Q: This was not a voluntary thing?

Adm. M.: No, no, However, before you could become an aviator, before you could go to Pensacola and take the flight course, you had to go to either San Diego or Norfolk and prove you could solo and then you had to become qualified in certain other areas - standing watches on deck at sea for instance. But they ordered you to San Diego or Norfolk without your requesting it. Now, I don't think you had to go if you didn't want to, but they ordered you there without your requesting it.

Then, if you finished successfully, you could request Pensacola, but you couldn't go to Pensacola unless you had successfully finished these preliminaries.

Q: It was really an aptitude test, wasn't it?

Adm. M.: That's right. In other words, if you can't solo in ten hours there's no use going to Pensacola.

I came back from my solo training and almost immediately

had an appendectomy. Then, about the time I got over that, I had a little gravel in the kidneys. The Mississippi went to the ship yard in Bremerton and left me in the hospital. I wasn't sick, but I had these pains and they had to take certain tests to see whether I had some serious affliction. Ultimately I was discharged from the hospital and ordered to the battleship Colorado.

Q: Because you'd had to leave the Mississippi?

Adm. M.: Yes, the Mississippi left while I was in the hospital. The Colorado was in the Navy yard undergoing overhaul, and the fleet was going to the East Coast. She was the only ship left and I was ordered there. I don't really know exactly what the word "traumatic" means, but I guess the experience I had on the Colorado was traumatic. The Colorado had a terrible reputation.

Upon reporting on board I found myself the senior man in the junior officers' mess and we were en route from Bremerton to New York. Without going into a lot of detail, we had problems of drinking on board ship while in Guantanamo of such a nature that two of my classmates were given general courtsmartial and kicked out, and one or two others were dropped in precedence.

I really avoided getting involved just by the skin of my teeth. I was sort of an innocent bystander. I was thankful to leave that ship when we got to New York and go back with the rifle team.

Q: It was a little safer there at that point, wasn't it?

Adm. M.: Yes. Poor fellows. One of my classmates who was kicked out was later killed in an automobile wreck in China. Another who didn't get kicked out but lost a lot of numbers later shot himself in China. One became a revolutionary in South America, then later in China and subsequently became a Civil Service employee at the Navy yard in Norfolk. He had an honorable career and finally retired.

Q: That was a very disastrous little party on board, wasn't it?

Adm. M.: Yes, but these same fellows had been in and out of trouble for years.

Q: From the Colorado and from the rifle team, you came back and went to Pensacola?

Adm. M.: Yes.

Q: Tell me about the course of sprouts there, the training at that point. It was an interesting time in Pensacola.

Adm. M.: We had primarily seaplanes to start with, "yellow perils," they called them. They were single-float seaplanes, and we had a certain number of hours in which to pass our tests. Concurrently we went to ground school (incidentally the only school I went to except the Naval Academy, and the National War College). But this ground school at Pensacola was really a course in aeronautical engineering, and we went about half a day, every day.

Q: Did you do flying in the other half day?

Adm. M.: Pretty generally, that was the routine. One interesting thing, we had the Bevo List then. If you were flying, you had to walk in and sign your name before every flight indicating that you hadn't swallowed one drop of alcoholic beverage in the last twenty-four hours. You signed up every day, and believe you me, people were honest when they signed that, too, because people were anxious to fly. You were next to the Almighty Himself back in those days, if you were an aviator! So it was very serious business.

From the seaplanes we went on to primary landplanes. Then we went to the oldest model of service plane, an observation plane, a two-seater. Then we went to big boats, and then to the single-seater fighter squadron. Here, again, I was very fortunate. Everybody wanted to go to fighters upon completion of their training. I never knew anybody who didn't. I've forgotten what the attrition in our class was, about half, I think. But we finished with about twenty-one people in our group and only three of us got to go to fighters and I was one of the three. So I was very fortunate.

Q: Most of the planes you were using in that time were versions of World War I planes, were they not?

Adm. M.: No. They were more advanced than that. We had in our single seater squadron one old observation plane, a two-seater, that we used to familiarize new pilots with the area. That could be considered to be, I guess, a World War I plane, but these others were basically built in the early 1920s, mid-1920s. We had the hell divers and Boeing F3Bs.

Q: The concept of the fighter was beginning to be developed at that point, was it?

Adm. M.: Oh, yes, but the fighters at that time, in the squadrons themselves, were fighter-dive bombers. So you not only did the dog-fighting in the air, your planes were the ones that did the dive-bombing.

The squadron that I went to was called VF-6, but a little bit later that same squadron with the same planes was called VB-2, and our insignia was the Felix cat. Whether it was

VB-2 or VF-6, we were fighter-bombers. We always called it the fighters, but one of our main jobs in addition to learning how to shoot was how to dive bomb. We had a skipper, Matt Gardner, who was quite a stunt pilot, and he taught us how to dive bomb. The way we did it, we'd roll over on our backs and just as we flew over the target on our backs we'd cut the throttle and drop dight down. But it was sort of hard to keep from getting in trouble on your back because these things didn't fly on their backs well unless you were sort of nose down to keep the engine from quitting.

Q: Did you have any close calls down there in Pensacola when you were training?

Adm. M.: No, I had no problems in Pensacola. I had a couple of close ground loops at North Island later on but I was one of those who about the time I started to lose respect for the plane I'd have something happen which would scare me, and my respect for the airplane would come back and I'd be a little bit more careful. But I never had any real accident.

Q: Who were some of the well-known pilots who trained with you?

Adm. M.: I don't know. Do you know of Jimmy Flatley?

Q: Yes.

Adm. M.: Jimmy came along a little behind me. Jack Raby came along a little behind me. I was just a little bit behind Jimmy Thach.

Q: What about Herb Riley? Was he there?

Adm. M.: Yes, Herb Riley. Herb Riley, Don Griffin, George Anderson. I would have gone to Pensacola about the time they did, but I had this appendectomy and I was in the hospital in Bremerton with pilitis, so when I got over that they said, "Now, look, we don't think there's anything wrong with you now but you've been fiddling around here and we think you ought to get all your health and your strength back before you go to Pensacola.

Well, when the skipper of the Navy rifle team found out about that, he got in touch with me and said:

"There's no place to get it back like coming with the rifle team and living in a tent. So, if you agree, I'll have you ordered there."

I wrote back and said OK. By doing that, I arrived at Pensacola considerably later.

Q: To go off shooting.

Adm. M.: And it enabled me to get married, too!

So Don and George and those boys were a year ahead of me at the Naval Academy and would have been about six to ten months ahead of me down there, but it turned out being nearly a year and a half because not only was there

McDonald #1 - 43

the delay due to illness but when I went there at the time I did I took JG examinations and they gave me time off to study for and take them.

But I must recall that my instructors in the fighters, those that really got me assigned to a fighter squadron, were John Crommelin and Little Bill Davis. You heard of Crommelin in later years?

Q: Yes.

Adm. M.: Let me tell you something real interesting about John. Did you ever hear of an outfit called the Green Bowlers.

Q: Oh, yes, yes, at the Academy.

Adm. M.: John Crommelin caused an investigation to be started into the Green Bowlers. He along with some other people were rather rabid about the Green Bowlers and said that they were people who put each other in various and sundry jobs, regardless of their capabilities, and this got to the point where in 1947 the Navy Department - assigned a Rear Admiral Lowery to investigate the Green Bowlers.

I went back there for duty about that time and I was called in by Admiral Lowery, and asked if I was a Green

Bowler, and I said:

"Well, Admiral, I don't know whether I am or not. I certainly was at the Naval Academy."

He said: "What do you mean, you don't know whether you are or not?"

I said, "I have never attended a meeting of anything called the Green Bowler Society since I left the Naval Academy. The boys who were my friends in the Green Bowlers at the Academy are still my friends, no more, no less, but I've never heard of a meeting since I left the Naval Academy."

Then Admiral Lowery said: "Have you ever been given an assignment that you felt was choice?" I was a captain in the Navy then.

"Oh," I said, "I think every assignment I've had has been choice, except going to a light cruiser one year, but I went over there at my own request in order to qualify as a top watchstander under way. I spent a year in that assignment, accomplished my purpose and was ready to leave, but it wasn't distasteful."

"Well," he said, "have you ever been given any particularly desirable assignments?"

So I said: "I think perhaps one of the best breaks I ever got was when I finished Pensacola I was one of only three in my whole group who got to go to fighters. I think that's one of the best assignment breaks I ever got."

McDonald #1 - 45

"Well," he said, "was there any particular reason, any particular individual that might have been responsible for this?

I said: "Oh yes, a Lieutenant named John Crommelin was almost solely responsible for me getting that assignment. He was my instructor."

Q: Tell me, Sir, about your tour of duty on the <u>Saratoga</u>. That was an interesting time in the history of naval aviation.

Adm. M.: Yes, it really was.

Q: It was kind of a watershed, was it not?

Adm. M.: Yes, I guess. It seems we were just beginning to think about using these carriers as floating air bases and really carrying, shall we say, offensive operations from them.

Q: They hadn't yet supplanted the battleship, had they, in the thinking of the naval strategists?

Adm. M.: Not exactly. In conducting our exercises, the battleship was still very much in the scheme of things. I think one of the historical exercises, if you want to put it that way, was conducted when I was in VF-6 aboard the <u>Saratoga</u>. I think our skipper Gardner had been replaced

McDonald #1 - 46

by Ofstie by that time. But this was the time that the carrier force launched attacks on the Hawaiian islands, which were repeated, almost maneuver for maneuver, by the Japanese in December 1941.

Q: This was a Sunday raid, was it?

Adm. M.: Sure, it really was. I happened to be there on that exercise, and I think this was probably one of the first large-scale exercises of its type. We initiated this type of exercise and we grew from there.

Q: Who masterminded this exercise?

Adm. M.: I don't know. I don't really know. I do know one thing. There was an observer on the <u>Saratoga</u> named Grover Loening, who built an amphibious plane and later built a little single-seater and he was quite an aviation pioneer and a writer.

Q: He's still about.

Adm. M.: He was aboard at this time and he wrote an article about that attack. I still have a carbon copy in my files and it was real interesting after the Japanese attacked in 1941 to read what Grover Loening wrote about our attack in,

McDonald #1 - 47

when was it, 1933?

Q: Somebody implied that the Japanese consul in Hawaii was not blind to what had taken place and had reported this.

Adm. M.: I wouldn't be surprised. You know we have no secrets in our country. Of course, back then some people tried to be careful but we have people today in the media who seem to take great delight in publishing everything especially if it is classified as secret and they don't seem to care whether it might have a bad impact on our country or not.

Q: Because their readers have the right to know!

Adm. M.: Look at what they're talking about what we did in Chile. What in the world do they think Russia's done in Cuba and everywhere else. But these same writers never say anything about that. Perhaps it was the same back in the 1930's, I don't know. I don't remember, but I doubt it.

I had three very enjoyable cruises in the fighter squadron aboard the Saratoga. But just before we came around to New York in 1934, there developed a little philosophy in the aviation community in Washington which said that in order to give the aviators broader experience we should start making some exchanges between those pilots who were in the aviation units aboard battleships and cruisers and those aboard carriers.

At that time I had a classmate who was in the aviation unit aboard the Detroit.

The Detroit was commanded by Captain Brainerd, whom I had known as the executive officer of Bancroft Hall when I was a midshipman. He came to my house in Coronado one afternoon and said that he had been following my career and that I was coming up soon for senior lieutenant and he knew that one of the requirements was that I had to be qualified as a top watchstander under way, and that my classmate who had been aboard his ship for two years was very anxious to get aboard a carrier and if I would like to come over there he would let it be known that, as commanding officer of the Detroit, he would be pleased to have me.

So, the shift took place. My classmate went to a squadron on the Saratoga, and I went to the Detroit, spent a year, and did a lot of watchstanding.

Q: Could this be considered in Crommelin's eyes one of those favored assignments?

Adm. M.: No, because it was being done generally. All you needed to do then, basically, was to get a swap. But many pilots, most of my contemporaries in fact, stayed on the carriers and qualified by standing watches on the bridge of the carrier, which one could do. But I figured as long as I had to qualify I might as well learn more than was required for simple qualification, so I went over and really learned how they operated in the cruisers.

Q: And there was no stigma against you on the cruiser?

Adm. M.: No. The Detroit at that time was the flagship of the cruisers and destroyers of the Pacific Fleet.

Q: Commanded by whom?

Adm. M.: Commanded by Admiral Woodward, and his flag lieutenant was a senior lieutenant named Hopwood. Hoppy and I became very good friends. He perhaps helped me more in my watchstanding than any other one man on the Detroit. We ultimately ended up with Hoppy as Admiral Radford's - (he was a rear admiral then) chief of staff and I was the operations officer. We still exchange Christmas cards with lengthy notes to Jean Hopwood, his widow.

Q: Tell me, on the Saratoga, I think this was the time when the communications were improving as far as aviators were concerned. Did you have two-way radios?

Adm. M.: I wouldn't really know about that because at that time the only planes that had any kind of radio in them at all were section leaders' planes; that is, only one plane in three. The rest of us didn't have any radio.

McDonald #1 - 50

Q: Oh, I see.

Adm. M.: And I don't think they could communicate, except for short distances. However, each squadron of single-seaters had a two-seater plane called a liaison plane, which was full of communication equipment and, basically, any long range communications were relayed through this liaison plane. Each 18-plane, single-seater squadron had one liaison plane.

Q: Also, someone pointed out to me this was the time when the larger machine guns were coming into being.

Adm. M.: Yes, I think they were, and this was a time when we started to get some unusual airplanes.

Q: Martin bombers, didn't you?

Adm. M.: I am thinking mostly of monoplanes, also Douglas built an experimental two-seater fighter. It had a closed cockpit and a 14-cylinder engine. The landing gear was not retractable. It had been to the East Coast but it landed so fast they sent it back to the factory to put some flaps on it to slow it down when it landed. Our skipper wanted to fly it back to Washington for further flight tests and fly one of the new Grumman liaison planes back to the West Coast but I got the job. And I think I was the first naval aviator that made the round trip from West Coast to Washington and back in a closed cockpit both ways.

Q: A little greater comfort!

Adm. M.: This must have been about January of 1934 and when I went up to Douglas to pick up this two-seater experimental fighter some Mexicans were there as the first prospective purchasers to go through the wooden mockup of the DC-3. We were all taken through by Dutch Kindleberger who later left and formed North American. On my return trip from Washington I spent two days and nights at Maxwell Field in Alabama because of inclement weather. Wiley Post, Amelia Earhart, Roscoe Turner, and other well known pilots were also there en route to the air races in Miami. A real interesting group.

Q: When you were operating from the Saratoga parachutes were in common usage, weren't they?

Adm. M.: Oh, yes. That was part of your equipment. You hooked yourself up to your parachute before you got in your airplane. They were the seat-back type.

Back then all our single-seaters were made by Boeing. Then along in there came the Grumman planes, and then, of course, about the time we got the Grummans, Chance Voight came out with the F-U.

After 3 cruises in Fighters and then one year aboard the Detroit I was ordered to Pensacola as a flight instructor. Upon reporting there I found that my one time skipper in VF-6, Commander Matt Gardner, was the skipper of the fighter training squadron and fortunately for me he had requested that I be sent to his squadron as Chief Flight Instructor.

During my second year as Chief Flight Instructor in the fighter squadron at Pensacola, I was asked if I would like to stay at Pensacola for a third year, and although it might seem odd for me to say I was asked, the fact remained I was asked because one seldom stayed there more than two years.

My third year, however, was spent on the main station. I went to the office of the superintendent of aviation training who was at that time Commander Gerry Bogan, who almost at the time I got there was relieved by Commander Tommy Sprague. The superintendent of training was really the director of all the Navy's training, and his office at that time was divided basically into two parts. One was called flight training and one was called operations. I was assigned to head up that portion called flight training and, while there, I received some of the best training of my life, I think, from Tommy Sprague. Soon after he arrived he informed me that almost all of my work would be with the commanding officers or the executive officers of the five training squadrons, and all of these individuals were considerably senior to me. So he said:

"When they call up and make a request, I don't want you to come in here and tell me that Commander so and so called up and wants to do thus and so and then just stand there. I want you to come in and tell me what they want and then tell me what you would say if you were the boss. I promise you that I will either say go ahead and do it or, if I disagree, I'll have you sit down and I'll point out to you why I disagree."

He did that for almost a year. Sometimes we had some pretty violent arguments. He made it very easy for me to argue with him. They were really almost knock-down-and-drag-out conversations. There were many times when he said, ok, I guess we've had enough, but we're still going to do it my way. I really learned a great deal from him. Instead of him telling me what to do in the beginning or instead of me making a recommendation and just having him disagree, cutting me off, it was really -

Q: Sort of hammering it out on an anvil, wasn't it?

Adm. M.: Oh, it was really great training, and it took a lot of time on his part. Over the years, I saw him a lot.

When he was at one time Chief of the Bureau of Personnel and I was aide to John Nicholas Brown who, as Assistant Secretary of the Navy for Air, had Personnel. We worked together a lot. And often I said to Tommy:

"Some of the things you taught me there and the time you took with me have just been invaluable."

Q: You said earlier that a Navy man is a school teacher and I guess this was an example.

Adm. M.: That's right.

McDonald #2 - 55

Interview No. 2 with Admiral David L. McDonald, U. S. Navy
(Retired)

Place: The Board Room at the Naval Institute
The Admiral is sitting in the same place where
he used to preside at the meetings of the Board.
Date: Saturday morning, 9 November 1974
Subject: Biography
By: John T. Mason, Jr.

Q: Well, Admiral, it's nice to see you this morning and it's nice to be resuming the story of your very successful naval career.

I think you want to talk this morning about flight training and your job in Pensacola in the years 1935 to 1938?

Adm. M.: Those three years were very pleasant years for me from the point of view of simply living and very rewarding because in those days and, I presume, today young men who wanted to learn how to fly, were crazy about it, and to find yourself in a position where you can help people attain what they so earnestly desire is a great feeling.

Q: Channel their energy.

McDonald #2 - 56

Adm. M.: Yes, it's a great feeling.

I spoke earlier about my third year over with Commander Sprague but my first two years I was the chief flight instructor in the fighter squadron. During these two years the Navy put into effect two far-reaching aviation policies. One was the Aviation Cadet Program in lieu of the old Reserve Student Officer Program. In fact the last class of reserve student officers finished Squadron 5, where I was chief flight instructor, two or three months after I arrived and then we began to get the aviation cadets.

Q: Tell me about that program in some detail.

Adm. M.: Basically the Reserve Student Officer Program had been in effect for a long time, certainly from the late 1920s at least, and these were young men who were college graduates who came to Pensacola, and underwent flight training as seamen, second class. At the end of their training period, if they finished successfully, they were given a commission as an ensign in the United States Naval Reserve and then ordered to the fleet, but generally only for a year. Then they were sent home and belonged to a Reserve organization.

Just why they changed from this and started to call them "cadets" I really don't know because all this took place in Washington. They took the same type of young man in the beginning but, of course, ultimately, during World War II, we got

McDonald #2 - 57

down to where we took high-school graduates.

Anyway, this was a change in policy and name, at least. But perhaps something that was more important took place, and that is this. Naval aviation was expanding and so was the Army Air Corps and we all remember, of course, that as the Army Air Corps expanded their younger officers were promoted rather rapidly.

Q: That was one of the characteristics of the Army Air Corps.

Adm. M.: The Navy didn't do this. The Navy's philosophy was that carriers were our most important aviation element. Although we had the observation planes on battleships and cruisers and we had big boats carriers were the real striking force. And those in charge of the Navy then felt that sea-going knowledge was important for carrier operations. So the Navy selected a certain number of either fairly senior commanders or junior captains and sent them to Pensacola and gave them what might be called a bobtail course in aviation. It wasn't very bobtailed though; in fact it was pretty generally the same.

Q: Did they get wings then?

Adm. M.: Yes, indeed they got wings and they had to pass their flight checks just like everybody else. They were given basically the same course. Ultimately they discontinued the advanced acrobatics in Squadron 5 after we had a couple of them parachute. I was there at that time and, as I said earlier, Squadron 5 was the last squadron in which a student was trained prior to graduation. So before these senior officers reached Squadron 5 I was called over to the office of the Superintendent of Aviation Training and was told that when these senior officers first arrived at Pensacola they were told to check their commissions at the gate; that they were going to be considered and treated as flight students and not as commanders or captains. Then the Superintendent said to me:

"Over in your squadron instructors do not ride with student pilots. They're all single-seaters. And I know that it is your custom to assign certain students to certain instructors, but I think that you yourself should handle these senior officers because it is a little bit embarrassing for a young JG to try to start telling a captain what he's done wrong. I want you to do this and I want you to know that these fellows have been told they're flight students and not commanders and captains, but of course I don't expect you to take advantage of it and start giving them hell.

Q: Rank does count, nevertheless!

Adm. M.: Yes, and as a result of this I got to know quite well various individuals who during World War II really became the leaders of carrier aviation. Chub Brown, who was later killed; Gunther, who had been gunnery officer on the <u>Mississippi</u> when I left to take flight training myself in 1930; Frederick Sherman, Buckmaster, Jack Reeves, McCain and many others. As a matter of fact, Frederick Sherman flew his flag in the <u>Essex</u> for, I guess, some eight months while I was executive officer. I'll always remember his arrival. When he reported aboard I went back with the captain of the ship to meet the new admiral - new coming aboard there, and I remember he said to me as I shook hands:

"Where was it I saw you the last time, McDonald?"

And I said:

"I hate to tell you this, Admiral, but I gave you a down in your flight check in Pensacola."

We later laughed about that on several occasions.

Admiral John Sidney McCain was one of my students too. So my tour at Pensacola was real rewarding and real interesting, and I had an opportunity just before my third year was up to get the next duty of my choice. I had been writing letters for Commander Sprague to the Detail Officer in Washington and along in the spring of my third year Commander Sprague asked me where I would like to go for duty.

I told him that I had been in fighters a long time and I had enjoyed my carrier operations very much but I would like to get into big boats to see what that was like and I'd like especially to go to Seattle and Alaska. I wanted to see what the northwest was really like. He kind of laughed and said:

"Write a letter for my signature just like you write these others to the detail officer, and tell him that I have a young fellow down here by the name of McDonald working for me who would like thus and so."

That's exactly what I did and within two weeks word came back that at the expiration of my tour I'd be ordered to VP-42 based at Sand Point, Seattle, Washington, operating out of Seattle and Alaska.

Q: You certainly had earned that kind of an assignment. When you were there as a flight instructor, you indicate that things were picking up. This was in anticipation of being involved in conflict, was it?

Adm. M.: I can't answer that. Carrier aviation was growing even in the early thirties.

Q: Yes, I know.

Adm. M.: So I think it was more a recognition, an early recognition, really, of the importance of carrier aviation.

McDonald #2 - 61

There was no hustle and bustle like we ran into in 1941, for instance, but there was, it seemed to me at least, a slow buildup. I don't believe that one could say in 1935 - and basically the decision about these senior officers must have been made about 1935 - I don't remember just when they went through Pensacola, but it had to be between July 1935 and May of 1937. But it seems to me that it was along in 1937 that they came through, so I would say that this policy decision was excellent long-range planning. Maybe it just turned out that way. But I don't believe one could say that it was because of -

Q: The imminence of war?

Adm. M.: I don't think so, but I don't know.

Q: Were we training any other nationals, like the Royal Navy?

Adm. M.: I seem to recall some, but I don't remember that either. But, since you mention this, I will tell you one rather interesting thing. When I was working for Commander Sprague, my third year, a fellow came over from England, a naval officer, to see how the U. S. Navy trained its pilots. I believe at that time all the Royal Navy people were being trained by the Royal Air Force. Anyway, he wanted to find out what training our naval aviators were getting.

Q: He represented the Fleet Air Arm, then?

Adm. M.: He did. And it was my responsibility to shepherd this fellow around for a couple of days, and it just so happened that his name was Lord Louis Mountbatten. So I got to know Dickie Mountbatten, as most people call him who know him, and in later years when I went to London for duty just prior to coming back as CNO, this gentleman literally went out of his way to be nice to me and my wife. When he found out that I was to return to Washington to be CNO and would be in London only two or three months instead of two or three years he wrote me a letter saying that "I'm enclosing herewith all of the events that are going to take place within the next six weeks which I think you and your wife would like to see if you stayed here for three years. You can't see them all, but if you will indicate which ones you and Tommie want to see (Tommie being my wife), I'll arrange it." And he arranged everything from a Garter ceremony at Windsor Castle right on down.

Q: Great!

Adm. M.: Shall we go on to the big boats?

Q: Yes, but I have one or two questions in addition. You said that when you went over to the main building you were in charge of flight training, but there was another section called Operational Training.

McDonald #2 - 63

Adm. M.: No, no, Operations, and that had to do primarily with the running of the airfields and the flight patterns and various things of that type, as differentiated from teaching people how to fly.

Q: I see. When you were there, in this period, the physical plant had expanded considerably, had it not? There was quite a contrast between what it was when you were there as a student?

Adm. M.: No, not too much. Corey Field had expanded and there were some new buildings there, but not really an awful lot. They'd been modernized more, but not too much expansion at that time.

I left Pensacola with a very good taste in my mouth. I enjoyed it, as I said earlier, from a purely personal living point of view. We could go fishing a lot and I did a good deal of hunting there, played a lot of golf, my wife and I. And also I felt that I had accomplished something. This was again, as I said yesterday, the first time since I had been in the Navy when I could really see the results of my efforts, and I really felt that I had done something quite worthwhile.

Then when we got up to Seattle and Alaska, I operated out of Lake Washington in Seattle. We had three big-boat squadrons to start with and later we got a fourth and later a fifth, and the operational schedule basically was to keep one of these squadrons in Alaska all the time, and

McDonald #2 - 64

the tour of duty in Alaska, if you want to put it that way, was for a three month period.

Q: Was this because of the severity of the weather?

Adm. M.: Well, we just didn't keep people away from home long then like they do now. If we'd think a little bit more about that today we wouldn't have so much trouble keeping people in the Navy. It just doesn't make sense to the average man to be away from home six months, back three, six again, back three when we aren't at war, and it doesn't make much sense to me either, although I recognize the reasons for doing this.

I arrived there in July 1938 and was very fortunate in making what they called an inspection trip in September with my captain and the wing commodore. This turned out basically to be a fishing expedition, I mean real fish, and this was fantastic to me where for the first time in my life I not only saw but I was able to stand in a stream with rubber boots on catching trout and if I wasn't catching trout I could throw my pole on the beach and pull out a 15-pound salmon with my arms. Simply fantastic!

My first 3 month tour however began on the first of December.

Q: You were assigned for three months then?

Adm. M.: Three months. We went to Sitka and at Sitka there's a little place called Japonski Island, right across a strip of water from Sitka, and on Japonski Island there was a wooden house in which the officers lived, a wooden shack where we all, the officers and men, ate, and then there was a converted coal shed which was a warehouse and the crews' barracks.

Q: How many men were accommodated in these places?

Adm. M.: If my memory serves me correctly, we had either seventeen or nineteen officers and about eighty-seven bluejackets, and we had six airplanes.

Flying conditions were dangerous. There were no radio aids then. When you got beyond the radio range of the beacon in Seattle there was nothing else, and when we flew from Seattle to Alaska we flew right on top of the water. You couldn't get up and get into cloud cover because we had no radio aids. We flew right on the water, we knew our speed, we'd throw float lights out the tunnel hatch and it would make smoke. We'd look at that and judge what the wind was and adjust our courses accordingly.

When we would go from Sitka on out to Kodiak we would send a seaplane tender ahead and on more than one occasion my section leader asked the tender to come out of the harbor and send what we called MOs; that is, dots and dashes on the radio key, and we would home in on that. One time the skipper of our squadron with three planes saw a lot of driftwood on the water and although he didn't exactly know where he was he knew he was close to the beach and they landed out in the middle of the ocean and waited for the tender to come out and send MOs and they taxied about five hours to get in. Exciting? You bet.

Why we stayed up there three months I don't know.

Q: And in the dead of winter!

Adm. M.: Well, we were learning how to operate in cold weather. It wasn't too cold at Sitka. It never got below maybe 15° or 18° because of the water that surrounded this island but it was probably 40° below forty miles from where we were, on the other side of the mountain range. But we learned how to get the ice off of our wings and various and sundry other things, so I think it was worthwhile. I enjoyed it.

Q: The main things you contended with were fog and wind, were they not?

Adm. M.: Yes. You didn't get much clear weather up there.

Q: The williwaws?

Adm. M.: Yes, it wasn't unusual to see the eggs or the coffee pot in the airplane suddenly fly up against the overhead when we hit one of these pockets. It was really rugged flying. Carrier aviation, I guess, has always been considered the most dangerous but I had far more hair-raising experiences flying out of Seattle and Alaska in those days than I ever did on a carrier. But with the advent of radio aids and things of that nature it is better but, of course, we were really pioneering. Kodiak, as you know, became a great naval air station, a great base, one of the largest really. It was very useful in World War II, yet when we went up there we would land in Old Woman's Bay and tie up to a buoy. There was only one little shack between there and the town of Kodiak and it was made of logs and was occupied by what they called government bear-hunters, two gents who were hired to shoot bears if the bears got in too close to the little town of Kodiak.

I well remember, I guess it was September of 1939, we shot some ducks one afternoon near the base at Kodiak, or what ultimately became the base at Kodiak. I doubt if a gun had ever been fired in the history of man in that particular spot. And fish! The creek or river or whatever you called the stream had just the most fantastic fishing. When we went up there to advance base, a tender would go up and set up a couple of collapsible shacks and about three tents. We'd stay about two weeks and usually in September. You could walk out in front of our little camp and throw a plug in the water for about ten minutes and you'd have a 15-pound silver salmon on the end of it.

McDonald #2 - 68

Q: Not much challenge in that, was there?

Adm. M.: The only problem was you had to cover yourself with a very fine net because they had these little things they called no-see-ems and they would practically pick you up and carry you off; oh how they would bite.

Q: What's the climate like on Kodiak?

Adm. M.: Well, I didn't stay there except during September. We stayed only at Sitka during the winter. But I imagine it's very similar. Not too cold. Not like one would think it would be in Alaska because you're so close to and surrounded by sea water.

Q: What was the overriding purpose of the big boats up there?

Adm. M.: Patrol, and they ultimately did this in WWII. We found the Japs, you know, trying a landing. In other words the patrol planes were there to see what they could find. These were patrol bombers too. We did drop bombs and we dropped torpedoes and preparing for this required a lot of training.

Q: Did our Russian counterparts maintain patrols up there?

Adm. M.: No. Not airplanes, anyway.

I enjoyed those three years. They were different. Where I had been flying single-seaters and had been completely on my own, here I was the pilot of a multiengine airplane, even though it was a seaplane, usually with three pilots, pretty generally myself and an aviation cadet and an enlisted pilot. Back then when these cadets finished Pensacola instead of being commissioned ensigns immediately they'd go to a squadron and serve as a cadet for about a year and then be commissioned. They later changed that and commissioned them earlier. I had one of these lads in the plane with me and also usually an AP, an enlisted man who was a pilot. Then we would have the plane captain and the radio man and a couple of mechanics, so we had about half a dozen people in the plane. Sometimes we'd advance base over on a little lake on the peninsula from Seattle and we six would actually live in this plane for a couple of days. We'd act as though we were on a mission with no support from anywhere. I learned from that this: that you can really be a friend or almost buddy, if you want to put it that way, with a bluejacket without really breaking down the autocratic barrier that must necessarily exist between officers and men in any military organization if its going to remain military. It can be done, and they never lose their respect for you. Today I am still in communication with one bluejacket who was in my plane in 1939 and also a man who was an aviation cadet, ultimately retired as a captain, and then taught school at the University of Wisconsin. Those are two people that I'm still in communication with.

Q: That experience in being close to your men must have been valuable and it must have been fruitful when you became skipper of a ship?

Adm. M.: Yes. I have often used a rather crude expression that says you can be nice to people without climbing in bed with them. Some people seem to be of the opinion that you must either be buddy-buddy or completely aloof. I don't think that's necessary.

One of the nice happenings for me in the Seattle area was that in my last year there we got a new wing commodore, we called him commodore, although he was a commander, and his name happened to be Andrew C. McFall, the same man who had been my seamanship professor at the Naval Academy when he was a lieutenant commander and I was a midshipman. I say it was fortunate for me because right after he arrived he called me up to his office and he said:

"Now, whenever I fly with this wing, wherever I go, I'm going to ride in your airplane. I think we ought to have an understanding. I'm going to tell you where I want to go, but I'm never going to tell you how to get there."

McDonald #2 - 71

And he and I had some rather scary rides during that year. But one of the reasons I'm living where I am today is because he's there and we often reminisce about our Seattle - Alaskan experiences.

Q: When you were in Alaska was the Coast Guard very active?

Adm. M.: Not right where we were. But it seems to me the Coast Guard ships were based near Juneau. They had a Coast Guard station at Sitka but it was primarily for weather.

Q: Did the Navy at that time have those oil lands that we hear so much about now?

Adm. M.: Without knowing, my answer offhand would be yes. I don't think the Navy has any so-called oil reserves today that they haven't had for years, as far as I know.

Q: They were acquired much earlier? When you were in the Seattle area, what was the mission of the flying boats there?

Adm. M.: That's a good question. I guess I never wondered what the mission was. I didn't concern myself with that. I just did what I was supposed to do, but basically we were learning how to get out of the airplanes whatever capability they had, and that involved search, patrol, bomb and torpedo. So basically we were there training for potential operations in that area and I'm sure when the war started with Japan these same boats were searching constantly an area out perhaps to a thousand miles and prepared to bomb or torpedo any ship that they thought was enemy. Coastal protection, I guess you'd say, and that of course is what a patrol plane is. That's the reason they call it patrol, they patrol large areas at sea and ensure that we can use them and deny the use of those areas to any potential enemy. And that's all we had in that area when I was there and when WWII started.

Q: Perhaps this is a good place to ask you about the flying boat, the merits of the flying boat, and what you think about its demise and all that?

Adm. M.: I think they're useful, but I think this is like everything else. You have so much money in the pot and how are you going to spend it? I happened to be in Requirements back in Washington when we decided not to pursue the boats any more.

Q: Was that the Seamaster, when that was done?

Adm. M.: Well, that was about 1955 to 1957. Airplanes today can be built with such long range built into them while at the same time requiring such a small amount of space in which to get off the ground. You see, this didn't used to be true. The beauty of the big boat was that we could get on Lake Washington and we could run for miles, two miles, if necessary. The landing field at Sand Point couldn't be built any longer because of the geographic limitations. So there were certain advantages to seaplanes then that aren't as important today.

But we did work with Martin on seaplane usage in the mid fifties.

Q: This is the Seamaster now you're talking about, isn't it?

Adm. M.: I don't remember whether that's what they were or not but I think so.

Q: Were there jet engines?

Adm. M.: I'm not sure. The idea then was that they would fly along and land and dunk a sonar to listen for submarines, take off and land somewhere else and dunk a sonar again, and infinitum. That sounded pretty good, except I remembered that once or twice when I'd had a little engine trouble and had to land off Puget Sound out in the Pacific in my PBY and I wasn't sure that I was ever going to get away with it. When you're sitting down on the water in a seaplane and get ready to take-off those swells look pretty big and you have to do some thinking about whether you want to try it or whether you want to wait and try to get somebody to tow you back in.

Q: They must look pretty big to seagulls too!

Adm. M.: Yes. All of these things are like so many things in the Navy and the military. It's a matter of opinion. We've got a hell of a lot of people today who are talking about reviving the airship.

Q: Lighter than air?

Adm. M.: Yes, and it makes a lot of sense in many ways but, I'm a Scotsman and believe that nothing comes free, and I think that we must be very careful especially in the military when lives are at stake. Some people say our job is to save lives and not to save money but that's not right in my opinion and I've said this. Our job is to save lives <u>and</u> money, not, however, to save money at the expense of lives. I think we just simply must deal with the economics of every situation and I believe right now that economics would not permit the revival of either the seaplane or the airship. At some future time, it might. That doesn't mean that they're no good but they have no place today since we just can't have everything.

As I said earlier, I enjoyed those three years. It was a different experience, and I left there with a pretty good taste in my mouth. It was really good until the final

McDonald #2 - 75

days and then for the next few weeks I would have sold the Navy for a nickel.

Q: Why?

Adm. M.: I was ordered to go down to San Diego, Coronado, to participate in the commissioning of a new patrol squadron. I was to be the executive officer. When I got down to San Diego imagine my chagrin when I learned that this new squadron was to have a number 4. With the number 4, that meant that we'd be a part of Patrol Wing 4 whose home port and base was in Seattle, and although our new squadron was to remain in in San Diego because of this peculiarity the Navy would not move my family from Seattle to San Diego. As fond as I have been of the Navy, I've always been more fond of my family.

So I communicated with my wife. She called in a second-hand furniture dealer and practically gave our furniture away, put the two children in the car, and headed for Coronado. I rented a furnished house in Coronado. They arrived -- at my expense. We moved in, and then in about ten days, I guess, or a week, on a Wednesday - Wednesday afternoon (we still took Wednesday afternoon off back in the old days and worked Saturday morning) we went from our house in Coronado, over to San Diego, bought a lot of things for the house, including a washing machine, a bicycle for each of the two children, came back home, had a big dinner and went to bed. About 10:30 the telephone rang. It was Washington, telling me to be in Norfolk to report as aide and flag secretary to Admiral A.B. Cook within I think it was twelve days. I would have sold my interest in the Navy, I think, for a nickel.

We forfeited the rest of the rent on the house. I think we took the bicycles and washing machine back, I'm not sure. Anyway in a couple of days we piled in the car and away we went.

We got to Norfolk, registered at a hotel, I went to the base and learned that the admiral was out at sea and wouldn't be in for three days, he and the staff. So I could have had three more days. I also learned that this particular admiral had had his third flag lieutenant within about eight months.

Q: That didn't look good!

Adm. M.: Oh, and I had a letter waiting for me. I wondered why this had happened. I didn't know why this Admiral had asked for me. I'd only seen him once. When he had AirPac, I guess, he came up through Seattle and inspected us. But this letter was from a man about six or seven years my senior who'd been one of those squadron commanders in

Pensacola with whom I worked when I was his junior. In his letter he said:

"I am leaving the staff. I am devoted to this admiral. I'm one of the few who are and if you want to blame anybody for your orders you've got to blame me because I recommended that you come here." At least I know why I was there.

That afternoon I saw a friend of mine that I'd been in VF-6 with and he said:

"Boy, we're betting on you but we don't know whether you're going to last three months or six months with A.B. Cook."

This was late September of 1941. During those three days I couldn't find a place for my family in Norfolk. When the flagship came in I reported. Two days later we went to sea and I left my wife and children standing on the dock. They got in the car and drove to my home in Georgia and spent six weeks with my family till they could find a place in Norfolk.

Q: Doesn't the Navy help under those circumstances?

Adm. M.: They do now but they didn't then. Well, I guess there wasn't any place available. Ultimately we found a place, an apartment house.

Q: In Norfolk, or Virginia Beach, or where?

Adm. M. In Norfolk. We put our name on the waiting list and people were moving pretty fast. I think it was either six or eight weeks before they notified my wife that there was an apartment available, so they came up.

This fellow Cook was a wild man in many ways, but a very smart fellow.

Q: Was he a sundowner?

Adm. M.: Arthur Byron Cook, simply had an ungovernable temper. One of the neatest men I've ever seen in my life. He looked like he had just stepped out of a band box. His family had a good deal of money. He was a rather outspoken man. He had been commanding officer of one of our two big carriers, the Lexington. After he became a flag officer he relieved Admiral Ernie King as Chief of the Bureau of Aeronautics. He'd had quite a career and was very capable, a very capable man.

I reported aboard and, as I say, two days later we went to sea, ended up in Bermuda, then without going into the details I guess within eight days he and I sort of had a showdown. We really had quite a discussion with it ending by him saying maybe I couldn't work for him. I was so mad by that time that my reply was:

"You know, Admiral, I didn't request this duty."

Then he changed his attitude completely and said he was glad that I came up to discuss this with him. (Incidentally, he'd thrown an inkwell across the cabin at the flag lieutenant.

In December I went with him to meet Mr. Churchill. We went up to Admiralty House and talked for a couple of hours and then had dinner with Mr. Churchill.

But let's get to something I think is most interesting. Around the 8th of November 1941 a small task force was assembled in Casco Bay, Maine, consisting of the USS Ranger, a cruiser, and some destroyers. I'm not sure whether the cruiser Savannah was with us at the moment or not. If not, she ultimately joined us. We sortied from Casco Bay early in the morning. Admiral Cook, my boss, was the force commander.

We went east and before daylight we were joined by six United States transports and we headed south. When we arrived at Trinidad only one man went ashore and that was the supply officer from the staff of Admiral Cook. Upon leaving Trinidad we were joined by a fast tanker. Just below the equator the tanker fueled all ships and the Ranger and the cruiser and I believe all but eight destroyers, turned around and headed back toward Norfolk. Then these six United States transports -- and listen to this -- loaded with over 20,000 British troops proceeded on to Calcutta and we weren't even in the war.

Q: You mean you were convoying them.

Adm. M.: Yes. These eight destroyers stayed with them till they got through the wolf-pack area off Capetown, then four of our destroyers broke off and the others went on with them. What I've said so far I know, because "I was there, Charlie," as the radio commedian used to say. And I think one of the transports was sunk before it got to Calcutta, but that I don't know.

Q: By a raider, perhaps?

Adm. M.: I don't know. Those of us who were returning to Norfolk were due in Norfolk on Monday morning, the day following Pearl Harbor. We were one day out of Norfolk when the message about the attack on Pearl Harbor came and, as the flag secretary, I of course got the message and took it up to the Admiral.

My immediate thought, and I think most of us had the same one was, I wonder if they'll turn us around and send us through the Panama Canal, and on into the Pacific? But we went on into Norfolk the next day, stayed there about a week, and then headed for Bermuda again.

We'd been chasing subs out of Bermuda for some time.

Q: This was the new Caribbean force?

Adm. M.: That's right and, of course, it was when we were in Bermuda during that Christmas that Mr. Churchill and company came over to see President Roosevelt.

Q: The policy had already been established, had it not, that when we were in the conflict we'd concentrate on the Atlantic first?

Adm. M.: I presume. One interesting little tidbit. Most of the messages going back and forth from England to the States about Prime Minister Churchill's forthcoming visit, were routed to us because we were going to be in the Bermuda area and although there was a rear admiral in Bermuda Admiral Cook was going to be there and he was the senior one.

So one day I picked up a message that listed the weight of baggage that was accompanying Mr. Churchill and his group. I looked at this and I said to Admiral Cook -

"What in the world have they got? This is a hell of a lot of luggage.

And Cook said:

"Well, I've always heard if we weren't careful the British would have our shirts. I guess they have our shirts packed up in those suitcases!"

Q: Tell me, Sir, how did you establish this kind of rapport with a man who was so difficult?

Adm. M.: I don't really know, but we got along real well and in March he called me in one day and said:

"Well, the Navy is starting a new project ashore. How long

McDonald #2 - 82

have you been at sea?"

When he said "how long have you been at sea" he meant how long had I been on duty which was considered sea duty for purposes of assignment. Of course I'd been in the Alaskan area three years and now I was on my fourth year.

He said:

"I know that with a war on no young man wants to go ashore, but Commander Radford in Washington is the head of Naval aviation training and he wants to set up a thing in the Florida peninsula called the Naval Air Operational Training Command with headquarters in Jacksonville. He wants to build a dozen or more air stations in this area to train young pilots in combat types of planes - let them get some experience in the same kind of plane they're actually going to fight in when they go out to a war zone. They want me to head it up. I guess one of the reasons is that I was chief of the Bureau for four years and I know a lot of people on the Hill and maybe can help them get some congressional support for this. You've been here with me a while and you've had some training experience in aviation over in Pensacola so I'd like for you to go with me and I'll take John with me also.

(Commander John Cassady was his operations officer.)

"I want to tell both of you I'll get you out of there in not more than a year and a half. I'll try to get you out of there in a year, but I need some help to get this thing started and you fellows..."

"Well," I said, "it's a pretty good idea. I wouldn't mind."

When I went home that afternoon I didn't mention this to my wife immediately. The children were playing on the living room floor and my wife was in the kitchen making biscuits. All at once a car drove up in front of the house and, by golly, here was Admiral Cook. My wife had on an apron with flour all over it. I don't think she'd ever met him.

He came in, sat on the floor and played with the kids. I mixed him a drink, and we chitchatted back and forth, and after about twenty-minutes he left. He'd no more than gotten out of the door when my wife said:

"What's up?"

I said:

"What do you mean what's up?"

She said:

"It's perfectly obvious the admiral came here to look over your family."

So I told her what he'd said.

"Oh, " she said. Wouldn't that assignment be wonderful.

The next morning when I went to the ship the admiral said:

"Have you thought any more about this Jacksonville thing?"

I said: "I told you it was all right with me. The war won't be over soon. I'll take a crack at it."

He said: "What does that Yankee wife of yours think about going down there?"

My wife was born and raised in Rochester, New York.

I said: "Admiral, we spent four years in Pensacola, one year as a flight student as bride and groom really, and three years after that and she loved it."

So we went, Cassady, Cook and McDonald, and I think today the best contribution I ever made to the Navy was in that Naval Air Operational Training Command.

Q: I think we should go back, perhaps, to the Ranger because there must be something more about the Neutrality Patrol, about that whole period?

Adm. M.: I can't enlighten you very much because the so-called Neutrality Patrol had been going on a long time before I got there. I really didn't get there, into the area, you might say, until mid-October, and we went out practically not at all until we went to Casco Bay, Maine, to form this group and take them south and then the war started. So you see I never really participated.

Q: What kind of an organization did we have at that point out from San Juan? Was Hoover down there then?

Adm. M.: I can't answer that. I don't know, because until that time I'd had sea duty only in the Pacific. The only time I'd ever been at sea in the Atlantic was on a midshipmen's cruise and in 1934 when the fleet came around. I'd spent all of my time in the Pacific. The nearest I'd come to being in the Atlantic had been the duty in Pensacola, Florida.

Q: Do tell me about that conference with Churchill in Bermuda.

Adm. M.: There was nothing really of particular importance, just a chitchat because his conference was really in Washington and all we did was just chitchat back and forth, have some drinks and have dinner.

Q: And then your recollection of him as a person? What was he like?

Adm. M.: Baby-faced, very jolly and with a drink always in his hand. But I've often doubted that he drank as much as indicated. It looked like he drank a good deal in the afternoon because of the drink constantly available but just before dinner he took a shower and came out completely refreshed, new all over again, like he'd had a full night's sleep and very vivacious. Quite an individual.

McDonald #3 - 86

Interview No. 3 with Admiral David L. McDonald, U.S. Navy
(Retired)

Place: The Washington Navy Yard, The Naval History Center

Date: Wednesday morning, 4 June 1975

Subject: Biography

By: John T. Mason, Jr.

Q: Well, Admiral, it's certainly good to see you this morning. I have been looking forward to this new chapter in your story. Last time, when you broke off, you had been asked by Admiral A. B. Cook to go with him to Florida to set up the naval air operational training command. This was in 1942, I believe. You had been somewhat reluctant to do it but you acquiesced, anyway.

Adm. M.: One had very little choice, when asked by Admiral Cook. To be perfectly frank with you, although he was considered to be somewhat of a wild man by many people, I enjoyed my entire tour with him. The purpose of the command being set up in Florida was to develop a group of air stations where we would train newly designated naval aviators in combat-type airplanes. Upon completing their course in flight instruction and being designated as naval aviators, either in Pensacola or Corpus Christi, these embryo pilots would be sent to the Naval Air Operational Training Command and given a short flying course in the same type of airplane that they would fly upon arriving in combat zones, so that at that time they would be at least familiar with the characteristics of the airplane.

This whole idea was the brainchild of Commander (I believe he was a Commander then, later, of course, Chairman of the Joint Chiefs), Arthur Radford. An agreement had been reached in Washington between the Navy and the Army whereby the Navy would be authorized to establish air stations in the Florida Peninsula, generally east of a line that was drawn north and south through the center of the state. The Air Force, or the Army Air Corps, which at that time had bases around Tampa and other places along the Gulf would operate to the west of that line. Of course, the Navy's major flight training base was then and always has been over at Pensacola, which was west of that line but so far west there was no interference.

Prior to the establishment of this Naval Air Operational Training Command, Admiral Cook, Commander Cassady, who was on his staff as operations officer, and I joined with some people from Admiral Radford's office in Washington and toured similar operational type training bases in Canada. The Naval Air Operational Training Command was commissioned, I believe around the 6th or 7th of May 1942. And there began the most interesting tour of duty I think I ever had and, in my own mind, I did the best job I ever did in the Navy while serving with Admiral

McDonald #3 - 88

Cook in that assignment.

Q: That's really something. You speak about the Canadian bases, what did you learn specifically from them that would apply down there? Was this the RAF having bases in Canada?

Adm. M.: Well, Canadian RAF, yes, RCAF. They had a similar setup and we wanted to see how they were doing it. We wanted to know how best to give combat indoctrination training to those who had already been newly designated as naval aviators; we weren't going to give them an up-check or a down-check, we weren't going to fail them necessarily -

Q: It was a finishing school?

Adm. M.: That's right, and we didn't want a syllabus set in concrete. Whether or not this could be done effectively was questionable, and this was one of the things we looked into in Canada. I'll speak of this a little bit later because it was very important, and we found out that things that work in theory don't always work from a practical point of view. Just before this command was established, Admiral Cook obtained two or three other people on his staff, not very many, and we started to work immediately. We took into this newly established

Command six or seven naval air stations which were already in operation. They were Jacksonville proper, Cecil Field, Lee Field, Banana River for big boats, which now is Cape Kennedy, and we had Opa-Locka, which is Miami, of course. Maybe Lake City. I'm not sure.

When I left about twenty-two months later and I think we had seventeen naval air stations.

Q: The measure of its success?

Adm. M.: Yes, very much. This NAOTC was commissioned, as I say, in May and the first air station we opened was in August at Fort Lauderdale, Florida. Then later at Vero Beach, Melbourne, and Daytona, Sanford and De Land, Boca Chica, St. Simon's Island in Georgia; Beaufort, South Caroline. In addition to these air stations, we developed something that very few people in this country know about even today. We created a thing at Glenview, Illinois, called the Aircraft Carrier Training Unit.

At that time, even in May of 1942, the Navy had a small group in San Diego and a small group in Norfolk - called Aircraft Carrier Training Groups. Young aviators who were going to carriers would finish their training in Pensacola or Corpus Christi and go to these groups and, while assigned to these groups, would learn how to fly on and off aircraft carriers because there was no training aircraft carrier at Pensacola then. When the Naval Air Operational Training Command was created, since these young aviators were coming to us to fly in combat planes, we thought well, why not give them carrier training, too. So the Navy acquired in Chicago two coal-burning, paddle-wheel-driven ferry boats. The tops were knocked off those ferry boats, planking installed for flight decks, and arresting gear installed. North American Aviation was asked to build hooks into a certain number of SNJ training planes, and when the boys would finish their operational training in Florida they would go to Glenview and learn how to get on and off carriers in an SNJ, flying on and off of these two old coal-burning, paddle-wheel-driven ferry boats by the name of the Wolverine and the Sable, hundreds of naval aviators.

This idea was really the brainchild of Rear Admiral Richard, or Dick, Whitehead.

Q: Many of these lads were actually fully combat ready when they went to their squadrons, weren't they?

Adm. M.: Reasonably so. Let's get to the syllabus. At first we thought there would be no specified course of instruction in the NAOTC. I didn't quite approve of this but I was sort of low man on the totem pole and was overruled.

McDonald #3 - 91

But we later modified this because if the idea was to let a man stay in this Naval Air Operational Training Command until he reached a specified standard of proficiency in this type of plane, that might mean that one man might have to stay there only two weeks whereas another might have to stay six weeks. Well, the people fighting the war had to have some positive figures for planning the flow of new pilots to them; a prediction had to be made ahead of time and maintained. So what we did was create what one might call a core syllabus which was of such a nature that even the least competent could complete in, shall we say, a month and if the man completed it in two weeks, then the next two weeks he would just continue to improve himself. So the fleet planners then knew when the pilots would arrive and, although a squadron commander getting a new pilot wouldn't be able to know ahead of time just how competent he was, in type, he would know that he was at least up to a certain minimum standard.

In the beginning, of course, I think my job was civil engineer and paymaster and planner and aide and everything else - but ultimately we settled down and my job was primarily deciding how many planes of what type we would locate at a particular air station, how many instructors we would need at that air station in order to get the most out of these airplanes, and, of course, how many students this number of instructors and this number of airplanes would process in a certain period of time. It was really interesting and I had as my primary assistant a young JG Phi Beta Kappa out of Yale who became one of my very great friends and became a very senior vice president of the New York Life Insurance Company until he decided he'd leave there and do something on his own.

We are still in touch with each other. This was a most interesting assignment and even though I was not Admiral Cook's flag lieutenant or his aide, I'm very happy to be able to say I don't think he ever went anywhere that I didn't go with him. This was rough sometimes but it turned out to be a great experience.

Q: Let me ask about the input to this particular job that you had. Did it also include a knowledge of the requirements of, say, the carriers in the Pacific using certain type planes?

Adm. M.: Oh, yes. Pensacola and Corpus Christi received the information on the kind of pilots that were needed and they would report to us. For instance, they would advise that a certain number of fighter trained pilots would be finishing on the 7th. We would determine then (if we had two different types of fighters), how many would go to each type.

McDonald # 3 - 93

Q: Exactly. I wondered if this was in the input.

Adm. M.: That's correct. We didn't have a computer then, but this was done by Western Union type messages. We'd get messages on specified days. Pensacola would report regularly on a certain day of the week. Corpus Christi would report regularly on a certain day of the week. One of the interesting aspects of the Naval Air Operational Training Command was our work week. Work went on seven days a week, of course, but each individual was given a day off out of every seven, and any man who was an aviator was supposed to fly on one of the six days he worked because we had to get in a certain amount of flight time to maintain our proficiency. And so I set up an arrangement whereby each week each aviator would turn in to me a slip saying what day of the next week he would fly and he would indicate which station or stations in the command he wanted to visit. I insisted that when they flew they had to visit air stations within our command. Then on each Thursday I would make up a list and I would send it to each of the air stations and they would know what aviator from the headquarters would be at their command on what day of the next week.

Q: This was an educational process?

Adm. M: And often the commanding officer of a station

would call up our office and say, "Look, some day next week will you have someone come who's familiar with thus and so?" Then we would arrange for a pilot who was working in that particular area to go to that station during his flying time the next week.

This ensured that the people who were running our air stations knew that the people at headquarters knew what their problems were, no question about it and they could learn of ours. It worked both ways. It was real liaison.

Q: A most effective system. Now, was any of this learned from the Canadians?

Adm. M.: I don't really think so. Of course, when you visit some other area you have to learn something, but to put it down in finite terms, I don't think so. It would be very difficult to do that.

Q: With all these air bases located in a relatively small area, the skies must have been filled?

Adm. M.: They were. And I might say this. Almost every air station had as a part of it two outlying fields where the boys could go practice their landings, and practice their carrier landing approaches.

McDonald #3 - 95

Q: Were there any accidents as a result of this crowding in the skies?

Adm. M.: I presume so, but not of a serious nature or I would remember it. Of course, we didn't have too much commercial traffic then but we had some. You see, by us being on the eastern part of the peninsula we could get right out to sea. Most of our practice areas other than just landing and taking off were out at sea. We had designated areas for various and sundry exercises, and, if I remember correctly, our pilots in proceeding from their base to their practice area at sea had to fly through certain designated channels, the channels being not only directional but also adjusted from an altitude point of view. So within certain areas commercial planes knew that we'd stay out of the way.

Q: This must have put a very heavy burden at the airports on the people in the towers?

Adm. M.: Well, yes, it did, but our tower people were very competent. And I almost forgot one of the most important aspects of the entire command. Our flight instructors were super. After the NAOTC had been operative for a few months our instructors came to us from the combat zone. Jimmy Thach, well known as the creator of the Thach

McDonald #3 - 96

Weave, came back and actually headed up the flight training at this Naval Air Operational Training Center. So the young embryo pilot was being told how he should learn to handle his airplane by the fellow who had been handling it against the enemy. It was quite an operation. I say to this day that in my humble opinion I did the best job there than in any place in my whole life.

Q: Did you use WAVES at the airfields?

Adm. M.: We didn't have such things until about 1943. The first WAVES in the Navy came to our NAOTC.

Q: The reason I ask is that Joy Hancock told me that the WAVES proved to be very efficient and very effective at the fields.

Adm. M.: Joy brought a couple of the first ones down there and at Admiral Cooks one evening (and I think Joy was there) I made the statement that it seemed rather odd to me to have 105-pound young ladies being mechanics on airplanes and 200-pound sailors baking cakes in the galley! But the gals did perform admirably.

Admiral Cook had promised John Cassady and me that he would arrange for us to get out into the combat zone, he wouldn't keep us there all during the war. And he did make those arrangements in 1943. I think it was the Wasp John was going as skipper and I was going as his navigator. This was going to be in late August or early September of 1943. However, Captain Gerry Bogan, had the Saratoga and I think Gerry fell on the flight deck or something and hurt himself and Cassidy was jerked quickly and sent out to command the Saratoga. I was still waiting to go to the Wasp. In August 1943 I moved my wife and two children out of quarters at Jacksonville. By that time I knew practically every grain of sand on the Florida peninsula, so I selected and rented a house for them at Hollywood. The Navy was running a radar school in the Hollywood Beach Hotel and Captain, later Admiral, Don Felt was the skipper over at Miami, a great friend of mine. Hollywood wasn't too far from there, in case my wife needed help. So I moved my wife and two children to Hollywood.

Almost concurrent with this move, Admiral Cook got orders to put on three stars and go to San Juan, and he was to be relieved by Rear Admiral Andrew C. McFall, the same man who had been one of my instructors when I was a midshipman and had flown in my airplane when he was our wing commander in Seattle. Admiral McFall arrived from the combat zone and the very day he took over he said to me that I was the only man on the entire staff that he had known previously and although he hated to do it I wasn't going to leave.

Q: That made sense, though, didn't it?

Adm. M.: It did to him, I guess! I explained to him my family situation, and he told me I could go whenever I could get a relief that would be acceptable to him. After a while we hit upon a man that we both knew, but to make a long story short I lived in BOQ for nearly six months and not only worked for Admiral McFall as I'd been working for Admiral Cook but I practically acted as his aide and the reception "Committee" to welcome all of his visitors. But he was very nice and most understanding. Since we took one day off each week doing nothing so to speak any one day to fly, during this six-month period I would get in an airplane about eleven o'clock Saturday morning, fly to Fort Lauderdale where my wife would meet me (she only lived five miles from the air station) and she'd drive me back to Lauderdale and I'd take off about ten o'clock Monday morning and I'd be in the office at one o'clock Monday afternoon. So at least I spent every weekend with my wife and children.

I certainly want to emphasize that no problem existed between me and Admiral McFall. We're living today in Ponte Vedra primarily because of Andy McFall. He's there also. He retired in 1946 and went there at that time because the man who built Ponte Vedra was a friend of his. We've always been in touch with him and I guess we see Andy and Dorothy (his wife) now more than anyone - they've probably been the best friends we ever had. But he did sort of upset my plans at the time. Incidentally, I did not go to the Wasp. I went to the Essex.

Q: May I ask if during the period you were in Florida you were less apprehensive than some men I've talked with, less concerned about getting out to the fleet because you were doing a job that obviously had to be done -

Adm. M.: No, I've never been one that beat on the desk and said that I was just dying to get to sea in peacetime. I always liked to be with my family. I really wasn't anxious to get to sea in peacetime. Of course, I didn't mind going to sea either; after all that was part of my job. I've heard people say they just couldn't wait to get to sea and I think a lot of them said that because they thought they were supposed to. In time of war everybody's supposed to say that they want to be in combat. Well, I think they do. I didn't want to avoid combat and of course I was anxious to get there, but I had the feeling that there was a job to be done everywhere. I really didn't much like it when I started down there with Admiral Cook, however, I felt all along that this would not be a short war and that I'd have my opportunity.

Q: I know, you said that.

Adm. M.: Then after we got going, although I wanted to get out and get aboard ship, there wasn't any question in my mind but what I was contributing as much to the war effort right there as I could anywhere.

Q: It was very obvious.

Adm. M.: And I knew it, I felt it. There were a thousand and one other jobs that I could have been in where I don't think I'd have had this feeling, but there I did and I think one reason was - and I'm not bragging when I say this - that I could deal with Admiral Cook, I think, better than anybody, unless maybe it was John Cassady. I think he relied on me. I think he had confidence in me and I had respect for him. He was a peculiar fellow, in some ways, and I think maybe that was one reason I felt that I was doing so much good and, let's just face it, he let me do a lot of things that I felt ought to be done that other people probably wouldn't have let me do. I thought they were right and felt good about it.

And let me say this. Radford in Washington, of course, was one of the keys and he had some people up there - I won't start naming names - but they were equally cooperative, and Admiral Radford and Cook could deal with each other. I always liked Admiral Radford very much. I later served with him, for him, several times and made some fantastic trips with him. So, we just happened to have a group that worked together real well. I was quite happy, though, when I got my assignment to the Essex because I had stayed at the NAOTC long enough.

Q: When you were down in Florida a lot of new plane types were coming along, weren't they?

Adm. M.: Yes.

Q: Did this complicate your training problems?

Adm. M.: I don't remember too much about that except for a twin-engine land plane. I think it was the Lockheed Hudson, a sort of military version of the Lockheed Lodestar, and we wanted to set up a training unit with these planes. It was very difficult to find naval aviators with appropriate background to be instructors. We finally got a man named Erdman whom I had known in big boats in the Seattle-Alaska area. He came down as the skipper of this twin-engine bomber training unit located I believe at Beaufort, South Carolina, and maybe Lake City, too.

We did get other new types but that's the only new one that I remember us having some problems with, and it was mostly getting pilots who had experience in this type to teach our young embryo aviators how to operate them.

Q: I would think one source would have been the pilots who had been operating at Anacostia at the Test Center. Did you use any of them?

Adm. M.: They were too few and far between. You see, when you start talking about the numbers of pilots to be trained and the number of planes to be used and then look at the number of individuals who had tested a particular type, the percentage was almost infinitesimal. I expect we probably did get some of those, but I don't recall.

Q: It occurs to me that they would have infinite knowledge of some of these new types?

Adm. M.: Yes, but as I say the only one I remember we had any problem with was this particular one.

Q: You made some reference to the great number of people who stopped by from Washington and I assume, from the commands out at sea.

Adm. M.: And allies.

Q: And you had to handle them. Tell me about that.

Adm. M.: Not necessarily me. All in all it was just the usual greetings and cocktails and dinner, but when you were working as hard as we were, why, a little of that went a long way.

Q: Were you training any of our allied pilots?

Adm. M.: I think so, but I just don't remember. I believe we did.

Oh, yes, we must have had some British because we had a British Naval officer, Charles Evans, who was one of our senior instructors down at Miami. I know Charles Evans had the British group at Miami, because in the beginning before he went out to the Saratoga, Captain Gerry Bogan was the commanding officer of Miami and Bob Pirie was his exec, and Charles Evans, who later became Sir Charles Evans, whom I got to know quite well in later years, was down there. So, thinking back now, we did have some from England and I expect we had them from other countries, too, but I just don't recall.

Q: I suppose like the Norwegians. They had no access to any of their own air facilities.

Adm. M.: I really don't recall, except I do remember Charles Evans. And I think that's about it for the NAOTC.

Q: Good. We go to sea, then, in the <u>Essex</u>?

Adm. M.: I might add one thing right now that irked me for years. For my work in the NAOTC I was recommended for a Legion of Merit, either two or three times. For reasons unknown to me, it was denied, except the last time. This last time it was reduced to a letter of commendation from the Secretary of the Navy and I didn't receive that until the war was over. Knowing what I'd done down there and knowing actually what I'd later done in the war zone, for which I had already received several decorations, I got so mad that I wrapped this letter of commendation up, wrote an official letter fo the Navy Department and told them what they could do with it.

I was on the AirPac staff at Pearl Harbor then and the chief of staff, Admiral Glover, said, "Is this what you really want to say in the letter?"

I said, "No, Cato, but I can't say any more without getting a general court."

He said, "You really want to send it?"

And I said, "I sure do."

So it went back to the Navy Department. About two

months later I got a letter from Admiral Radford, who I think was DCNO Air then, saying, "I think fortunately for you this letter arrived at my desk. Since I was in Washington when you were down there with Admiral Cook and since I am thoroughly familiar with what went on down there, I understand why you're mad and I thoroughly agree that what you did hasn't been recognized, but I don't really think this letter will do you any good. If you will agree to withdraw it, I will promise you that I will have the matter investigated."

The letter was sent to me via the chief of staff. He called me in, the same chief of staff knowing how mad I had been about it, and said:

"Well, are you going to withdraw it?"

And I said, "Look, Cato, I have so much respect for Raddy I'd do most anything he recommends. Yes, I'll withdraw it."

I never heard any more about this for some time. Then, a couple of years later, I happened to be the aide to the Assistant Secretary of the Navy for Air, and one day a retired senior naval officer came to my office and said he wanted to talk to me. I had never known him although I had known of him.

Q: A naval officer?

Adm. M.: Yes. We had a cup of coffee and we chatted a little bit, and finally he looked at me and said:

"I'll tell you why I'm in here. You remember that letter you wrote about the letter of commendation some time ago and told them what to do with it?"

I said, "Yes."

"And Admiral Radford wrote you and said if you'd withdraw it he'd have it investigated?"

I said, "Yes."

He said: "I've got to tell you, fellow, he told me to investigate it. I never did a thing about it. I forgot all about it and I don't reckon I'd have ever remembered it again if I hadn't seen the other day where you got this job, and I apologize."

Real interesting.

Q: It certainly is! It reached a dead end, didn't it?
Well, you got plenty of other awards.

Adm. M.: Yes, and ultimately I got this, too.

Q: The Navy was somewhat behind the Army in handing out awards during the war, in the early phases of the war.

Adm. M.: Yes, but I think the Navy was right. When I was executive officer of the Essex, I made a request of my commanding officer, that the various requests that were being made up for medals by the squadron commanders and the air group commander not be routed through me, because I did not agree with them and I would not approve them. It got to the point where they were getting medals for taking off and landing without breaking their necks even though they didn't even engage in combat, air medals. We started trying to catch up with the Army Air Corps. I didn't approve of that and fortunately I had a very fine commanding officer. I just simply laid it on the line that it would be just wasting time because I was not going to approve these things. So they bypassed me pretty generally and he approved them. I felt we were downgrading them.

Q: But you do approve of awards?

Adm. M.: Yes. But I don't really think a man should get an award for doing something that he's just expected to do normally. But when Dave McCampbell, our *Essex* group commander, went out and shot down nine Japs in 90 minutes or eliminated them, that's something else, and most worthy of recognition.

This thing of getting an Air Medal for every five flights, just because you take off and fly in the war zone is no good. Sure, you run a danger, but, hell, everybody on the ship is in danger of being torpedoed every minute. I think you can go a little too far.

Q: And perhaps this has been true of the Purple Heart also?

Adm. M.: That I don't know. The only people that I know who got the Purple Heart got hit with something, including our chaplain who was hit in the behind. I laughed at him and told him he was running down the hatch when our ship was hit by a kamikaze.

Q: Well, you went out to the Essex as air officer?

Adm. M.: I went to the Essex as air officer and was very happy, of course, to report to the then commanding officer, Ralph Ofstie, who had been my commanding officer in Fighting Squadron Six in the early 1930s.

Q: You went out in April of 1944?

Adm. M.: I guess, March or April, I don't really know. I served under Ralph Ofstie as air officer for only a few months. When I reported in, he said, "I'm glad to have you aboard. When are you ready to take over as executive officer?" He explained why, which I'd rather not

McDonald #3 - 109

put in here, and I said, "Captain, I think I'm more qualified to be exec now than I am air officer, because the exec's job is more administrative and the air officer really has to handle the operation of these planes and I haven't been on a carrier now for some time."

Well, he laughed and I presume that he initiated a communication forthwith to the Navy Department, but I don't know. Anyway, I hadn't been air officer very long until I became executive officer. Then, I hadn't been executive officer very long when Captain Ofstie was selected for rear admiral and was relieved by Captain Weiber. I was selected for captain the next March, but, of course, I couldn't put on my four stripes until I got off the ship. So I stayed on as exec until we came in to Leyte around the very early part of June of 1945, incidentally, not having seen land for 79 days.

Q: Where was the Essex operating when you first joined her?

Adm. M.: When I first joined her she was in the Navy Yard in San Francisco getting either a new radar or a radar overhaul and the day I joined her or the day after I joined her we went west, and I think we launched some of the first strikes, not counting Doolittle's, against Tokyo. We said the Essex had more combat days than

many other ships that were glorified because some of those
that were glorified were glorified because they were hit.
We used to laugh and say the skipper of every ship that
gets hit get promoted when those who don't get hit don't.
The reason the Essex had so many days of combat was because, at least from the time I got there to the time I
left, we never missed one hour of operation because of
any damage. We were hit by a kamikaze but he hit a gun
turret and while he killed about 17 or 18 people, it
was the side of the ship this Jap plane struck and it
happened within seconds after our last plane was launched.
And although our next launch was scheduled forty minutes
later, we had the fire out and a piece of steel over the
hole and made the launch on time. So it was a very efficient ship.

Q: What battles were you in?

Adm. M.: I don't really know. We were at Guam, we were at
Saipan, we were at Tinian, we were at Iwo Jima, we were
at Okinawa. I talked about another one not long ago where
we were up north and the battleships took on the Japs
coming through the straits but I can't remember the name
today. I can't recall specific instances but I do believe
I can say without fear of being in error that from the
time the Essex reached the combat zone after I got aboard,

McDonald #3 - 111

which must have been in late April or early May 1944, there was no battle of any type that she wasn't involved in up until the time I left in early June of 1945.

I believe that the first air group we had when I was aboard, Air Group 9, probably shot down more Jap planes than any other air group. I might be wrong on this, but I believe that Dave McCampbell, the group commander, came out as the Navy's No. 1 ace, and certainly his action in the battle in early November 1944 in which he shot down nine Japs in ninety minutes stands as an all-time high. I also remember that we were among the first in the Saipan and Tinian escapade because two days after we had secured things I went ashore. On Saipan I obtained a little piece of wood which was out of the wing root of a Jap Betty that had been shot down and I later installed a clock out of a fighter that participated in this attack in that wing root and I have that as my one wartime souvenir. The clock came out of the fighter because when the fighter returned to the carrier, although the pilot was able to land aboard safely, the fighter was so shot up we had to push it over the side, and the mechanic who had given me the clock installed it for me in the wing root of the Betty.

Q: Since you were constantly changing fleet designations between Halsey and Spruance, the Third and Fifth fleets, was there any noticeable difference in tactics or anything of the sort when you were with these two commanders?

Adm. M.: I don't really remember because you see I was executive officer most of the time, and as executive officer I was more concerned with housekeeping details and personnel matters until the battles actually started, at which time I became part of the fighting machine instead of the housekeeping machine and took my station in the combat information center where I acted as what was known as the evaluator, making recommendations to the captain, or admiral whom we had on board, as to how many and what type of planes should be sent where. Once a particular battle was over and we secured from general quarters, I went back to the business of taking care of the ship, and, of course, in the middle of the battle I don't think you could notice a difference in tactics between two commanders. The tactics would depend upon the type of battle and not necessarily upon the commander. So where they might have done different things at different times, I'm quite sure the situations were different.

Q: You spoke about handling personnel matters. Were there any specific problems that came about with personnel because of the battles?

Adm. M.: No, not aboard the Essex. The only problem that

McDonald #3 - 113

I had was caused because of a kamikaze killing many of our stewards. Our stewards were not Filipinos. They were nearly all black.

Q: Negroes?

Adm. M.: That's right, Negroes, nearly all of them. It seems like we had some seventy odd and they were good. With the commanding officer's permission, I arranged to have a battery of antiaircraft manned by these blacks and I think that it only took some twenty-odd or maybe into the thirties to do it. This was considered quite an honor and these stewards really fought and worked hard for the privilege of manning these guns at general quarters, instead of going somewhere else. Unfortunately, when we were hit by the kamikaze, he landed right in the middle of this particular aircraft battery and most of our casualties were blacks. They were, of course, outstanding blacks and we had a little difficulty then trying to get - (I think we lost 17 or 19, I'm not sure, killed and wounded, maybe more) - replacements and we had a few problems until we could get proper replacements.

Thinking back, it seems to me like that's the only personnel problem I had.

I remember one rather funny experience. We had some stewards that had put shoe polish on the shoes of other stewards who were sleeping with their shoes on and then they would put a match to the shoe polish. Two or three of these culprits were reported to me by one of the senior Negroes who was pretty old compared to the rest of them, and when I held what you might call preliminary mast to decide whether or not they should appear before the captain, these three lads denied that they had done a thing like this, whereas the older Negro insisted that they had. But in view of their denial, I turned to the older one and said:

"Charlie, because of the lack of evidence, I just can't take them to the captain. I'm going to have to let them go." And he asked me if he could make a statement. I said, yes, and - I'll have to modify the words a little bit - but he said:

"Commander, I wants you to know and I wants them to know if any black so and so ever puts a hot foot to me he's going to get his damned throat cut."

That was all that was said and we had no more hot foots!

Our chaplains were interesting, too. Our senior chaplain wore naval aviator's wings. He'd been a naval aviator in World War I, a Presbyterian. Our junior chaplain was a Catholic. He'd been in China and he'd been repatriated on the Gripsholm.

And, while I'm talking about people, I must say that one of my greatest helpers in my role as evaluator was a fighter-director officer who sat on my left, hour after hour, in our battles with the Japs, his name was John Connolly, who later became, of course, Secretary of the Navy, three-time governor of Texas, and Secretary of the Treasury. He was a senior lieutenant, one of the most competent officers, regular or reserve, that I have ever worked with and, although he was only a lieutenant and I was the senior man in the wardroom and No. 2 on the ship, when we weren't fighting the Japs John and I would often take on all comers playing bridge. This is another friendship, like Admiral McFall and the vice president of New York Life, that I have kept over all these years and cherish very much today.

Q: You might say something about Reserve officers because you had a lot of them?

Adm. M.: Aboard the Essex it didn't make any difference, one way or the other, whether a man was regular or reserve, and, generally, speaking, the individuals performed their assigned tasks regardless. Now, granted that when you assign them a task you should give great consideration to their background and their training, and, of course, there are some jobs that Reserves can't do as well and there are some that they can even do better. Nearly all of our intelligence, the people the pilots would talk to when they returned from a flight, were reserve officers. One of our outstanding young men was assistant flight deck officer, a young Reserve named Donnelly, who's today the head of Donnelly Press in Chicago. I guess he's probably retired from that now, but he was very outstanding.

When the chips are down, you don't ask them where they went to school. I, for one, had just as fine performance from one group as from the other. You get a misfit now and then most anywhere. Of course, you probably get more misfits in the Reserve because the regulars basically are there because this was their chosen career and it's not quite as difficult for them. They're inclined that way in the first place, whereas the others aren't necessarily. You need both. I think a core of career officers is absolutely essential, but I think it's just as necessary to have an adequate Reserve.

Q: You spoke about being at sea for so many days. This in itself must have presented a fatigue problem, did it not?

Adm. M.: Yes, but, during times like these you don't run your ship on the same kind of a routine that you run in peacetime. If a man isn't working he'll sleep if he wants to whether it's one o'clock in the afternoon or not. In peacetime you have taps and you have reveille, but in times like this pretty generally the men realize that their lives might well depend upon what their shipmate does, and vice versa.

I've often said, the Navy is peculiar in a lot of ways. I think some of the things we've tried to do in recent years have failed to recognize this. We have tried to make everybody equal time after time. Over in the Pentagon efforts are often made to treat the Army and the Navy and the Air Force all the same. Well, you can't always do that. In certain areas you can, but as I've so often said - in the Navy the man next to you, working next to you, isn't just a worker, a fellow worker, he's a shipmate and, as such, you've got to be able to share his success and his failure, his joys and his sorrows, because you never know when your very life might depend upon how well he performs his duty. Furthermore, in the Navy aboard ship you not only have to learn how to work with a man but, by golly, you have to learn how to live with him. I don't know that you have to do that anywhere else unless you're going to be a monk. People in the Navy must realize and understand and appreciate this.

Q: That's the best definition of a shipmate I've ever heard.

Adm. M.: You've got to, and only by knowing these things

McDonald #3 - 118

are you able to live with him and get along. It's easier in wartime, I think.

Q: Yes. You did use various islands for R and R?

Adm. M.: Yes, we used islands for R and R.

Q: Ulithi was one?

Adm. M.: Ulithi and Mogmog. Oh, gosh, any number of them, mostly for baseball, swimming, and drinking. When I say drinking, I don't mean just going over and getting dead dog drunk, but playing ball with beer or having some whiskey, but basically, swimming and associating together off the ship.

I left in June of 1945, hoping, as I had all along, to go as commanding officer of the Naval Air Station, Fort Lauderdale, which I helped establish and where my wife and children were residing only five or six miles away. But I was informed that I was to go on the staff of Commander, Naval Air Forces, Pacific, located on Ford Island.

Q: Quite a different locale!

Adm. M.: I flew back from Leyte to Alameda about, I believe, three weeks before I had to report and then I flew from there on down to Florida for a couple of weeks with my family, then back to Honolulu, where I reported to Commander, Naval Air Forces, Pacific.

Q: Who was he?

Adm. M.: Vice Admiral George Murray. This is another thing I think is rather interesting. When I was working with Admiral McFall in the NAOTC, Admiral Murray was the boss of all naval aviation training with headquarters in Pensacola. He had a conference over there and I went over with Admiral McFall to this conference. During the course of the conference some things were proposed that I didn't think were right and I said so. On the way back to Jacksonville, Admiral McFall very nicely said to me that he didn't think that I should have talked to Admiral Murray the way I did, and I remember telling him that when I saw someone with the ball in his hand and he's about to drop it I couldn't help but get excited, and I was convinced that Admiral Murray had the ball in his hand and he was about to drop it. So I got excited and said what I said.

I often wondered whether I really had spoken in a discourteous manner to Admiral Murray, but when I was told on the phone from Washington, (and I was on the phone in Alameda) by Cassady, who was in Washington at the time trying to get me sent to Fort Lauderdale, that I was going to go back to Ford Island at Admiral Murray's specific request, I no longer worried.

I went back and became plans officer. We were planning the invasion of Japan, but that didn't get very far because very shortly the war was over.

Q: Was this the Olympic designation?

Adm. M.: I don't really remember. This was July of 1945. Then as quick as the war was over, of course, the planning then was how to unwind.

Q: May I ask one question about the planning for the invasion of Japan? How big an operation did you anticipate this to be?

Adm. M.: You know, that was thirty years ago and I haven't thought about it or read very much about it since, and I just wouldn't have the faintest idea.

Q: Some men have said that they looked upon it as a possible holocaust. I mean tremendous loss of life.

Adm. M.: Well, we were prepared for that, but, as I say, I hardly remember what we were doing then, but I didn't feel that that might happen. I felt we had enough power, the plans were of such a nature with the bombardment and the air strikes, etc. I just didn't believe these fellows could stand up under this much more. You know, I'm just talking from hindsight now.

When the war was over I was there and then, as I say, our planning was for the rollback. Then after six or eight months I also became operations officer, because the planning and operations became all one and the same. So I became both the plans and the operations officer, and then about that same time our boss changed. Admiral Murray was relieved by Vice Admiral Montgomery, who had been A. B. Cook's chief of staff when I was with Admiral Cook at sea before we went to Jacksonville.

Q: Interesting interweaving of personalities, isn't it?

Adm. M.: Speaking of personalities, this is rather interesting, I think. I guess it's all right to record it.

Admiral Cook used to scream at people. He had an ungovernable temper and he'd really scream at you. Captain Montgomery, then the chief of staff, often said to me, "If I ever get to be an admiral, I'm not going to do that. I hope I never do that." Well, from that time until Admiral Montgomery came to be AirPac as a vice admiral, not only had a few years passed but he had been through a lot of trying times in the war, and he wasn't quite as calm and serene as he once was. He hadn't been there very long when I went in to see him about something he really screamed at me. I'll never forget it. I waved my finger and I said:

"Admiral, don't you remember when you used to say about Admiral Cook that you'd never do that?"

And, gosh, he laughed and he said, "Gee, Mac, you trumped my ace!"

He was very fine to work with and I stayed on there under a more pleasant environment for the next year because my wife and two children came out to Hawaii in May of 1946 and were with me then until our departure for Washington in June of 1947.

Q: Admiral, that's an interesting aspect of your character, your ability to speak out and say the truth, as you felt the truth to be, without fear of any consequences.

Adm. M.: Well, I guess. From what I've said here, you might think that but there have been an awful lot of times when I wanted to speak out but didn't. I think I've been lucky that the timing and, I guess, the individuals with whom I was dealing all just happened to be right. I got away with it, if you want to put it that way. But I do think that if you are working for an admiral if you are on the staff of an admiral, I think it's your job to tell him whenever you think he is about to make a mistake, and I don't believe that it will be resented, provided he turns to you and he says, "I don't care what you think. This is what I'm going to do," and then you say aye, aye, Sir.

Q: Yes.

Adm. M.: I don't think to warn a superior is wrong. It's the unwillingness to swallow your own point of view later on and carry out his instructions even though they're contrary to what you've said. If you can't swallow and go ahead and do his bidding, then you'd better not warn him because he can see later that you still are unwilling or unable to give him full support. And I think there are people like that. Their nature is like that. I'm of such a nature that if you want to assume the responsibility, then I feel a little different about it, and I think that it's my responsibility to notify my boss when I think what he proposes is going to be wrong. But once I let him know my view, then I think that part of my responsibility ceases. From that point on, it is my responsibility to do what he says.

Q: I would think that a man in authority would want this facet to a problem?

Adm. M.: Well, some people - Admiral Cook, I think I have recorded this once before, told me "If I ever ask you what you think, I want to know what you think and not what you think I'd like for you to think." So, some people welcome this and some people don't.

Q: Admiral Burke told me, one time, that he sought this out in somebody on his staff. He wanted somebody who would say no.

Adm. M.: Well, I think one can pretty well determine if he's on a staff, whether or not the admiral has complete confidence in him. If you have the feeling that there's no doubt in your boss's mind but what you're working for him and not for yourself, then I think that you can feel pretty free to speak up to him. But there are some people that I don't think I could have worked for very well. Fortunately, I never had to, but if I had I think I'd have kept my mouth absolutely shut unless they asked me. Had I been working for them and got to know them better, I might have changed my mind. Of course, I seem to have gotten along well with what a lot of people that others think are sundowners. I might have recorded this before, but somebody once said, "You do because you're as big a sundowner as they are."

Q: Immediately after the war you, like all the rest, were faced with the problem of demobilization of the fleet units, were you not?

Adm. M.: Yes, and it was a very interesting time, bringing the things back through Pearl, bringing our carriers and planes, and, of course, the Reserves were being demobilized rather rapidly. And, incidentally, the man who had helped me in the Naval Air Operational Training Command, this young junior grade lieutenant who later became a vice president of New York Life -

Q: You never did give me his name.

Adm. M.: His name is Baker - Richard D. Baker, Jr. He lives at 1 Armour Road, Princeton, New Jersey. He tried to get out of Jacksonville and get to the war zone but my successor wouldn't let him leave. Just before the war ended, when I came from the Essex down to Hollywood, Florida, to visit my family, on the way back to Pearl Harbor I stopped in Jacksonville and made arrangements to have young Baker sent out to Pearl Harbor to help me out there, but before he got out there the war ended. He got to San Francisco and they wouldn't send any Reserves farther west than San Francisco, but we communicated with each other and I communicated with somebody else and Baker came out. Very fortunately, he was able to stay for almost a year and was extremely valuable during the most critical part of this demobilization.

I don't really remember any particularly interesting things that happened. I couldn't say that the work was routine, but certainly there were no problems that we couldn't take care of.

Q: Were there any guidelines that came from Washington on demobilization?

Adm. M.: I presume, but I just wouldn't remember.

Q: Admiral Radford had worked on that problem.

Adm. M.: Yes. However, there was nothing, shall we say, that was so helpful or that was resented to the point that I remember them today. It seems to me that things went quite smoothly.

Then, in May of 1947 I was going to be ordered, I thought, to be the commanding officer of the Naval Air

McDonald #3 - 127

Facility at Annapolis, which sounded very good. At that time the Navy was trying very hard to get an airfield at Annapolis and before I got orders it became quite obvious that they were not going to obtain an airfield.

Q: The citizens prevailed?

Adm. M.: I don't know whether it was the citizens, or money, or what. Anyway, they weren't going to get an airfield and under those circumstances the commanding officer would be a commander and not a captain. The new plan then was for me to relieve Captain George Anderson in Strategic Plans. But before I did it was decided that Admiral Anderson (whom I'd known for a long time) would be retained in his present assignment because of the terminal illness of his wife and I was ordered to aviation military Requirements, working for both DCNO Air and the Bureau of Aeronautics.

Q: What did Requirements, aviation military requirements, entail?

Adm. M.: Drawing up the specifications for the airplanes that we felt the Navy should have and, at that time, drawing up the specifications for an aircraft carrier that would be large enough to handle airplanes that would have no difficulty in carrying the atomic bomb. Basically, plans for the *Forrestal*; a carrier that was first called the *United States*, and which was later killed by the Secretary of Defense, one Louis Johnson with, I'm sure, the consent of many above him.

Those were the things that we were working on primarily and one of the little problems, of course, was trying to find out what airplanes we could use from a cost-effective point of view and, concurrently, keep these aircraft companies, some of them, at least, alive. After all, they'd been building airplanes by the thousands. The war was over and the needs relatively minor by comparison, but you couldn't let every aircraft company in the United States go under. Yet you couldn't just come out and subsidize them with something that you couldn't use. So, trying to figure out something that you could use, that would enable the taxpayer to get his money's worth, while at the same time keeping certain companies alive. This was quite a problem.

Q: Like a juggler, balancing all these things and working under Louis Johnson.

Adm. M.: Well, I didn't even know him then. I was at the Navy Department and I didn't know who the Secretary of Defense was -- no, Forrestal was Secretary of Defense then.

You see this was 1947. Mr. Sullivan was Secretary of the Navy. On one occasion, I remember, we were to buy a few planes of a particular type, not very many, and I said to my superior that I wouldn't agree to such a purchase because these planes were no good. That while I realized it was important to keep the producer of this plane alive, that such was a policy matter and that I wasn't in the policy making business. My superior then talked to me about twenty minutes or more and said:

"Don't you understand that under these conditions, you too are a policy-maker," and I said, "Give me the pen. I'll agree." We ordered six of them. It was essential, at the time.

After I'd been in this job not quite a year, I started another very interesting and somewhat different career.

Q: A question or two, if I may, about that particular job?

Adm. M.: Yes.

Q: How did the Congress view the situation in terms of appropriating money for it?

Adm. M.: I can't answer that because it wasn't my job to go before the Congress, and I literally don't know. Maybe

McDonald #3 - 130

unfortunatlely, but most of my life I haven't concerned myself very much with things that weren't any of my business. My job was to try to figure out, as I said, what our needs were.

Q: When you were working in this area, were you working with a firm policy on the part of the Navy as to the number of ships, carriers, they intended to retain and to keep in operation? Was this a fixed policy or was it in a state of flux?

Adm. M.: Well, no, it was a fixed policy, but if I remember correctly my particular job didn't get too involved in that. To sort of explain my job; I know we needed fighter planes. I didn't know how many fighters, that was somebody else's job. My job was to figure out what kind of fighter planes we should have, what they should be capable of doing? What can technology give us? Somebody else was figuring out how many carriers and, consequently, how many fighters we should have and whether or not they could get the money from Congress to buy that number of fighters. Later I was somewhat involved in that, but I was low man on that particular totem pole. Although I was a captain I had several younger and very active pilots working for me who were trying to come up with what kind of fighters and other types we should have and their characteristics.

McDonald #3 - 131

Q: You had been operational in the Pacific in combat, so you had that knowledge, but was there available also the input from others, a great number, on what was needed?

Adm. M.: Yes. You see, I had been in combat but I had not been flying in combat but I had people under me who had been. For instance, let's take the fighter desk, so called. That man had been flying fighters in combat. And here is the dive-bomber desk. Here is the torpedo desk. Now, these desk officers were pilots who had recently been in combat in these types of planes. I was the fellow who was sort of a devil's advocate; who would ask them all kinds of questions and try to bring out the advantages and disadvantages and try to get agreement on the optimum. Then, of course, we would go on up to the Chief of the Bureau of Aeronautics for the final decision.

Then the DCNO side. They were the people who would figure out numbers and be concerned with the budgetary aspects of it.

Q: I know that immediately following World War II there was an effort to make a composite study and report of the experiences gained. Was this available to you?

Adm. M.: I presume. I don't recall.

Q: Hank Miller was involved in that.

Adm. M.: I really don't recall. I didn't get involved in it, I know.

Q: How cognizant were you of the status of the Russian situation?

Adm. M.: None.

Q: Was that not something of consideration to you? You had to consider a possible enemy.

Adm. M.: I think, for the record, we must realize that we're talking about something that happened thirty years ago and that I really haven't thought about since then! I'm hesitant because I don't want to record misinformation. I think I would only remember if they had a particular impact, good or bad, and at that time the Russians had been a recent ally.

Q: That was a very strategic spot you were in.

Adm. M.: Very interesting.

Q: And you said there was another phase of your job, which you started to talk about.

Adm. M.: I said after about a year I started on a different sort of job. One day I was invited up, or directed to go up, to the office of the Assistant Secretary of the Navy for Air –

Q: Who was that?

Adm. M.: John Nicholas Brown. And to explain to Mr. Brown and describe to him somewhat in detail aircraft carrier operations, how they were conducted, et cetera.

Well, to make a long story short, all I was sent up there to do was to let Mr. Brown look me over because very shortly I was ordered as his aide.

Q: He was fairly knowledgeable anyway, was he not?

Adm. M.: I presume so, although Mr. Brown hadn't been there too long. But he was a very interesting man.

I found Mr. Brown to be one of the most gentlemanly gentlemen that I have ever been with. He was a very wealthy man. I think very shy, extremely conscientious, and he loved sailing. At that time, the Assistant Secretary of the Navy for Air was the civilian secretary who concerned himself with personnel matters and he always thought that there was some way he could "salvage" a bad boy. I didn't always agree with him. And once when he said that he often wished that he had gone to the Naval Academy and became a naval officer, my comment was (I used to call him "Boss"):

"Well, Boss, I'm not sure you would have made too good a naval officer." When he asked why, I said:

"Because maybe you're just a little too much of a gentleman."

He had quite a laugh about that!

I accompanied Mr. Brown to many places. His great failing in that job, as he himself said, was his distaste for politics. His relations with Capitol Hill were minimal. He just didn't like that back scratching. I'm not telling tales out of school because when he was relieved by Dan Kimball in about March of 1949, this is what he told Dan. He said that if he'd fallen down, he felt it was there but it just wasn't in his blood.

I enjoyed being with Mr. Brown. I visited a lot of

places with him. We visited a lot of naval establishments. The going was relatively easy in those days. Of course, we in the Navy were a little bit subdued because unification had taken place, most of us not liking it at all. But the decision having been made, we were, of course, going along with it. So life during those months was relatively easy and quite pleasant. Then Mr. Brown made it known, at least to me, prior to the election that fall that he was going to leave early the next year. He didn't make this decision because he, like many others, thought Mr. Truman might not win. That didn't enter into it at all. Of course, Mr. Truman did win and Mr. Brown left.

Once again, here's a man (Mr. Brown) that I have continued to see over the years. He and his wife called us up when they were on a chartered boat in Jacksonville, not long ago and, odd though it might seem, when I arrived at my daughter's here in Washington yesterday, I had a letter from him. He's a wonderful man. His younger boy is head, I think, of the art gallery here in Washington. His older boy went to Harvard for three years, was on the dean's list each year, then left Harvard and came to the Naval Academy. He had an outstanding record and today is a captain, the skipper of - I think it's a missile frigate.

Q: So what the father had hoped for himself his son has achieved!

Adm. M.: Yes.

Q: How did Mr. Brown deal with Capitol Hill, if he wanted nothing to do with the political side of the job?

Adm. M.: He didn't deal with them very much.

Q: Did you, as his aide, have to?

Adm. M.: No. Mr. Sullivan, I think, did most of that when he was the Secretary.

Q: And he was politically minded?

Adm. M.: Yes. I don't mean to infer that Mr. Brown, if he had been asked to do something or given a particular thing to do that involved going up that he, would not have gone. He just didn't like back-scratching, if you want to put it that way. But I think the record will show that Mr. Brown was a very fine Assistant Secretary of the Navy for Air. People were very fond of him and he was an extremely competent man.

Q: Did you stay on with Kimball when he came?

Adm. M.: Yes. After the new administration came in, in

1949, Mr. Brown left and was replaced by Mr. Kimball. This was an entirely different type of man. Whereas Mr. Brown was what I presume one might say highly-intellectual, a man of great wealth, extremely gentlemanly, not interested in politics, Mr. Kimball was a sort of hell-for leather businessman who finished high school and then took the flying course with the Army Air Corps in the same class with Jimmy Doolittle. Then when he was demobilized (World War I) he started on the West Coast with General Tire and Rubber Company and pretty generally stayed with them. His formal education was rather brief, but he was extremely long in practical experience. Although I don't mean to infer that Mr. Kimball wasn't a gentleman, he was the rough and ready type and enjoyed very much what we call the political aspects of the job. He enjoyed people, being with people, having a drink, back-slapping, talking, telling jokes. He was a hail fellow well met.

Both of these gentlemen were wonderful and yet so different. I got much closer to Mr. Kimball because Mrs. Kimball stayed in California most of the time. Consequently, both my wife and I were with Mr. Kimball much of the time after working hours if he had any entertaining to do. I was very fortunate, I think, in the beginning. I had convinced Mr. Kimball that my job was to look after him, and I did. He hadn't been assistant Secretary for Air very long when he and I went to California, flew out there.

While there, we got a telephone call notifying us that Louis Johnson had canceled the carrier United States, Secretary of the Navy Sullivan and Under Secretary Kenny had turned in their suits. I was told on the phone by Mr. Sullivan "you and Danny Boy" as he called Mr. Kimball "get in that airplane and come right on back." So Mr. Kimball and I got in a DC-3 and came back without stopping, except for gas.

We hadn't been back very long, when Mr. Kimball became Under Secretary. That involved a move from the Navy Department to the Pentagon. He asked me if I wanted to go over there and my answer was "Yes, Sir, if you'll let me run that office the way I want to run it." His answer was, "You run it here the way you want to. I don't know why you won't over there."

I said, "I wanted to ask you that, Boss, because the way that office is being run over there now isn't my way.

Q: What changes did you intend?

Adm. M.: The main change was the buffer between the Under Secretary and those who wanted to see him. The way it was running then - the person between the visitor and the Under Secretary was a female stenographer. The way it was over in the Navy Department in our office and the way it was over in the Pentagon after I got there, was that no one, absolutely no one, ever went in the Under Secretary's office without coming at least in sight of me, unless they went through the Secretary of the Navy's office and into Mr. Kimball's office through the back door.

I don't mean by that that they had to come by me and tell me what they were doing or what they wanted to do, and why. He might even have called for them. But there was a door they had to go right by where I could see them and often I would go in and ask him if anything transpired between him and the person he saw that I ought to know about, because I think in the job I had it is essential that you know what your boss is involved in. That's the way we operated. I often said, when I was Chief of Naval Operations, that I came nearer running the Navy when I was aide to Dan Kimball and he was Under Secretary than I did when I was CNO. Of course, one reason is that when I was CNO I often felt that I had no more authority than a Lieutenant Commander and sometimes said so to Paul Nitze, the Secretary of the Navy.

Q: Also you'd lost actual command of the fleets, too, by that time?

Adm. M.: Well, that wasn't what it was. When I was CNO we had too many whizz kids that people were listening to.

Mr. Kimball took me with him almost everywhere he went. He introduced me to more people in the civilian world than I knew existed. Everybody. I spoke earlier about how nice he was to me and my wife. He was also devoted to our children. Someone once said, "He is such a diamond in the rough. What do you like in a fellow like that?" This was years later. I replied:

"Well, when my daughter was married and Kimball was no longer connected with the Navy, he flew from Los Angeles to Cincinnati and rented a car and drove forty miles out in the country to be with my daugher at her wedding. That's typical of why I like him."

He and Mr. Sullivan were very close. I think Mr. Kimball did the Navy an awful lot of good. I did not think they were going to make him Secretary. I felt they were sort of using him as a fall guy there for a while and I told him so, but I was wrong. They did make him Secretary.

Q: How effective was Sullivan as Secretary?

Adm. M.: I can't answer that because I was working with Mr. Brown then. We didn't have too much to do with him and I think I would have known more about him if he'd stayed on with Kimball there as Under Secretary. From reports, I guess very good, but I don't know.

Q: What kind of relationship did you have with the White House? Bob Dennison was over there.

Adm. M.: Dan Kimball had real good relations with Bob. I didn't have much to do with him. Nearly every morning when Kimball would come to work one of the first things I would do after we settled down a little bit, I'd ask, "Have you got any plans for lunch?" and if he didn't, I would recommend who I thought he should invite for the purpose of discussing various and sundry specific things. He often had naval officers such as the CNO, Chief of BuPers, et cetera.

Q: He had a mess, had he?

Adm. M.: Yes. Often people would tell me that they wanted to talk to him about thus and so and I would say, "Well, gee, maybe you'd come in for lunch?" If he didn't have any plans, why, he's say, "Have you got any ideas?" Sometimes I'd say no and we'd eat together. I always ate with him, and I always ate with Mr. Brown.

But often - and you spoke of relations with the White House - when he had no plans and I had no plans up my sleeve, I'd say, "Why don't I get the admirals?"

The admirals I was referring to were Louis Strauss and Sidney Sauers. They'd both been rear admirals in the Supply

Corps during the war. I don't know whether Louis Strauss was on the AEC then or whether he was chairman of the AEC. He later became that, anyway. Sidney Sauers, however, was Secretary of the National Security Council, if I remember correctly. He was over in the White House and he and Mr. Truman, you know, were both from the St. Louis area. And very close friends.

So we'd get Sidney Sauers and Louis Strauss over for lunch, the four of us. I'd hesitate to say how many times the four of us had lunch together. Of course, I'd just sit there with my mouth open, listening to some of the things they talked about. One time we were working on some China problems and Admiral Strauss began to talk about the Chinese national railways. After a while, I said:

"Good gracious, you know almost where every spike is driven."

"Well," he said, "I ought to, Dave, I felt I almost owned them at one time."

Kimball changed my life in one way. My name, of course, is David Lamar McDonald and when I was a boy I was always called Lamar, never by any other name until I went to the Naval Academy. Then I became Mac and no one ever called me anything but Mac, except those in my home town when I would go back and my relatives who called me Lamar.

Not long after we arrived at the Pentagon and Mr. Kimball was Under Secretary, he was standing at the door of my little cubbyhole while I was talking on the telephone and as I put the phone down, he said to me:

"You know, there's nothing sillier than to hear you pick up the phone and say, 'This is Mac McDonald.' All McDonalds are Mac. You have a nice first name. Do you mind if I call you David?"

I said, "You know, Mr. Secretary, you can call me anything you want to."

Dan began to call me Dave, introduced me to everybody as Dave, and now nobody that I haven't known prior to 1949 calls me anything but Dave, and the majority of those who used to call me Mac call me Dave. I think there were some who said, "Well, after he got high rank he thought he'd be fancy and didn't like the Mac, so he changed it to Dave." But that wasn't the way it happened at all. Dan Kimball started that and that's the name, I would say, that of all the people in the world today who know me at least nine out of ten of them know me as Dave.

It was a wonderful experience with Dan because he very rarely failed to let me do what I recommended. This was a little bit difficult at times because, once we reached the point where I was pretty sure I could do whatever I wanted to, I had to be real careful about what recommendations I made, much more so than normal. If you've got a boss who just listens and says sometimes yes and no sometimes you might try something out on him, but if you find yourself in a position where the odds are almost 100 percent that he's going to do as you suggest, you then find yourself assuming the responsibility that he has. It's a different ball game.

Dan used the *Sequoia* a lot, the boat, and it would nearly always be my decision as to whether or not the party planned should be a stag party with me not present, a stag party with me present, or a mixed party with me and my wife present. I'd just go in and say this is what I think you ought to do. That didn't necessarily mean that I selected his guest list all the time. He'd tell me who he wanted to have and what he had in mind, if he had anything in particular. He was a gregarious fellow. He liked to be with people. He didn't always invite people to come to the *Sequoia* for the purpose of trying to sell them a bill of goods. He just liked to be with them. That's the kind of a fellow he was. Sometimes he did have a specific purpose in mind. I would sometimes say to him, "what do you have in mind? Any particular reason for this?" And sometimes he would tell me and, as a result, I would say, "I think I'd better be there and listen in." And sometimes I'd say, "Oh, no, I think I'll go home." Sometimes, I'd say, "Maybe we ought to have the wives. I'll bring Tommie," and he'd always agree.

Q: But his wife still was not here as a hostess for him?

Adm. M.: She came very seldom and at times when she was in Washington the two of them would come to our house and we'd play four-handed gin rummy. But she didn't like Washington. Ultimately, they were divorced.

Q: He married Doris Fleeson, didn't he?

Adm. M.: He married Doris, and this was real interesting for various reasons. I think Doris knew that I didn't exactly approve of his new marriage and Doris was a little rude to me and my wife a couple of times when the four of us were together over in Paris, when I was on duty in Paris.

Later, in Washington, one evening Doris was so nice to us butter couldn't melt in her mouth, and I made a comment about some of our previous evenings together. I said, "You're so nice now - what in the world turned you around?" She looked at me and my wife and she said:

"You know, I finally came to the conclusion that if there's anybody in the world that loves Dan any more than I do, it's you two."

From then on we were real friends. My wife and I were in the mountains of North Carolina when Dan died.

Doris called me on the phone. She was in a wheelchair then, you know. She asked if I could get to the funeral. Then within twenty-four hours she, too, was dead.

Q: Yes, I know.

Adm. M.: My wife and I went to the double funeral. Kimball was a great guy.

Q: Speaking of his going on the Sequoia, the President was very fond of the Williamsburg. Did you get invited over there, to the Williamsburg?

Adm. M.: Yes and no. We get back to Kimball again. Along in the late fall of 1949, x-rays showed a growth on the diaphragm behind my heart. They didn't know whether it was malignant or not, nor how long it may have been there. Anyway, they left the operation up to me and I said, "Let's take it out."

So I went out to Bethesda in January of 1950 and they took this thing out, after a lot of tests and what not beforehand. It wasn't simple. They had to take a rib out to go in and take this growth off the diaphragm, but when I came out of that operating room Dan Kimball was there and he came out there to see me every morning before he went to work. About two weeks later, I guess, I became ambulatory but it was too cold to get outside. Dan came out and he said:

"Well, Tommie and I have an agreement." (Tommie being my wife.

"What?"

"Mr. Truman, the President is down at Key West. His yacht's down there. They send a mail plane down nearly every day. I've made arrangements for you to ride down in the morning in the President's plane and they will put you in the Navy hospital down there, where it's warm."

And that's what happened.

And on several occasions during the month I was there I went down to the Williamsburg and had lunch and saw President Truman. I stayed there a month. When I came back to Washington, I had my strength back, I had my weight back, and I was brown as a berry.

Q: All fixed up!

Adm. M.: Yes. An odd thing, though. My throat felt very very dry and I said there was something wrong, even though I felt fine. Then when the throat specialist examined me he said I had an ulcer on my vocal cord. It had been caused by all these tubes. I said, "What do you do?"
And he said:

"We'll have to cut it out."

I said, "Gee, I'd just as soon jump out of the window

as go back to that hospital."

So I went over to see another throat specialist at the dispensary in the old Navy Department. He said, "I might fix that thing up without cutting it if you'll do what I say."

I said, "What's that Cecil?" I'd known him for years. He said, "Don't smoke, don't drink, don't utter a word and come to see me twice a day."

I said, "You've got a patient."

I went back to the Pentagon and I told Dan. I said I thought I was all set but this is what's happened. I said, "I can come over here but I can't talk."

Dan said, "Good God, come on whether you talk or not."

I had a secretary who'd been with me over in the old Navy Department and who came over to the Pentagon with me. She knew my thinking, so I went to work with her very valuable assistance. I wrote notes and talked sign language. But after a week Cecil Riggs told me I could whisper, after two weeks I could talk quietly. With this gal's help we did all right. In later years when Tom Gates was Under Secretary, she became his secretary and when he became Secretary she went with him, when he was Secretary of Defense she went with him. She went with McNamara and she's still with McNamara today!

Q: With the International Bank?

Adm. M.: Yes.

But this was typical of Kimball. Gosh, I mean he didn't have to arrange to have me flown down to Key West and then let the President know that his aide (me) was down there. That's the sort of fellow he was. A diamond in the rough but wonderful.

We went down to Norfolk one time where he was to talk to a group of civilians who were being indoctrinated as to what the Navy did. They had a dinner and Dan made a talk. I'd written him a speech and he'd had about a drink too many because he got up and said I'd written this speech for him but "you know what I'm going to do with it," and he put it in his chair and started talking. The next day I told him that I thought he had made a perfect fool of himself, and I meant it.

He was scheduled three weeks later to make a talk at Madison Square Garden and he was to follow Trygve Lie of the United Nations. Dan felt badly about what he'd done in Norfolk. He knew he'd talked after a lot of martinis and wasn't very impressive. He said to me: "I've got to go to the Garden and make that speech. Can't do up there the way I did in Norfolk.

I said, "No, you can't."

"Have you got any suggestions?"

I said, "I sure have. I've got the speech all ready.

Boss, I took a course in public speaking over at George Washington at night. I'd like to bring a Professor Stevens over here to your office and have you get up there and give this speech and let him give you some instruction."

He agreed. Stevens came over twice. I guess Dan gave the speech to me three or four times. We went up to New York, we went to the Garden, he made his talk, we got in the car and on the way back to the hotel he said, "How did I do?" I didn't say anything for a moment and then he said,"I was afraid so." Then I said:

"Look, I was proud to be sitting there today as your aide." He was absolutely fantastic and he said, "You know, I'm going to keep doing it," but he didn't.

He was a very impressive looking fellow, you know. I told him when I left - I left in July or August of 1951 and went over to the National War College. I said:

"You know, the only place you let me down, you started with that speech instructor and you were doing so well, but you didn't keep it up. You should have kept it up."

Well, he said he didn't have time, and that's right. It took a lot of time.

Stevens had been my professor at George Washington. Then when I went to the National War College where it was voluntary and you had to pay for it yourself, I took it again. Professor Stevens was also my prof there.

McDonald #3 - 151

Q: It's a useful asset, isn't it? The ability to speak in public?

Adm. M.: Oh, yes. Uniformed people speak a lot now, but when I was coming along we didn't. In 1947, before I went with Mr. Brown, someone came by along in August or September and said:

"If you want to take a course in public speaking at night over at George Washington, the Navy will pay for it." It wasn't really at night. It seems to me it was about 5:30 or 5:45 or something like that. I took it.

Q: Late afternoon.

Adm. M.: Yes. But to get back to Mr. Kimball, I enjoyed working with him very, very much. It was almost like the Naval Air Operational Training Command. There were times when I felt that I was doing a lot of good. He had to take certain types of advice from somebody. You can't spend your life in the business world and be capable of facing every Navy problem immediately and I felt that I was helpful because he let me be helpful.

Q: That's the purpose of having a military aide, I guess?

Adm. M.: Well, no, not exactly. I used to cross my fingers every now and then when I'd be giving advice that perhaps he should be getting from the CNO or the Chief of BuPers or someone like that. Most of the time I think I cut them in on it. One particular case was with the Chief of BuPers, Mr. Kimball didn't approve of a recommendation and the Chief seemed to have a hard time getting to see Mr. Kimball so I talked to him. It was Johnny Roper and I said, "Well, if you can convince me you won't have to talk to Mr. Kimball. I'll be perfectly frank about this thing. I don't necessarily disagree with you but I don't know enough about this to convince him, to get him to consent. He wants to know more than I am able to tell him. Consequently, he won't sign this. But, hell, you don't have to see him. If you can sell it to me. Now, if you can't sell it to me, I'm not going to go in there and try to sell your thought if I don't agree with you. You can go in later." He convinced me and it was signed by Mr. Kimball that day.

Usually, it worked like that. I didn't try to undercut my seniors. I had to be careful about that. I had to live with them a lot of years!

Q: For quite a long time, yes!

Adm. M.: There has never been any doubt in my mind but what a lot of the contacts that I made there with senior people that I'd never known before and maybe some civilians were primarily responsible for me continuing to climb the promotional ladder. There's no question about it.

McDonald #3 - 153

Q: Certainly being in a job like that and being skipper of the Coral Sea. All of these were advantageous places.

Adm. M.: Yes. I left Mr. Kimball in the Pentagon with great regret and went over to the National War College.

Q: Was this something you wanted to do?

Adm. M.: I guess. I was probably unique in that at that time I'd been in the Navy, man and boy, for quite a few years and I'd never been to any school after I left the Naval Academy.

Q: You hadn't been to PG school?

Adm. M.: No. As you know, for the last two days I've been meeting with the board of consultants over here at the National War College and a young man who's the educational boss over in the Pentagon now asked me what schools I had been to - we were talking about whether they should to to the Naval War College and then the National or whether they should just go to one or the other - he asked me what schools I'd been to and I told him I hadn't been to any except the National War College. He really couldn't believe it. Then I did say, "Well, I took a course in flight training which

McDonald #3 - 154

lasted as long if not longer than an academic year. I flew a half a day and went to ground school a half a day, which was really, in effect, aeronautical engineering. I didn't want to go to school. I was offered postgraduate school, not directly but asked if I wanted it, and I said no. And when asked why not? I was wrong probably, but I said:

"Why should I go to school to study strategy and tactics when I can get out on a ship or else in an airplane squadron and practice the real McCoy? "Now," I said, "I would like to take either a course in law or go to Harvard Business School." But I said, "As far as going to a Navy school is concerned, I don't want to." And I didn't.

Now, when it came time for me to go to the National War College we'd reached the point where we started "going to school" crazy. Perhaps the "Unification" after World War II caused the Navy to begin to emphasize schools more. You see, prior to World War II not many people in the Navy went to school, not like they do now, because we had many ships. The Navy operates in peacetime just like they do in wartime, except you don't shoot at somebody. It takes the same number of people to run the ships in peacetime, practically speaking, as in wartime. You've got to have the same bases to support them. So the only people available for school are the surpluses. If you put a lot of people in school you'd have to increase the size of the Navy.

The Army, on the other hand, and they wouldn't like to

McDonald #3 - 154A

hear me say this, but back in those days they were not mechanized and in peacetime about all they did was cut the grass and put a little fertilizer on it. Nothing much else to do, so they went to school, which was good. But Navy schools were aboard ship. They didn't have that.

Along came unification and we all had to do the same

thing. So the Navy started more and more schools. Now, Dr. Carr, or Tom Carr, from the Pentagon told me yesterday that the Navy is still having a little harder time than the other services getting people to fill these school billets. I said to him:

"Tom, it's very simple. The secretary of Defense, the Congress, and others determine how many ships and planes the Navy will have and they determine what bases they're going to have. Those must be manned. Now, if they only have ten men left over, that's all they can send to school. And if they want to send 100 to school, all they've got to do is increase the size of the Navy by ninety more."

The Air Force is faced with a somewhat similar situation and, since the Army has become more mechanized, they are a little more like the Navy in that respect than they used to be. But in my younger days I felt that unless one wanted to be a civil engineer or an engineering duty only officer or an aeronautical engineering duty only officer or a Supply Corps officer, why go to PG school, right out of the Naval Academy? A lot of people today who don't go to the Naval Academy go to PG school for the line course to learn some of the things that we spent a lot of time on at the Naval Academy.

But, you see, golly, back in my early days 97 or 98 out of every 100 officers were out of the Naval Academy. I don't think I did wrong. But if I could put myself in a position of being graduated tomorrow instead of in 1928 I might do it differently.

McDonald #3 - 156

But to get back, you asked if I volunteered to go there. I felt that maybe I was - no, I think I asked for it.

Q: It was in its early stage then.

Adm. M.: Yes. I believe that I had come to the conclusion by that time that not only for promotional reasons but for my own broadening that I should go to a college, and I had a great desire really to go to the National War College. I felt I'd be more on my own there than anywhere else and I could do some of those things that I like to do without having to punch a bell and conform to a rather strict curriculum.

Q: Tell me about the War College set up when you went there in 1950.

Adm. M.: Of course, it was a fairly new school.

Q: Who was head of it? General Bull?

Adm. M.: That's right. General Bull was the head of it.

Q: Was George Dyer there?

Adm. M.: George Dyer was the deputy. I don't remember

McDonald #3 - 157

very many others by name. There was an English professor from somewhere up around the vicinity of Harvard or Yale whose face I can see but I don't recall his name.

I felt that at that time in our group (the Navy) we had quite a few who were a little older not only than I was but perhaps the average age was older than the average age of those in the Air Force and the Army.

Q: What were they, captain rank?

Adm. M.: Yes, we were all captains. I had been a captain for five years and was at that time 44 years old, and we had a few people in there three or four years older than I was, in the Navy. I think those in the other services were a little bit younger.

I enjoyed it very much.

Q: Was the State Department represented?

Adm. M.: Yes.

Q: Any of the other agencies?

Adm. M.: The State Department was represented, CIA was represented, and, for the first time in the history of that school, one civilian was there from the Department of of Defense. I've often wondered why, but he was, and he was quite young.

The course, if you want to put it that way, was basically domestic, the first part. I know my little paper, so called, was on the Point Four Program. I remember that. Then, in the spring, it was more strategic and I well remember that because the paper I wrote was how to fight a war with Communist China. I turned in my paper one afternoon and the next morning the headlines said that MacArthur had been fired by the President. So it was very interesting for me to read later on what General MacArthur said before the Congress. I could see how the State Department wanted to fight the war and how General MacArthur felt it should be fought and how I thought it should be fought! And I must say that I came nearer agreeing with him.

I indulged in one favorite pastime while at the College. At noon we would take some exercise and then a bite of lunch, and then have some free time. After a couple or three weeks someone asked me what I was researching. I said, "What do you mean?" And he said:

"Well, just as quick as you finish lunch you head straight for that library." We had about half an hour, "and I just wondered."

I said, "I'm doing something that I've always wanted to do."

"What's that?"

"I go back there and I pick up The Wall Street Journal,

I sit down in a chair, and I put my feet up on the desk and I read. You might laugh at it, but you know and I know we fellows in the military are supposed to save lives instead of dollars but I sort of think we ought to save dollars, too."

I learn a lot about the economy of this country and I think that has a lot to do with what is happening, what's going to happen here, and it might have something to do with what we have to do, and I enjoy it.

Q: What was his reaction?

Adm. M.: He just laughed. He couldn't believe it. But, by golly, that's just what I did and I enjoyed it.

As you know, I've been on the board of consultants of the National War College for the last three years now - the first year I was unable to get up here, but I have for the last two years - I have said there and I still believe that the most important thing I gained at the National War College was learning why my contemporaries in the other services plus the State Department, CIA, et cetera, thought the way they did. The contacts I made, the friendships I made, were far more important than anything else to me and, as far as I'm concerned, that would have been worth the year.

Q: Most of those men were on the way up, weren't they?

Adm. M.: On the way up. There's been some criticism of the National War College. Some say they don't work hard enough, it's sort of a sabbatical. My answer is no, it's not, but I wish it was. Why shouldn't it be? Why shouldn't a man - for instance my case, coming out of the Naval Academy in 1928, plug, plug, plug day after day, year after year, and then when you reach the rank of captain, as I had then, I'd been over in the Pentagon working very long hours, not necessarily productive all the time, but being so busy with routine matters that you really couldn't think, what's wrong with taking a year off, putting your feet up on the desk and thinking?

I realize that in a case like that there would be some who might take advantage of it, but basically those who go to that school have a pretty good background. They're selected for it. And even so, there'll still be maybe one or two, but that's a pretty small percentage. I'd love to see it somewhat of a sabbatical, but it's getting more and more like a routine school. Maybe that's necessary. They have to get money from the Congress and there are a lot of people who, anytime you ask for something want to put it, even if it isn't finite, on the scales and have it balance with something that is, and if you're talking about money and a sabbatical you can't do it.

I had the great good fortune later on of having ambassadors that I had known there in areas where I operated. I later went over to Paris with General Norstad and there I found some of my friends in the Army and the Air Force that I'd known. It's a great feeling. We talk about unification in the military - there never will be complete unification nor should there be, but it's a wonderful thing if you're in the Navy to sit back and say, "Look, I know so and so in the Army and the Air Force and I don't care what's happening, I can get the straight information from them." Not that other people will lie to you but, you know, there are some things that they're unwilling to tell you. To me, the National War College is the one place where unification works. I don't believe, if you go down there today, you'll find a single one of those people, at least while they're there, who acts in a parochial manner, less parochial, I think, than any other place. I might be wrong but that's my view.

When I went there I had the view of it as a sabbatical, if you want to put it that way. There were certain things I wanted to do, like reading The Wall Street Journal. Well, we're not going to pay you your salary and spend a lot of money to send you to school to read that, somebody might say. But, you know, maybe that helped me in later years. I even took another course in public speaking. I think that helped too.

McDonald #3 - 162

Q: Was that at the College?

Adm. M.: Yes. That was the second time I took it.

Q: One man told me he got great benefit from the fact that he lived out somewhere and was part of a car pool?

Adm. M.: Well, this is part of getting to know others. Yes, I was in a car pool with two Army officers and an Air Force officer. We lived on Lee Highway - out towards Falls Church, so it was about a 30-minute ride, and we got to know each other quite well and there was a reasonable amount of social association, not too much, just enough. I enjoyed it very much. However, I would not have wanted to stay and be an instructor. At the end of a year, I'd had it.

Q: This was a possibility, was it?

Adm. M.: I guess for some people. I don't know that it would have been for me. Even today I don't know whether or not they're asked whether they want to be instructors. Of course, there are some jobs in the military about which I don't think you ought to be dictated to all the time. I think it was wrong for me to be appointed CNO without discussing it with me first. I didn't want it, and I think it was wrong. And I believe a student at the Na-

McDonald #3 - 163

tional War College, for instance, who is being considered to be retained as an instructor should be consulted. I don't necessarily mean that if he doesn't want it you're going to comply with his wishes, but he should be consulted. If he doesn't want it and you think he should have it, you can explain to him why and even if you haven't changed his mind he will be more satisfied than if he'd just been told he's being so ordered come hell or high water. We have to do that enough in the military, so I think we shouldn't do it in those cases where it isn't really required.

Q: In your times at the War College they didn't have the jaunts in the spring, did they, that they now have, the junkets?

Adm. M.: Yes, they did but I had the same misfortune there that I had at the Naval Academy. I believe I said earlier that I went to the Naval Academy because I thought that I could go to Europe in the summers as a midshipman but I never got there. One of the nice things about the National War College was that they took trips abroad and, lo and behold, this was the one year they didn't do that because of the Korean crisis.

Q: Oh, I see!

Adm. M.: So we made trips within the United States. Since then and within the last two days we've had some discussions down at the National War College about these trips. I don't know whether they'll continue these or not. Some views have been expressed along this line: on these trips you spend a lot of time trying to find out what they're thinking in other countries but do you spend any time trying to find out what the people in this country are thinking? If you get south and west of the Washington, New York, Boston axis, you'll find the thinking is a hell of a lot different. Why not make trips into these areas?

In my case, where did we go in the United States? Nowhere except to military installations. I think they should perhaps go out and meet with community leaders let's say in Houston, have the editors of the papers and the owner of the TV station and the president of the junior college, and the bishop of some church? Why not go and stay a couple of days and have conversation and a little banter back and forth? There are people who think lines of military thinking are very narrow, who slowly but surely are going into their shells toward isolationism.

We in the military just don't spend enough time trying to find out what John Q. Citizen is thinking. And if we spend more perhaps he would also have better appreciation of our thinking.

Q: That's a valid point.

McDonald #3 - 165

Adm. M.: Why hasn't this been done in the past? Simply because when you do a thing like this you can almost say that you're getting involved in politics, and we in this country have always been very proud of the fact that the military stayed completely aloof from politics. I can speak freely now and I would say maybe it's high time we got involved in politics. I'm a taxpaying citizen just like anybody else, and I don't like some of the stuff that's going on in this country. Do I have a right to try to change it? Well, as long as I'm not going counter to the policy of the commander-in-chief, I don't know what's wrong with me as a military man expressing some views about why I think military aid should be given to Timbuktu, if I think it should. Why shouldn't I go to the Congress and express myself even if on active duty? But it's a very, very ticklish point because, as I said to a group the other day, if you start doing this some of you are going to get fired. However, any time you get yourself into a difficult situation, you aren't going to get out by continuing to do the same thing that you've always done. To wit, today everybody wants to cure the energy problem but nobody wants to even drive 55 miles an hour. They seem to think that we can get over this recession or whatever you call it by continuing to do the same things we were doing that got us into it. Sombody's going to get hurt or have to change their ways. Anyway that's the way I look at it. Maybe the military ought to start trying to find out what John Q. Citizen is thinking because John Q. Citizen, after all, is the man who pays the taxes and if John Q. Citizen doesn't want a military, let's get rid of it.

McDonald #3 - 166

Q: Well the junkets abroad were precisely to find out what the heads of government were thinking about, weren't they?

Adm. M.: Yes. As I say, we don't put many strings on trying to find out what they're thinking in a foreign country. Of course, on these trips they usually only talk to the top dog and there too one would learn more I'm sure if they talked to some of the lower echelon people. Coming to Washington very seldom as I do today I'm convinced that this place isn't even halfway in touch with what the people in the country are thinking.

Q: The Navy has for a long time had a policy of this sort, have they not, in terms of, say, the CinCLant, the VIPs who go out there and other people who aren't VIPs but community leaders from all over the country were taken out to a carrier and that sort of thing?

Adm. M.: Yes, but they're generally from Coastal areas and also I'm saying why don't we go to them instead of having them come to us? Let's meet with them in their environment.

Q: Where they'd be more likely to talk freely?

Adm. M.: They might be, yes. Why don't we try it for a change? So that more people will get to see those in uniform. The image of the military man today isn't very high, I don't think. And I think one of the reasons is people don't know them. The average citizen out in the boondocks forms his or her opinions from what he reads in the newspaper or sees on the idiot tube, and most of those people who are either printing or talking are primarily interested in sensationalism, and maybe if those in uniform got out into the hinterland it might help. I don't know.

But, of course, that has nothing to do with my history, so called.

Q: When you were at the War College, what kind of relationship did you have with the Industrial War College?

Adm. M.: Very little. If I remember correctly, periodically we would have joint sessions to listen to a lecturer, but not much more than that. The coordination and the intertwining of the work done between the two has been, I think, increasing all along, but very little back then.

Q: Well, there was some sort of athletic exchange, anyway?

Adm. M.: Well, we had athletic exchanges but I didn't pay

much attention to what they were doing over there academically because I was interested in what I was doing over at the National War College. We were mostly operators and they were materiel people, more or less. They have to work together ultimately but not necessarily at school. We were studying two entirely different things. One is geo-politics and one is resources. Ultimately they come together because perhaps one of our greatest strengths is our economy and our technical capability, but you don't have to mingle in school and we didn't down there, we didn't mix.

Q: Well, it was certainly a year not wasted, it was a profitable one?

Adm. M.: Very good. I was ready to leave and when I left there I was ordered to what they call a jeep carrier, a ship that had at one time been a large oil tanker then converted into a small aircraft carrier which was not only the flagship but the only carrier at that particular moment that was engaged in carrier-based antisubmarine warfare.

Q: On which coast?

Adm. M.: The east coast. The ship had just come out of overhaul and had gone to Guantanamo to undergo certain test and training with what they call the Underway

Training Command. I flew to Guantanamo and took command down there.

Q: And she was the Mindoro?

Adm. M.: That was the Mindoro, and during the time that I had the Mindoro, which was until the next June, we were at sea a large amount of time compared to the way ships operated at sea then. They didn't stay at sea like they do now, not nearly as much, but I thought enough then and I think too much now.

We engaged in some very fine antisubmarine warfare exercises which I found most beneficial. Of course, I enjoyed the ship very much. I had no particular experiences, good, bad, or indifferent that I recall.

Q: What was the state of the equipment, the ordnance at that point?

Adm. M.: I don't remember. I think the planes were TFs. I do remember there was one operation where we kept airplanes in the air continuously twenty-four hours a day for ten days. That was quite a record. It might have only been two or three at a time that were running antisubmarine patrol, and there were basically three of us who stood watch. We had a captain aboard who was acting as an admiral and he and I and my exec would stand one watch in three on the bridge. It was really very pleasant.

I left there and got a very fine assignment as operations officer on the staff of Admiral Radford out in Hawaii. That was in 1952 and, you may recall, that when I left there in 1947 I'd been operations officer for AirPac in Hawaii.

Q: Yes.

Adm. M.: So I went from operations for the Air Command over on Ford Island to operations for the entire Pacific command over at a place called Makalapa. One of the highlights there with Admiral Radford was accompanying him on a trip which took us first to Japan, Hong Kong and then Saigon, where the French were involved. Admiral Radford and I went up to Hanoi and had dinner with General Salan, the French commander. There were a lot of briefings and then we took a little time out and went over to Siemreap, where we saw the great ruins at Angkor Wat, back down to Pnom Penh and then back to Saigon, and from there we flew to Delhi, took a little side trip to Agra to see the Taj Mahal. Then we went to Karachi, on up to Peshawar, where we got in cars and drove to the top of the Kyber Pass and had a meal with the Kyber Tribal Chieftans which was rather interesting. I wrote my wife about it and said that we had great ribs of sheep barbecued over what I thought was camel-dung fires.

We came back and went to Rawalpindi where the head of the armed forces (whose name I don't recall right now) later served as President of Pakistan for quite some time. We inspected a lot of things there, hospitals, various engineering maintenance plants and maintenance facilities. From there we went to Ceylon and stayed there a couple of days. I might say that on this trip was Admiral Radford and his wife, his aide, a yeoman, an Army colonel, an Air Force colonel, and a civilian from San Francisco who was a public relations man for Pacific Gas and Electric and me.

Q: Oh, his name I should know.

Adm. M.: Bob Gros.

Q: He was a friend of Nimitz.

Adm. M.: I was the senior among the military and Bob and I were usually paired together. Why was he on the trip? Well - During the so-called revolt of the admirals in the late forties, Admiral Radford was on the spot and Bob helped him a lot with his writings. Later Bob used to come out to Hawaii and, without charge, give a lot of instruction in public speaking to people on Radford's staff. Admiral Radford felt that newspaper editors and reporters and what not were often taken on trips like these and he saw no reason why he shouldn't take this fellow because this particular man worked for Pacific Gas and Electric only a certain percentage of the time and during his free time he would give lectures in the eleven western states on various and sundry things. When we were in Ceylon Bob and I went up to the Gem City where we rode an elephant and bought star sapphires for our respective wives. Then we came back to Singapore and after going through all the formalities there we later had a very informal swimming-pool luncheon with Sir Malcolm MacDonald over in Johore, which is right across the border. He was living in the palace that the sultan had built for the sultana. This luncheon was very interesting. I would always try to find out what the uniform would be through the aide. At a cocktail party in Singapore, the afternoon before the luncheon at Sir Malcolm's the aide was standing next to me when the Army colonel came up and asked me "what's the uniform tomorrow for the luncheon?" I said:

"Bill, look, we're going to be the guests of a MacDonald. Wear a pair of slacks with your shirttail hanging out."

"Oh, yeah," he said,. About that time the aide turned

to me and said:

"How did you find out, Captain? That really is the uniform, that is, slacks and an aloha shirt."

Q: He was the son of the one-time prime minister, wasn't he?

Adm. M.: Yes, son of Ramsay MacDonald.

From Singapore we came back to the Philippines, then Guam, and then on home.

Q: And the purpose of this trip was to get acquainted, was it?

Adm. M.: Yes.

Q: Was Radford new to this assignment?

Adm. M.: No, no, he'd been there for some time. When he lined this trip up he sent for me and told me about the trip. Radford then was wearing both hats, CinCPac and CinCPacFlt. I was operations for CinCPacFlt. The Air Force and the Army fellows were on the so-called CinCPac staff.

He told me he was going on this trip and was taking these two fellows and he wanted me to nominate someone from CinCPacFlt. Well, for some reason, he said he wanted an aviator, so I nominated a captain in my shop. After some discussion Raddy said:

"I thought you might go," and I said:

"Well, Admiral, I haven't been out here very long," (I got out there in July and this was late August, and we were going in early October) and "I think I ought to go out and visit some units of the fleet."

"Why," he said, "are they having problems out there?"

"No, Sir."

When I came home later that day and told my wife I said:

"I'd give my right arm to make this trip but I just don't have the guts to nominate yourself."

About two days later he sent for me again and said:

"Have you given any more thought to that trip?"

"Well," I said, "Not particularly, Admiral."

"I mean about the nominee."

"Oh," I said, "I think the man I nominated is really ideal."

He said, "I still wonder why you shouldn't go," and that was it. I walked out and the next morning I got a telephone call from the duty officer saying:

"Captain, I think you might be interested in a message Admiral Radford has sent to Washington. It's a message requesting clearance for certain individuals he wants to

McDonald #3 - 175

accompany him to the Far East, and you're the Navy representative." So I went.

We had a wonderful time and I got to know Raddy and Mrs. Radford extremely well. Raddy, God bless him, died without ever knowing how much I wanted to go, and I don't know how many times he said to my wife, talking about that trip, what a wonderful time we had, "and you know, Tommie, I'll never forget, Dave didn't want to make that trip!"

But it was a wonderful trip in all respects. Of course, just to see the places and talk to the people and the sightseeing was unbelievable.

Q: This was before SEATO came into being, wasn't it?

Adm. M.: Yes.

I stayed on with Admiral RAdford and when President Eisenhower came through to make the trip to Korea -

Q: That was December of 1952.

Adm. M.: I was the man who had to do a lot of the plotting of the journey. As operations officer I recommended where the planes would land and how we'd station destroyers in case something happened to the plane if it went down, safety measures, and what not. I worked on that and, of course, got to see those fellows with the President. Although the President stayed over at Kaneohe, quite a few in his party stayed just two doors from my house, which was pretty close to Radford's there in Makalapa.

Then, of course, later Admiral Radford came on back as Chairman of the Joint Chiefs and Admiral Stump came out.

Q: Tell me a little more about the President's visit. Who briefed him?

Adm. M.: I don't know. I wasn't involved in that.

Q: Admiral Radford went with him, did he not?

Adm. M.: He did go with him. Although I did much in connection with this trip, I wasn't present at the briefings. I think I went to a couple of parties, maybe, cocktail parties. I don't think we even went to a dinner.

Q: Wasn't Don Griffin out there also at the time?

Adm. M.: Yes. Don was - he had plans, I believe.

Q: Because he had something to do with the President's trip.

McDonald #3 - 177

Adm. M.: Yes, and I think other people - Eddie Layton probably did a good deal of the briefing on this, but I'm not sure.

Then Radford came back and went to Washington and Admiral Stump came out.

Q: When Radford was on this particular duty, was this when he decided upon the airfield in the Philippines?

Adm. M.: No, no, that was already - that was beforehand. He had this brainstorm back in the mid-forties, and Subic was going, it was a going concern at this time, Cubi Point and Subic Bay. We landed there. When I say it was a going concern, it had been constructed and was operating, but nothing like it is now.

Stump came. He was a different sort of a fellow. I'd never known him very well but I enjoyed working for him.

Q: And your job for him was the same?

Adm. M.: Same thing. Admiral Stump hadn't been there very long when he indicated that Oley Sharp had worked for him before and he wanted him to work for him again.

McDonald #3 - 178

Sharp was a year senior to me. We had a lot of conversation, Admiral Stump and I, about Sharp coming out. We established what I thought was a most necessary position. We had three independent divisions: operations, administration or plans or maybe communications, I'm not sure. We thought, and I had talked to Admiral Radford about this, that these three divisions should have a capstone. These division officers were all going to the chief of staff and others independently and yet they were so interlocked that maybe it would be better to make a little pyramid and put a top dog there.

So I talked to Admiral Stump about Sharp filling such a spot and said:

"I think that would be ideal, Admiral, because Oley's just a year senior to me, and I'll still be completely free and independent, as will the others, but he'd be the coordinator." So that job was created and Oley came out and, of course, that's where Oley and I got to know each other real well, so well, I guess, that nobody thought Oley would get CincPac any more than I did because he was the man I supported for the job when I was CNO.

Nothing particularly unusual happened while Admiral Stump was there. With him I went through the Mr. Kimball and Mr. Brown experience again. Admiral Radford and Admiral Stump were quite different but both were wonderful people.

I did have one strange experience while he was there. President Eisenhower made retired General Van Fleet an ambassador at large, gave him a sizeable staff and sent him out to the Far East to make certain studies and recommendations. In addition to his aides and military personnel there were quite a few civilians. If my memory serves me right there was the dean of law school from Columbia; a man from Dun and Bradstreet; and some people from the Department of Defense headed up by Secretary McNeil, who was the comptroller. Then, off to one side, were three, almost you might say nonworking military advisers one each from the Army, the Navy, and the Air Force.

Somewhere along the line, in Korea or later and for various or unknown reasons, the Navy man's presence was no longer desired and he was released. Admiral Stump called me in, told me that the Navy man had been fired and that there seemed to be much friction between members of the group and that I was to go out and "pour oil on the troubled waters," as he put it. Gosh, I'll never forget it.

I took my handkerchief out of my pocket and dropped it on the floor, and Admiral Stump said, "What's the matter?" I said:

"I give up, Admiral. I don't want to get mixed up in this."

I went home and I guess it was two days later when he called me in again.

"Well," he said, "Here are some more communications that have been going back and forth between Van Fleet and

Radford and me. You're it."

Oh, my.

He said, "I want you to go out there and I want you to know that any advice you give General Van Fleet or the ambassador, it's your advice. You're out there as an individual. But, you know, I think it might be helpful if you knew what I thought about certain things. How do you think we ought to go about this?"

So I said: "Well, Admiral, why don't you just let me start by asking you a bunch of questions and if you'll answer them then I think that I'll know your views."

And that's what we did and, by golly, I went out -

Q: Where was Van Fleet based?

Adm. M.: I met the group on Formosa. We stayed there a month - and I'm telling you it was sort of unhappy duty.

Q: Why?

Adm. M.: Well, I don't really think I ought to put this down because it goes into -

Q: Personalities?

Adm. M.: Yes, and it was about to explode and fly apart.

Q: What was his real mission as ambassador at large?

Adm. M.: How to settle the fate of the Far East, really. Sort of a far-flung thing. Most of the time on Formosa we were figuring out, trying to figure out, what the Chinese would have to have in order to invade Formosa and what Chiang needed to stop them, a lot of that, and spending a lot of time with the people. I don't really know just what the exact mission was and I think this was one of the problems.

We were to go from there to the Philippines, then to Saigon, Indochina, and then back.

Q: Japan wasn't involved in all this?

Adm. M.: They'd already been there and, actually we never went to Saigon.

But I'll never forget when we got back to Hawaii I was greeted with basically this statement:

"You didn't stay in the Philippines but five days instead of two weeks and you didn't even go to Indochina, but you all came back in the same airplane together and, by God, that's something!"

Q: Whose observation was that?

Adm. M.: I'll pass on that one. The entire group stayed there in Hawaii for about four days, wrote up some form of a report, then the others came on back to Washington and I stayed in Honolulu. I don't know what ever happened to the report.

Q: You mean this was an ad hoc ambassadorship that was just for a study?

Adm. M.: Yes.

Q: What relationship did this Van Fleet mission have to the CinCPac command?

Adm. M.: I can't answer that, none so far as I know. I think that eventually a copy of the report was sent to CinCPac for such comment as he might make. CinCPac was to support them logistically while they were in the far east but this was purely a Washington deal, as I remember.

Q: It was almost an intrusion on the CinCPac command?

Adm. M.: Well, yes and no. It could be an intrusion, yet it might not be provided it was agreed before any of it

McDonald #3 - 183

was implemented that CinCPac would have his day in court. And I think that was the way it was intended. Frankly, I don't believe that one line of that report was ever put into effect. I think it just died down and that was it, so far as I know. I never heard any more about it - ever. I never made any more inquiries because as far as I was concerned it was a very happy day when the mission was completed.

Q: You were glad to get out of it!

Adm. M.: Yes, and it wasn't too much longer after that when the word came that I was still slated to be the Commanding Officer of the new Forrestal but there had been another delay. Later, came word from Washington saying that from the messages and communications I'd been sending it looked to them like I was getting itchy feet to get a carrier and if I didn't want to wait for the Forrestal the Coral Sea was returning from the Mediterranean and would go in the Navy Yard in Norfolk in December and I could take command about the 22nd December and sail to the Med around March, if that's what I'd prefer.

I went in to Admiral Stump and asked "What is your advice?" He wouldn't give me any. I went to Rear Admiral Putt Storrs, an aviator, and he said, "I'd wait forever and take that Forrestal. I went to, I think it was

Admiral Hopwood, who was CinCPacFlt chief of staff, and Hoppy said "Bird in the hand." I said, "I agree with you," so I sent back, "I'm ready. I'll take the Coral Sea."

So I came on back, took command of the Coral Sea –

Q: Before you tell me that story, let's go back to CinCPac. It being one of the early attempts at a joint command, how did it work?

Adm. M.: It worked out all right, I thought. Both the Pacific Command and the Pacific Fleet Command were under the same commander. You didn't have two entirely separate commands out there then. CinCPacFlt handled the communications for CinCPacFlt and CinCPac. Pretty generally the CinCPacFlt administration handled both. Only a few of the divisions were duplicated. Admiral Radford was the boss of both. He had a Rear Admiral Storrs, who was his chief of staff for CinCPac, and he had Phillips, and later Hopwood as chief of staff for CinCPacFlt.

Q: I was thinking of the Army and the Air Force serving together with the Navy?

Adm. M.: I don't really recall how that worked. I didn't pay much attention to it because I hadn't gotten involved in unification then. My attitude was if I'd wanted to be a soldier I'd have gone to West Point, and I was in the fleet, I wasn't involved.

But there was a lot of discussion about the organizational set-up. Should we be completely split with two admirals each with complete staffs, et cetera, which of course it ultimately was. But I'm not sure today (1976) that the Air Force has a full general out there, or the Army either. They're sort of throttling back now to where the Army and the Air Force don't have so much to do with that area.

Q: At one point, when Stump retired, was it not thought that the Air Force would get the top command?

Adm. M.: I don't know this but I've been told that when they abolished CinCFE - Far East - and put in under CinCPac, that it made Max Taylor so mad he was bound and determined that the Army was going to take over CinCPac. CinCFE, of course, had been an Army commander. When I was in the Joint Chiefs and they would talk about an Army or an Air Force officer as CinCPac, I'd say it makes about as much sense to me as sending a naval officer over to be SacEur. I said, "After all, we've never had a naval officer as SacEur because it's primarily Army and Air." Except for logistics, of course, I said the same thing applied out in the Pacific which is primarily navy.

McDonald #3 - 186

Q: The story about the establishment of SEATO. I know that Admiral Stump had a lot to do with it.

Adm. M.: I presume so, but I don't know that story. I really don't know it. In trying to explain why SEATO - I often referred to NATO which most people understand. I've pointed out to people that right after the end of World War II Russia began to take over more and more of Europe, and there was a thing called NATO created in Europe and subsequent to the creation of NATO Russia hasn't taken one inch of ground nor has, as far as I know, one soldier been killed in anger.

Now, along in the early and towards the mid fifties, it seemed to certain individuals at the top of our planning policy-making that the same thing was about to happen in Indochina, a gradual encroachment by Communism. And so this same group of people said, look, this is the way we stopped it in Europe without any difficulty. Why not create a NATO over here to do the same thing? And it sort of seemed logical. So these countries all came in. I've forgotten which they were now, I think Britain, France, Australia, New Zealand, the United States and SEATO was formed. That was the genesis of the thing.

Q: In this time was not the Taiwan Defense Command in being?

McDonald #3 - 187

Adm. M.: I guess, but I just don't know. I just don't remember whether the Taiwan Defense Command, as a command, was in being. It sounds sort of silly because I spent a month there with Ambassador Van Fleet, but I just don't recall.

Q: What about Korea? The talks were going on interminably, and still are, I understand.

Adm. M.: Can't answer that, either. You see, during all of these periods I was never involved in planning. I would have gotten involved deeply if we'd started shooting, but I wasn't involved in either the planning or the intelligence. I was involved at the time in seeing that our forces were maintained and trained to the best of our capability.

Q: In the area of operational planning and forces, I know that under the aegis of SEATO there were demonstrations of weapons and so forth on our part. The CinCPac command would entertain representatives, military representatives, from all these countries to show them this and that.

Adm. M.: Well, it seems to me there were a lot of them coming through there but trying to dig back thirty years

McDonald #3 - 188

again, I just don't remember much about that. In Hawaii, the year round you've got all kinds of groups coming in from countries farther to the west and particularly those allied with us or who are getting our military assistance and what not. It seems to me they were coming through there almost daily or weekly, some for a particular purpose and some not.

Q: Do you want to go now to the Coral Sea and your command of her?

Adm. M.: I came back from Honolulu in the late fall, took command of the Coral Sea in the Norfolk Navy Yard just before Christmas 1954.

Almost immediately, just before the ship was ready to leave the Navy Yard, I went by airplane down to Mayport and went out to sea a couple of days on the Midway because I had never been aboard that type of aircraft carrier before and I thought it would be nice to at least ride on one for about a day before I had the responsibility of taking one from the shipyard on out to sea. I'm glad I did. When leaving the shipyard in Portsmouth, the system is to take a Navy Yard pilot to a certain point, the name of which I can't recall right now, and at that "point" a Naval Base, Norfolk, pilot will pick you up and take you on till you get beyond the piers at the Norfolk Naval Base.

Well, this particular time, when we got to the "point",

McDonald #3 - 189

the shipyard pilot had to get off because there was another ship coming up that he had to get aboard to put into dry dock, but for some reason there was no Naval Base pilot to relieve him. I'll never forget, he asked me:

"Do you think you can take it by yourself?" And I said:

"Well, if I can't, I'm in a pretty bad way because there's nobody to help me."

I think the only thing I did wrong was that I probably went a little bit faster than I should have gone because I wanted to have plenty of rudder control. Anyway, I went on out to sea.

Within about three months, then, I think it was in March, we went down to Mayport and picked up our air group and headed for the Mediterranean.

Q: How large an air group did you have?

Adm. M.: I don't really remember. I think about ninety planes, but I don't remember.

I headed for the Mediterranean saying to myself that at long last I'm going to get to Europe. And I think it was about the 5th of April that we went in to Gibraltar and I put my foot on European soil for the first time in my life.

McDonald #3 - 190

Q: You'd been all over the world but not to Europe!

Adm. M.: From Gibralter we went to Barcelona.

By this time of my life, our childred were married and my wife went over and met me in Barcelona and then followed the ship for six pleasant months. Once again, my old skipper from VF-6, who was my first skipper on the Essex, (Ralph Ofstie) was at that time commander of the Sixth Fleet and he very kindly asked me to write him a letter and list the ports that I wanted to visit. He had only two caveats. One, you cannot visit any port on the African coast, you cannot go to both Istanbul and Beirut, but you can go to one or the other. I selected Istanbul because I wanted to see if an entire civilization had really changed in a generation.

And I really did get to see fascinating things in Istanbul thanks to a very fortunate break. Before our arrival there I received a letter from a friend of mine who had spent some time in Istanbul. He told me that there was a lady in the American Consulate there who had been there for many years, knew everybody and everything worth knowing and that she was a very good friend of his and his family and for me to be sure to contact her. Of course she was present at the very first reception. I immediately spoke to her about our mutual friend and the conversation went on from there. But before the reception was over she came to me and said that she was interested in a young lady there in Istanbul, about 18 years of age, that she would like

McDonald #3 - 191

to have see the ship. She said that she knew that visiting parties were going out every day but she'd rather not have this young lady go with such a large group. I then suggested that she herself bring this young lady to the dock about 11:30 the next morning where the two of them would be met by my wife and then the three of them could come out to the ship in my Gig and have lunch with me. I further said that in the meantime I'd find a nice young Ensign, have him to lunch also and then after lunch he could show the young lady the ship. This was exactly what happened and then imagine my surprise when I later learned that this young lady was the daughter of the Mayor of Istanbul. Believe you me during the next five or six days we were privileged to see more of that city and its environs than one can imagine; everything from visiting the belly-dancing gypsies in their native homes which were caves in the hills about 25 miles from the city on down to viewing jewels galore from the old Ottoman Empire.

We had a delightful cruise although on our very first day in to the Mediterranean we had an unfortunate fire.

Q: On board ship?

Adm. M.: Yes. We had a Marine squadron aboard, fighters, and they had something called a donkey engine, a little auxiliary power unit used to crank the planes. They were using one of these and a part broke, flew off, and hit an auxiliary gas tank on the wing of another plane and it burst into flames, and this was in the middle of the pack and I felt we'd really had it. I didn't see how in the world we could keep from buring up a dozen planes or explosions or what not. However, we only lost one airplane and partially burned another. Don't ask me how. We had a strong wind and I had time to maneuver the ship so as to use the wind advantageously and the boys who did the firefighting did a wonderful job.

Q: It speaks a lot for your firefighting crew and damage control.

Adm. M.: An awful lot.

We had a most successful cruise. We were fortunate in that we returned with every pilot who went over there. In those days it was sort of hard to operate for six months without losing one. We did a lot of operating and, of course, we did a lot of entertaining, which I guess was expected.

If my memory serves me correctly, we didn't operate too much with our NATO allies during this particular period, compared with what we did when I was over there later as Commander of the Sixth Fleet. We joined up with Commander, Sixth Fleet, I remember in Cannes. As I said, I'd never been to Europe before and my former boss - Ralph Ofstie had also spent most of his time in the Pacific. I remember when we both were at this particular party in Cannes, France, he motioned to me to come over and, although he had three stars then, I never called him anything but Captain because he was my captain when he was a lieutenant commander and I always called him that to the day he died. I went over and said:

"What do you want, Captain?"

He said: "I just want to tell you I think you and I have been in the wrong ocean all of our lives!"

He was an old bachelor, had been, and he later married Joy Hancock, of course. He'd been trying to marry her for quite a few years.

Q: And it didn't last very long, did it?
Adm. M.: No, he died soon after coming back to Washington. I was very fond of Ralph. No one could have been nicer to me over there. I also had a fine admiral aboard for a while, not all the time but a good deal of the time.

Q: Was he commander of the carrier division?

Adm. M.: Yes, Cornwell first, and then it became Bat Cruise and that was rather interesting because Bat Cruise was the man who taught me how to solo an airplane in Coronado in 1929, and here he was my admiral and me the skipper of the flagship.

Our job over there was what I guess you'd call familiarization, training, showing our flag and our faces to our allies. At that time, the presence of a United States ship in a port in that area just meant an unbelievable amount to the local people.

We were in Naples when the selection board was meeting for admiral. I wasn't really concerned because I didn't think they'd get to my group. But the report of the Board seemingly was being held up. While people were wondering why the delay, we were at a party attended, among others, by a general officer in the Army who said he had all the dope that there were problems with the Navy selection board, it had been turned down by the Secretary of the Navy, there'd been some discussion, and it probably wouldn't come out for two or three months. But, as I say, I wasn't too concerned because I didn't think they'd get to my group.

My wife was there and we were staying in a hotel. When I went aboard ship the next morning about a quarter of eight, a half dozen fellows lined up there, sticking their hands out, and I said:

"What in the hell is this?"

They handed me a message and I realized it was a message from Admiral Fechteler, who was on duty there in Naples and he had sent his Marine orderly out, saying "Congratulations. You've just been selected for rear admiral," which was a very happy moment, of course. My wife had lunch with Mrs. Fechteler that day and when I came in I asked her if she had a nice lunch - she said yes, then I said:

"You know, Admiral Fechteler did a wonderful thing this morning."

McDonald #3 - 195

She said, "What?" So I told her and she said:

"What! And you didn't come and tell me." Happy though she was she was annoyed that I hadn't let her know immediately.

Q: It meant your tour of duty on the Coral Sea was cut short, didn't it?

Adm. M.: Yes, but not too much because I probably wasn't going to make my number until the next spring - this must have been in June or July - and we were returning about the last of September. A little bit later, though, I did receive a message saying that shortly after my arrival back in the United States I would be relieved and to proceed to Washington and take over as Air Warfare and be frocked as a rear admiral without the pay.

Q: Tell me a little more about the Mediterranean at that point. You said earlier you were told you couldn't go in to North African ports. Were you able to use Wheelus base?

Adm. M.: Oh, I'm sure, if we'd had to put our planes in there, but we had no occasion to. In other words, what Commander, Sixth Fleet, was saying to me then was that during the period you're going to be over here we have no visits scheduled to North African ports.

Q: Oh, they weren't just barred?

McDonald #3 - 196

Adm. M.: As far as I know, no, but as far as I was concerned yes. Now there are some, of course, where you can't get a ship that big in. At that time, the Coral Sea was the largest warship in the world, because the Midway, the FDR, and the Coral Sea were sister ships and they were the largest, but the Coral Sea was the newest and when they built her she was a few inches longer than either of the other two, so that made her the largest warship in the world.

Q: What about the Israeli ports? Was that off base?

Adm. M.: I guess. I don't know. I don't really remember. I didn't have any desire to go there anyway compared to the other places. The only thing that sticks out clearly in my mind is that I had to select either Istanbul or Beirut. There weren't any other places that I had any desire to go to that I didn't go to.

Q: Was there a political reason for that?

Adm. M.: Not that I know of.

Q: Either one or the other but not both?

Adm. M.: Oh, no, no, no political reason. At that time

McDonald #3 - 197

when we swung around to the eastern Med, part of the Sixth Fleet would go up to Istanbul and part would go to Beirut. Then we'd come back and come together and work back toward Villefranche and Cannes and that area. If my memory serves me correctly, that was the reason for that. There was never as far as I know any political reason for that. There was never as far as I know any political reason for not going to both. There were a couple of times when we didn't go into Beirut as scheduled because of a little uprising which they had periodically. But later on we'd reschedule and go in.

Q: What was the status of the Turkish Navy at this time, or did you get a glimpse of it?

Adm. M.: I don't really remember. You see, I was thrilled at operating my air group at sea and seeing the European ports and these larger issues didn't occupy my time very much. I was a captain and my ship was my main interest. In most of these places, of course, we would be entertained, by the French when we went to Toulon and by the Italians in Genoa and particularly by the Italians in Livorno, or Leghorn, if you want to call it that, because La Spezia, up there a little bit farther, is one of their antisubmarine warfare bases and Livorno, or Leghorn is where they have their naval academy. I can say that I've been at their naval academy graduation three times. That was the first time, that year (1955) and then again later when I was with the Sixth Fleet, and once when I went down there from Paris.

I don't really remember the navies, on that trip, in either Turkey or Greece. I do in later years, but not on that trip. I remember Barcelona very well.

Q: Yes, you said at lunch that Spain was your favorite country. Did you get your introduction to it at that point?

Adm. M.: Yes, and then when I went over to Paris to work for General Norstad the first vacation that I took from there, ten days, I guess, my wife and I drove down to a little place called Sitges, about 25 miles south of Barcelona. Later, when I had the Sixth Fleet, I visited Spain many times. Then, when I was Chief of Naval Operations, it was the first country I visited as a guest of the government.

I still communicate with a fellow named Nieto. And I used to know Munos Grandes who was vice president. Nieto was an admiral but he was secretary of the Navy. And the man who was really doing his stuff with Franco was Admiral Carrero Blanco. I had Munos Grandes and Carrero Blanco out on my flagship. Nieto, as Secretary of the Spanish Navy and the Secretary of the Navy from Peru were both invited by our Secretary of the Navy to come to the U. S. but in both instances they almost became my guests because of our rapport. They were both admirals. Maybe that accounts for it. I don't know. But over the years we've kept in touch with Admiral Nieto, and also with the

Spanish CNO until just three years ago when he died. Of course, Carrero Blanco was assassinated, unfortunately. He was a very fine individual.

But back to the Coral Sea and Norfolk, very pleasant, and, of course, to me, very enlightening. I think we learned a lot on that trip. The crew behaved nicely. There were no real problems that I can recall and if we'd had real ones I'm sure I would not have forgotten them. I had just a wonderful group on there and a fine operating outfit. I left the Coral Sea with an extremely good taste in my mouth. It was quite a different feeling from the Mindoro, yet the Mindoro was my first ship and I don't think I ever had any sad moments on her either, but she was small and we were limited as to what we could do. And the ship was hard to handle. She was a tanker with a lot of oil, a small rudder and not much power. Then, when I had the Coral Sea I felt I was really in carrier aviation. By golly, we had a fighting air group, complete in all respects. Here was a ship big enough, fast enough, to do what we were supposed to do if we had to do it. You feel a great sense of satisfaction and you know, in your own mind that if something happened tomorrow, we're ready and capable.

Q: A sense of confidence.

McDonald #3 - 200

Adm. M.: Yes, so I left there, as I say, with a real good taxte in my mouth. I wasn't too concerned at leaving early, about the first of October, and I'd had her nine or ten months and you only got about twelve or thirteen anyway. And having just returned from the Med we probably wouldn't have gone anywhere for three or four months.

So, it was a good time and, of course, if there are good jobs in Washington I was getting one, getting a real good job, and putting on a broad stripe. It was all real good.

Q: Let me ask a question about the Coral Sea. A young chap at the Institute some years ago went out on an aircraft carrier and came back and he observed that there was such a sense of overwhelming power experienced on board a carrier that he sometimes had fear that maybe a naval officer would lose his sense of humility because of this.

Adm. M.: No, I never felt that. The greatest feeling to me on a carrier is the sense of teamwork. You watch those planes, especially at night, operating off and on that deck, with the sailors running in and doing this and that and the other. Many years ago on the old Saratoga we had the Junior Chamber of Commerce of San Francisco out to observe our operations in the morning. As we sat down to lunch the

McDonald #3 - 201

man next to me was silent for some time, then he turned to me and said:

"Lieutenant, I never knew what the word 'precision' meant until this morning."

Today everybody's talking about all this individual stuff, you've got to do it your way, doing your own thing, et cetera. There's none of that on a carrier. The way you have to rely on each other, the teamwork, is just unbelievable. And these men do this night and day. They'll work on into the hours of the night and they'll still run up and down the flight deck goosing each other. Aboard ship one gets away from a lot of sometimes unfortunate distractions.

I've taken some civilians out on a carrier down where I live and they're absolutely pop-eyed to see how these things are done - landing at night, and, gee, before you know what's happened, the flight deck men are on the wings, the hook's undone, it's retracted and the plane is taxied forward - plane after plane.

I think it's marvelous, just marvelous.

Q: And the secret of that is not only training, but discipline isn't it?

Adm. M.: Yes. That's right. The man has to do it the way he's told. He can't do it his way. When I was in command of the Sixth Fleet, of course, my flagship was a cruiser, but I took every opportunity, within the realm of reason, to go to the carrier. It's just absolutely fascinating. To me, it is to this day. It's quite a thrill. And regretably, a lot of people who deserve so much of the credit are those you never see, those in the combat information center, and the people in the engineroom et cetera. I guess that's the reason they call a ship's company the crew.

One of the things that has disturbed me a little bit in recent years is giving certain ratings more pay because some people say they're more important. What they really mean is because they're harder to get. This is unfortunate. People say, well, you're an aviator, you always got extra pay. I got extra pay because I might not live as long, because of the hazard and not because an aviator was more important. I regret that it has apparently become necessary to have aviators with one pay scale, doctors with a pay scale just simply out of this world, and nuclear-submarine people who get this, that, and the other. Well, you say, in the civilian world you do. Yes, but you don't require the cooperation among individuals in the civilian world that you must have on board ship. It is an essential.

I don't question the necessity for those variations in pay but I think it's regrettable. I think you ought

McDonald #3 - 203

to be paid because of your rating and your length of service. Longevity raises are necessary because I don't care how good you are, unless there's a vacancy, you can't go up and, after a certain length of time, I think you should cease to have to suffer from a lack of increased pay because there's no vacancy, and that's where length of service comes in.

McDonald #4 - 204

Interview No. 4 with Admiral David L. McDonald, U.S. Navy
(Retired)

Place: Naval History Center, Washington Navy Yard, Washington, D.C.

Date: Tuesday morning, 7 October 1975

Subject: Biography

By: John T. Mason, Jr.

Q: It's great to see you, as always. You lift the spirits. Last time, you told me about your tour of duty in the Coral Sea and about your selection to rear admiral.

I want to ask you one question about the Coral Sea. You served in the Essex also.

Adm. M.: Yes.

Q: The other day I was with John Niedermair, who had a great deal to do with the design of the Essex and somewhat less to do with the design of the Midway, and he was extolling the virtues of the Essex as a carrier over those of the larger ones. Do you want to say something about that?

Adm. M.: Not particularly, Jack. We must remember that during the time that I was aboard the Essex we had no jet aircraft whatsoever. They were all propeller aircraft, whereas aboard the Coral Sea we had a certain number of jet aircraft. And at the time I was on the Coral Sea, the Coral Sea was a straight deck, too, and I think she had quite a few advantages over the Essex operating that type of aircraft.

In subsequent years, they started, of course, operating jet aircraft from the Essex class but, pretty generally speaking, those Essex-class ships had been modified to include an angled deck.

Q: Yes, so the deck comes in.

Adm. M.: That's right. I think in many ways the Essex was more efficient, but with a different type of aircraft. If you had tried to operate from the Essex, as originally designed, the same kind of aircraft that were being operated from the Midway and the Coral Sea, at the time I had the Coral Sea anyway, I think it would have been much more difficult. So it would be very difficult for me, after having been away from it this number of years, to indicate that one was more efficient than the other. I'd rather have the Coral Sea.

Q: All right! I'm glad to have your comments on that.
Now, you came back to Washington and you were made

McDonald #4 - 206

Director of the Air Warfare Division, Office of the Chief of Naval Operations, and this was in the year 1955. Tell me about that job. What was involved?

Adm. M.: I think perhaps the most important part of that particular division, if you want to call it a division, was the requirements for naval aircraft. And, of course, along with it went requirements for aircraft carriers and we also concerned ourselves with operating efficiencies of the various aircraft. It was aircraft requirements and readiness, basically. I think the most important phase was really looking ahead trying to see what type of aircraft we thought the Navy should have in the future.

Q: About ten years hence or somethinglike that?

Adm. M.: That's correct. Of course, let's not forget BuAer, the Bureau of Aeronautics. We, over in the office of CNO set up the requirements and then they, of course, tried to fulfill them. Nevertheless, we worked very closely together in all phases.

Looking back, after my two years in that job, there were two things that really stood out in my mind, (1) that our efforts during that period ultimately resulted in the F-4 fighter, which turned out to be the finest, I think, the world has ever known, and (2) the P-3 Orion

ASW airplane. Interestingly enough, there were a lot of arguments about these aircraft. The F-4 was the first real two-seater fighter that the Navy ever had, and the real contest was between the F-4 and a modification of the F-8, the coca cola shape plane, which was a single-seater. People were quite opinionated in the Navy then, especially fighter pilots, and they probably still are today. There were those who absolutely felt it wouldn't be a fighter if it had more than one seat.

Some of us felt, I was one of them, that we'd reached the point in technology where there was so doggone much stuff in the cockpit that you could jolly well use a second man. If my memory serves me correctly, we carried the F-8 and the F-4 designs along together, quite a while before a final decision was made. It was made for the F-4 which happened to be the plane that my helpers and I generally supported. I can't say the decision turned out to be the best one because we don't know what would have happened if it had been the other way, but it turned out to be very successful.

The P-3 was in a similar category in that there were those who thought that we could still effect more modifications to the P-2, that the time hadn't come when we had to build a new plane.

Q: Were they economy-minded?

Adm. M.: Well, I presume economy-minded but to answer what I think is in your mind, I don't think their feeling was dictated by that. But there were some of the rest of us - and I had perhaps the strongest feeling on this - that we'd hung everything we could on the P-2. There just wasn't any real growth left and the time had come to get not only a different airplane but an airplane that would not just suffice for the time being but would have a great deal of growth left in it. And, of course, ultimately we did buy the P-3.

Q: Did your job constitute something similar to the Ships' Characteristics Board?

Adm. M.: Somewhat, yes, somewhat. Although I think that my shop had a lot of influence and I don't think the Ships' Characteristics Board ever had much influence, and I've been a member of it. In the Air Warfare division we had desk officers just like they had in BuAer. We were the operating people and we really came up with the designs and BuAer fulfilled them. As I said, we tried very hard not to dictate to the people in BuAer but rather to coordinate with them, but it was more our responsibility to come up with the requirements than it was BuAer's. It was BuAer's responsibility to fulfill those requirements and in doing that they also, of course, coordinated with the desk officers in my division.

If my memory serves me correctly, we had a lot of argument with BuAer on the P-3. As a matter of fact, I got a fellow down from Canada who was the boss of their ASW, an officer, and one civilian who was really their design man, and asked them in front of some of my friends in BuAer who weren't ready to go for the P-3, what kind of plane they would prefer. I did this because Canada had taken the Britannia and made an ASW plane out of that, which was a little bit too large. I asked this officer and this civilian designer, "Now that you have done what you have done and have had the experience, if you could do it all over again, sit down and get exactly the airplane you would like to have, what would it be like?

And they came up with something that was pretty well what our P-3 turned out to be. Thinking back to our arguments with BuAer, this little conference just about settled the question. The single-seater and the two-seater fighter discussions were more within the Op-Nav group, rather than arguing against the people in BuAer.

Q: I take it there was no British or Canadian counterpart to the two-seater?

Adm. M.: There probably was but we didn't pay any attention to that. We would not have paid any attention to the other either

McDonald #4 - 210

except I got in a bind. I was trying to prove a point and I had people against me. I went out to get everybody I could -

Q: To substantiate what you - ?

Adm. M.: Yes. So that was the reason for it, for taking what really was a most unusual step. We never did anything like that before, or after, I don't imagine.

Q: Do you recall any particular experience of yours in the fleet which was a feed-in?

Adm. M.: No. To the single-seater two-seater thing?

Q: Yes.

Adm. M.: No, I don't, Jack, because this was 1955-6, and actually I got out of fighters myself in 1938, as far as flying them personally.

Q: There'd been a world of change since then.

Adm. M.: Yes.

Q: Were there any other new type planes coming on stream

McDonald #4 - 211

at that time?

Adm. M.: Yes. I remember when I had the Coral Sea over in the Med just before I came back to this job we were visited by a man that I had known for a long time named Ed Heineman, who was - I don't really know his exact title but basically he was the chief designer at Douglas Aircraft Corporation. And Ed discussed with us and gave a presentation to us about a small, light, inexpensive airplane that he was going to build, which turned out to be the A-4 and which we're still flying.

So that was in the mill at the time. I don't recall others, though. I can't remember any specifics except that helicopters were becoming quite popular - people were becoming quite interested in helicopters along about that time. You see, this was about 1956 and some of the first A-4s didn't really start flying, I don't believe, until about 1961 - not in the squadron, anyway.

Q: Yes, there is a considerable time lag from the drawing board to the squadron?

Adm. M.: Always, yes. Back then we gave them a lot more testing before we let a contract than we did under the McNamara concept, and I think we were more successful in the past.

McDonald #4 - 212

Q: It's interesting what you said about the increased interest in helicopters at that point. The Coast Guard, I understand, had been interested a long time before.

Adm. M.: Probably, and also various people in the Navy. When I was in Military Requirements in 1947 I had a similar job to Op-55 except I was a captain and the set-up was a little bit different, but it was still requirements. And at that time a Navy Captain Marcy thought the whole world was rising and falling on the development of the helicopter. There's no question about it. He ultimately, I think, probably pushed them about as much as anyone in the Navy.

Q: I suppose the Coast Guard's early interest was an obvious one.

Adm. M.: Oh, yes, rescue. And I think the seaplane sort of went out the window during my regime at Op-55.

Q: Do you think there's any possible future for the seaplane in the Navy?

Adm. M.: No. But if you want to make me prove it with a slipstick like Mr. McNamara sometimes did, I couldn't do it. That's just my opinion.

Q: You mean that it filled a need at a certain period?

Adm. M.: Yes, and I had three years' experience. I was in a squadron that got the first PBYs then operating out of Seattle and Alaska. I operated in that area for three years. I left, as a matter of fact, just about three months before World War II started. Yes, large seaplanes filled a very great need then. Back in those days, if you had a big airplane, you had to have a lot of room before you could get in into the air. Of course, in Lake Washington we had plenty of water room but the adjacent field there at Sand Point was limited. Of course, we know that this isn't necessarily true any more; we can probably get large planes off the ground quicker than we could get them off the water.

Q: What about lighter-than-air?

Adm. M.: That's something with which I'm not really too familiar. I never concerned myself with that field.

Q: That didn't come up as a subject in your shop?

Adm. M.: Yes. I had a man that had a lighter-than-air desk.

Q: Rosendahl was always around wasn't he?

McDonald #4 - 214

Adm. M.: Yes. I don't say he's wrong, but I can't quite see the practicability of the thing. Many things which are good aren't the most practical. We had a lot of people, you know, who wanted to make a submarine aircraft carrier. I couldn't see the practicability of that either. But we actually did try a sub in this role.

Q: Tell me about that one. When did that happen?

Adm. M.: Oh, golly, I don't remember now. Maybe some time in the mid-50s. But we really had people who thought you could build submarine aircraft carriers. And we probably still have people who want to build submarine transports.

Q: What happened to that experiment, submerging?

Adm. M.: I really don't remember, Jack.

Q: It's a novel idea!

Adm. M.: You know you only have so much time in a 24-hour day and some things that you'd like to get interested in seem, on the surface, less practical than others and since you have to eliminate something, you eliminate those that at least seem to you to be less practical. That's sort of the way I've been about the lighter-than-air ship and

McDonald #4 - 215

about building submarines to haul airplanes or large numbers of people.

Q: Rosendhal, I recall, has assembled a great number of facts to prove the effectiveness of lighter-than-air during World War II off the coast.

Adm. M.: Well, we had people who assembled a lot of facts that proved that you could build a TFX for the Air Force and Navy, but it didn't turn out that way. You can prove most anything with figures if you're clever enough but it can always, pretty generally, be disproved, too.

Q: That's a very devastating comment!

Now, you said one other phase of your job was to think in terms of aircraft carriers?

Adm. M.: Yes, but these were pretty well locked in by that time. The <u>Forrestal</u> class was already out. I guess we were working on the <u>Enterprise</u>, but I'm not really too sure. I do recall that when I was in military requirements back in 1947, we wanted to get a carrier big enough to operate an airplane that could take an atomic bomb. I was an anti-big-carrier because at that particular time, of course, the war had just ended and I, like so many others, was absolutely in love with the Essex class.

McDonald #4 - 216

Q: Meantime you'd served on the Coral Sea?

Adm. M.: No. I'm speaking of 1947 and 1958. However, in 1948 we set out to build an aircraft carrier big enough to take an airplane that could take an atomic bomb, because unless you could carry an atomic bomb, politically you were out of business, so we in Naval Aviation had to go "big" carrier.

Many things have been developed for odd reasons; from necessity, you might say. I well recall, again back 1949-50 when Dan Kimball (who was Assistant Secretary of the Navy for Air or Under Secretary) and I got aboard a carrier in Norfolk - I was his aide - and we went out to sea. The two of us got in the back end of a P-2 which had been hoisted aboard at Norfolk and took off from the ship and flew to California, nonstop. We got headlines the next day which said the Navy could launch planes at sea in the Atlantic and go 2,000 miles and bomb a city. This helped the aviation part of the Navy stay in business.

Q: That was selling the Navy in a spectacular way.

Adm. M.: That's right.

Q: That was public relations.

Adm. M.: Exactly right. I think we've just about covered, Jack, the 1955-1957 period.

McDonald #4 - 217

Q: All right, except perhaps you would comment, since you've had a tremendous amount of experience, on this continuing controversy over the big carrier, the super aircraft carrier, its feasibility and the cost involved, all that sort of thing?

Adm. M.: I think the only comment is that it is first necessary to determine what the job is that you think you're goint to have to do. Next, what kind of an airplane, then, will you have to have in order to enable you to do that job. Then, what kind of platform is necessary in order to operate that airplane in the most efficient manner.

Q: The objective.

Adm. M.: That's right. You don't really start with the carrier. The carrier's just the landing field, basically. It's the thing that takes the weapons, really. What kind of a job is it that you perceive having to be done let's say out in or from the middle of the ocean.

Q: Am I right in thinking that the opponents of the big carrier based their arguments on the cost involved and the vulnerability of the carrier? All the eggs in one basket, so to speak.

Adm. M.: Yes, I think that they probably do, and these are two factors that certainly cannot be overlooked. A lot of people say the military man says it isn't his business to save a dollar, it's his business to save lives. Well, I think his business is both, cost-effectiveness. I think you've got to think about both of them. However, I do think that since no two things can always be exactly equal, unless it's two and two, that the effectiveness must be given priority over the cost. Sometimes people have a hard time seeing that and we have to admit that there are those who really go four bells and a jingle and to hell with what it costs if we need it.

Well, you can't criticize them for going for what they need but, by golly, I think you can criticize them any time they fail to take a good, hard look at the cost. Otherwise, we'll have a Navy ending up like New York City. There is a limit. I think that there are those who sincerely believe, and I'm not sure they aren't right, that we can develop aircraft to do the necessary job without having to have such a large, expensive, complicated platform. I'm inclined to think that we've seen the largest carrier we'll ever see, how much smaller I don't know, but I think we've probably seen the largest. When I say "the largest," I don't mean to nit pick like when I say when I had the Coral Sea it was the largest warship in the world because it was a few inches longer than the Midway, but I mean an appreciable difference.

Q: When you were in this job Arleigh Burke was CNO and he was interested in every aspect of the Navy. Did he get involved in aircraft requirements and carrier requirements?

Adm. M.: I don't really think so, Jack, but I had very little contact with Admiral Burke. If he got involved in aviation matters he got involved with a vice admiral named Bill Davis who was DCNO Air. Interestingly enough, Burke's Vice Chief most of the time was Don Felt, and many people, maybe the majority, of the naval officers in the Pentagon when told that Admiral Felt wanted to see them would practically start quivering in their boots before they ever went up there. I was just the other way. It didn't make any difference to me when he sent for me. I liked Don Felt immensely. I'd known him for years. He was a little rough, maybe, at times but I always knew exactly where I stood with Don. Most of my business, as an individual or as Op-55, was with DCNO Air. But when it became necessary for me to go higher, I would usually go and see Admiral Felt.

Q: When you were concerned about the P-3 and ASW, did you work with the submarine boys, and did they have any deep feelings?

Adm. M.: I'm sure we did. I had an ASW officer in the division but I can't tell you today who this ASW officer was. But, yes, we worked with the submarine people all the time. We had many different liaison set-ups in Op-55. One of my jobs, for instance, was as a member of the Military

McDonald #4 - 220

Liaison Committee to the Atomic Energy Commission. We'd meet with the AEC Commissioners every other week or so and we'd make visits to Hanford, Savannah River and various places like that. There was a group in my division spending a lot of time on the development of an atomic-powered airplane. We often visited the General Electric Company plant just north of Philadelphia, where they were trying to build an engine for an atomic-powered airplane. Such a plane would look almost like a blimp, a big airplane, not just a normal patrol plane. But with a nuclear-powered engine, gosh, the thing could fly for an awful lot of hours.

I had a desk officer who really spent most of his time on that. It was really being pursued, no question about it. As a matter of fact, I think the officer was Eddie Outlaw. I'm not too clear but it seems like Eddie was the fellow who was quite interested in it.

Q: Something like that, did our research and development people put funds into the GE effort?

Adm. M.: I would doubt it, but I don't know. I expect that GE put them in. Then, of course, if they had sold it to us they would have gotten them back. That's the way a lot of that works, you know.

Q: Sort of a gamble, isn't it?

Adm. M.: Oh, yes, but let me tell you, Jack, we see a lot of criticism now and then about the boys in the Pentagon getting pretty close to the manufacturers. I said earlier that Martin came down and tried to sell us a strategic concept on using this big seaplane. And Ed Heineman I spoke of, he was over when I had the <u>Coral Sea</u>, showing us his idea of this little light attack plane. A lot of aircraft companies do these things and this is one reason that they employ retired officers sometimes. It isn't to come down to the Pentagon and get their friend to buy the product. This fellow might have had an idea when he was on active duty that he couldn't sell.

On the other hand, as a friend of mine he might be able to find out what I'm thinking, if I'm in Op-55. Then he can develop, or his company can develop, a concept which can be best fulfilled by a plane they propose to build, and that's the way the military get an awful lot of their things and thank goodness we do.

Q: That's very interesting. The military is to be the buyer of some of these special type planes?

Adm. M.: We don't have to take them but, gee, after all,

the boys in the Pentagon don't have all the intelligence in the world. Most aircraft companies have excellent planning groups. And we should be happy to benefit from their efforts. Holy smoke, look at the planners Mr. McNamara had. I don't think any of them had ever been in the military. They weren't always right, but they weren't always wrong either.

So, this togetherness with the people that ultimately produce the military hardware for you, I think it's just worth its weight in gold. Of course, you do make a lot of very close friendships, and this makes it pretty rough to avoid a conflict of interests.

For instance, I came back as CNO about the time they put out the directive where you couldn't take anything worth more than $25 or something like this and you couldn't accept this, that, and the other from anyone doing business with the Defense Department. Well, I went in to the Secretary and I said, "Look, this is ridiculous."

He said, "What do you mean?"

I said, "Probably one of the best friends I've got in the world is a former Secretary of the Navy. His name is Dan Kimball. I was his first aide. Dan's the head of Aerojet, and they sell many things to the Navy. What if Dan invites me out to Burning Tree to play golf or out to dinner? What am I supposed to do? Of course, it's a favor if I go, but it's as a friend."

Some of these things are a little bit difficult and I think the people who make up such regulations don't really understand or appreciate the situation. I just noticed the other day where somebody had been going over to Northrup's shooting preserve and the inference was that they were really cooking up some crooked scheme.

Q: People are involved and -

Adm. M.: Sure. When I was a Captain in Military Requirements I used to fly up to Grumman once every week or ten days, to see how they were progressing on various things, what they had in mind, what they were doing here and there, and, of course, when I did I'd go out to lunch, I didn't pick up the tab. But I didn't feel obligated to them either.

Q: Tell me about the atomic engine that GE was working on. What Happened to it? Why was it not feasible?

Adm. M.: Couldn't get the weight down to any practical size. It was too heavy by the time you got all the shielding, et cetera. There'd have to be many breakthroughs before you could get it down to a satisfactory weight. That, of course, is what they were hoping.

Q: Was Rickover interested in that?

Adm. M.: I don't remember or recall that he was at all. I wouldn't say yes or no on that. As a matter of fact, as far as I was concerned, I'm not sure I even knew Rickover existed at that time (1955-57).

Q: That was the period when the Polaris was being developed and he was interested there.

Adm. M.: Yes, the Polaris started along in there because I was one of those who recommended Red Raborn for the job.

Q: Oh, you were? Tell me about that.

Adm. M.: Well, Red's a classmate of mine. I'd known him for a long time. They had quite a few names on the list and I just put my two cents' worth in and said I thought that Red would probably handle that job in pretty good fashion because everything he went about he devoted all of his time to. And he'd been in missiles with Dan Gallery during the latter part of the war, or subsequent to the war and had done real well there.

Q: Gallery and Sides, too, I guess?

Adm. M.: Yes. I think maybe Red was more with Savvy than with Dan.

Q: Next comes an assignment which was quite different in nature and must have been vastly interesting. In November of 1957 you became Deputy Assistant Chief of Staff at Supreme Headquarters in Europe.

Adm. M.: Yes. In late 1957 I was called in I believe by Admiral Felt or Bill Davis - I think Admiral Felt - and told that I was being considered as the officer to relieve Paul Ramsey over in Paris. I had relieved Paul in Op-55.

Q: Oh, you had?

Adm. M.: Yes, and my comment about the Paris job was that I'd just about as soon jump out the window as go to Paris and work for the Boy Wonder. The Boy Wonder being General Lauris Norstad, U. S. Air Force.

Norstad finished West Point about two years after I finished the Naval Academy and probably got four stars three or four years before I got two and I had no particular desire to work for him under these circumstances. Whoever it was talking to me, either Bill or Arleigh or Don, said:

"All right. You go home and think about this and come back tomorrow. This is something you and your wife can discuss and you come back tomorrow and tell us who's better qualified."

I came back the next day and I said: "All right, you win."

So I went.

Q: You had a complete concept of what the job entailed?

Adm. M.: Not too much, but like most of those jobs, you know, the world wasn't coming to an end whether you did a good, bad, or indifferent job. The job over there was sort of political, getting to know NATO allies, you know. It's not really an operating job.

After it was announced that I was going, many people began to give me a lot of advice; most of it the same kind of advice. In those days many naval officers, especially Naval aviators, were seeing Air Force aviators under every desk. Don't trust 'em many said to me; be real careful.

The day before I left, I walked in to say goodbye to Don Felt and I said:

"Don, everybody else has been giving me advice and you haven't opened your mouth. Don't you have some advice?"

I saw Don in Honolulu just two and a half weeks ago and I repeated this to him. I don't know exactly what he said at that time but basically he said, "When George Anderson was over there in the early fifties working for Eisenhower, George and Eisenhower had great rapport and that was wonderful. If you will go over there and develop a personal relationship with General Norstad like that, you will have done a good job."

That's the best advice I had received. I went over there with a determination not to be suspicious of what they were saying or what they were doing. I'd been there probably less than two weeks when a message was brought down to my office for me to initial and I wouldn't initial it. A little bit later I got word that the General wanted to see me and I went up to General Norstad's office. I don't remember his exact words, but basically Norstad kind of smiled and said:

"I understand I'm about to make you unhappy if I send this message?"

I said: "No, you're not about to make me unhappy, General. You can send it if you want to but I'm not going to initial it until I have my say."

He said: "What's your say?"

And pretty generally I told him that he wasn't very popular in the Navy and if he sent this message without some preliminary explanation everybody in the Navy would say, "I told you so." I said, "I don't object to the contents of this message per se but it would be far better if you will let me call the Navy boss in London first" - that's where it was going, to CincNelm - "and explain the reason you're sending this." And then I added, "General, I'm working for you and I think part of my job is to let you know whenever I think you're doing wrong."

I'll never forget Norstad said: "You're working for me? All the others who have been over here have been working for the Navy."

I said: I'm working for the Navy too, but I'm working for both as long as I'm here."

Norstad said: "Make your telephone call, release the message."

From that day to this, I think, I became one of Norstad's best press agents and I expect some of the things Norstad said and wrote about me had as much to do with my being CNO as anything.

Q: And this came from Don Felt's advice!

Adm. M.: That's right. Norstad and I became very good friends during my time there and I stayed about twice as long as any of my predecessors. I had a little heart problem, a cardiogram abnormality while there. It turned out not to be serious and I've been all right ever since, but as a result of that, instead of leaving after a year and a half, I stayed nearly three years at Norstad's request. During those years I did a few things for General Norstad that no one ever knew I did.

We were about the same age and I wasn't in his Air

Force. He had me do things that people never suspected he would have asked me to do.

As an example, one Saturday noon I had my cap in my hand and was going to play golf and I was told, "The General wants to see you," so I went by his office with my cap in my hand, and he said, "Where are you going?"

I said, "I'm going home and go play golf."

"Oh," he said, "You just thought you were going home and then to play golf." Without going into all the whys and wherefores, I did not play golf. I got into an airplane at Orly, in civilian clothes, after dark. It landed me in Bonn, Germany, I stayed there for twenty-four hours. It picked me up after dark and brought me back, and I had taken a message to "Garcia" and nobody ever suspected.

I did a lot of little things like that that I think were helpful to the General and were certainly most interesting to me, most interesting. I enjoyed the duty. We were sort of working in a vacuum, you know. The countries weren't supporting NATO the way they said they would or the way they should and there was a lot of flim-flam and all of that, but that's part of the game.

Q: The French were still active members?

Adm. M.: The French were still there. My immediate boss,

first, was a French Army major general, later, a French Air Force Major general named Puget, whom de Gaulle ultimately made head of all the French armed forces. Subsequently, he retired and became head of Sud Aviation. I also became very close friends with the man who was the first three-star German officer to ever serve at SHAPE, an Army officer who had been a prisoner of the Russians for nearly eleven years. He himself later became chairman of the Joint Chiefs for the Germans.

At one time, the three top people in the Plans and Policy set-up at SHAPE were: the German Army officer General Foertsch, who later became chief of all the German armed forces; French Air Force General Andre Puget, who later became chief of all the French armed forces, and McDonald, who became CNO.

Q: That looks like a national war college crowd, doesn't it?

Adm. M.: Yes. Not too long after my arrival over there I was assigned a most interesting job. We'd get reports that had been filled in by these various NATO countries indicating what their contributions to the alliance were going to be. Then I would go to the capital of a country accompanied by several military people and two or three civilian economists and we would spend a week trying to decide in our own minds whether the country was devoting enough of its gross national product to the military. That was sort of ticklish ground we were walking on, but very interesting.

Q: Yes, and if you decided they were not, then what was the step to take?

Adm. M.: Nothing, just tell them. All that would do, you see, was give the commander, SacEur, Norstad, more ammunition when he went before the NATO civilian ministries. I think that was the reason for it. I don't remember which countries I visited now but I remember going to Copenhagen.

Q: You were really getting a dose of Europe, weren't you? You told me that when you went over in the <u>Coral Sea</u> it was the first time you'd been in Europe.

Adm. M.: That's right. But during these three years at SHAPE my wife and I put 30,000 miles on our Volkswagen travelling in Europe and mostly in NATO countries. I hate to say this - but at the National War College (now they're going to call it the National Defense University) they're putting more and more emphasis on pure academics in order to better convince the Congress that this school is necessary. When I think that the real value there (like my work at SHAPE) is the friendships you make and the understandings that develop. Why not say so and if the Congress won't buy it, do away with it. This stuff of trying to make students out of 40 and 45-year-old men irritates the hell out of me.

Over at NATO, I felt that the greatest benefit was becoming friends with the people of the various countries, the top military people. If they weren't the top then they were going to be, becoming close friends so that you can get to know and trust each other.

I think the contacts that you make in places like this are worth more than all the damned strategic plans you try to draw up because, you know, when the war starts you throw the plans out the window, anyway, pretty generally speaking. Not that you shouldn't have them, but knowledge of people is still more important I think. And to go back to the National War College. They're so terribly afraid somebody's going to think this year is a sabbatical. Why not? Why shouldn't these top leaders of the future who have been immersed in routine paper work year after year have a year to just "think" for a change. Congressmen aren't stupid and I believe the majority will support such a concept. As you might know by now this is a pet "peeve" of mine.

Referring again to the importance of knowing people, at one time there was at least one individual in the capital

of each European NATO country that my wife and I knew
well enough to pick up the phone and call up and say,
"Look we're coming to spend the night." That was in
the NATO countries plus Spain and Sweden.

Q: Naturally in Spain because that's your favorite country!

Adm. M.: Yes. For some time after I left the European
area we kept in contact with a lot of these people. Of
course, when I left Paris I went right on down to the
Mediterranean as a CarDiv Commander and then Commander of
the Sixth Fleet. On our first trip to Venice, a fellow
who used to work for me in Paris was the admiral in charge
of the whole Italian area of Venice. He was the boss
and that certainly made life a little more pleasant for us
during our stay there.

Q: What was SHAPE's relationship with CincNelm?

Adm. M.: Very little. About the time I got there and
before I got there, SacEur, Norstad, did not have control
over the Sixth Fleet. But later something happened back,
I don't remember just when, but the Sixth Fleet came under
him. I'm not sure whether it was through CinCNelm or not.
Anyway, some in the Navy got all jittery and exercised

about the change. The U. S. Admiral who was in Norfolk liked no part of it, of course, because he was the Navy NATO commander and their only real striking force was the Sixth Fleet. He sent his chief of staff over. I well remember that. I met him at the airport. He was coming over to discuss this and I told him, "Keep your shirt on. Norstad's not going to do anything about this, but if you fellows start raising the devil, he might. He's not going to change anything. I'm here and I know." And, of course, he never did. He didn't want to run the Sixth Fleet. But if we went to war, there was some tie-in through the Joint Chiefs. I don't remember the details of the organization now.

Q: That was an amendment to the National Security Act, wasn't it?

Adm. M.: It might have been, when they took all the forces away from the CNO and put them under a unified commander and so forth.

Q: Yes.

Adm. M.: That was what it was because CinCNelm was not a unified command. CinCNelm gavé me my logistic support however, I had a DC-3, which was used by the Naval aviators, not only at SacEur, which was the NATO command, but also by those assigned to CinCEur, which was the big U. S. command about ten miles away. Norstad was the boss of both, but he had a Deputy at CinCEur headquarters. He was sort of like Jimmy Holloway, senior, who was at one time the Chief of BuPers and DCNO Pers at the same time, but he had somebody else over at DCNO to run that office for him. We had quite a few naval aviators in the area and this DC-3 enabled them to get in their flight proficiency time and it was supported by a Navy unit over in London. The plane had to go over there now and then for overhauls and checks and what not, and we got all our logistic support from CinCNelm.

My contingency money was a bit more than the $30 a quarter I got when I had the Coral Sea and it came out of London. The first CinCNelm was Admiral Boone and then Admiral Holloway. I had known them both for a long time. Both appreciated the rather unique position that I was in over there at SHAPE. Being the senior U. S. naval officer on Norstad's staff and being No. 2 in a division where we had 52 officers from twelve different countries, I had to entertain quite a lot and both CinCNelms were most helpful.

Q: What about the NATO fleet exercises? There was one, I recall, about that time, I think it was 1958, Strikeback, off the Norwegian coast. Did you get involved in that?

McDonald #4 - 236

Adm. M.: No. The only ones we would get involved in would be in the Mediterranean. The politics of the thing were rather interesting because periodically SacLant would hold exercises over there and would want at least one of the carriers and some destroyers to come out of the Med and join them, but that was never permitted.

Q: That was not permitted?

Adm. M.: No.

Q: What was the overall objective of the Mediterranean exercises? To get these various fleet units to work together?

Adm. M.: That's all primarily, and they did it quite well, especially the French and Italians; sometimes Greeks but not much with the Turks. Generally French and Italians. The Italians have a lot of good ASW facilities at La Spezia and they had some rather interesting underwater things, you know, swimmers.

Q: Oh, yes, in World War II that was carried on, wasn't it?

Adm. M.: Yes. It was really interesting down there. They were exceptionally good at this.

McDonald #4 - 237

Q: Do you recall any one of those exercises?

Adm. M.: No, not particularly. I was more involved when I was down in the Med as Commander 6th Fleet than I was while at SHAPE.

Q: But you were, at that point, able to use some of the French North African ports, weren't you?

Adm. M.: Oh, yes. Sure, the French were completely in NATO when I was there.

Q: Was there any indication at that point of the future French action in withdrawing from NATO?

Adm. M.: No, I don't think so. I think this was done by de Gaulle. But I'm not damning de Gaulle. At times I have wished we had a de Gaulle in this country - someone who would let all other countries come after the U.S.A. I also often wish we had a Franco who'd take some of these people who try to shoot our president and, without all the fanfare, shoot them. Why fiddle around? No wonder we have no respect for law and order. I liked de Gaulle because he said after France, all my friends come first. I'm all for that. That's what I used to say in the Pentagon. Yes, I'm for unification, after the Navy. I made no bones about it. This doesn't mean that I'm discriminating against other services. Just like I say, "I'm a white, Anglo-Saxon Protestant male." I make no bones about that. I'm also a capitalist. I was born white, I was born an Anglo-Saxon, I was born a male. I elected to be a Protestant and I like capitalism. If its a question of Protestants or Catholics, it's going to be Protestant. If it's to be male or female, it's going to be male. If it's to be black or white, it's going to be white. No bones about it. But this doesn't mean that I'm going to be against this or that for no good reason. I think my record in the Navy shows that nobody ever treated minority groups nicer, but, hell, that doesn't mean that I like them as well as I do my own people. Some of us have gotten ourselves to the point where we're afraid to speak up as to what we believe. So-called minorities don't hesitate to speak up for themselves and I see no reason why others shouldn't openly support the groups to which they belong. If they don't, we'll soon have minority rule.

There is a school of thought that says if you really support NATO the way I think the agreement requires you to, you give up some of your sovereignity and de Gaulle said I won't do that. But this is an issue I never heard anything about during the three years I was at SHAPE.

Q: Was IberLant in existence then as a NATO command?

Adm. M.: No. That came along a little bit later.

Q: During your time there, was Spain trying to come into NATO? Was she interested in doing that?

Adm. M.: That's hard for me to answer. I don't know. It didn't come to my attention. The only thing that came up that I can recall that seemed to almost rock the boat a little bit was when the Germans made arrangements with Spain to have some training areas in Spain, maybe firing ranges for their airplanes, target areas, or something like that. That sort of got headlines with, shall we say, the wrong connotation. That seemed to exercise the top people a little bit.

Q: Because of World War II associations?

Adm. M.: Yes, but it quieted down. This was some of what was involved in my night trip to Germany.

Q: I see.

Adm. M.: That's the only time I ever heard it, but that didn't mean Spain was or wasn't trying to come in.

Q: Well, simultaneously, we were negotiating for the bases

over there.

Adm. M.: Yes.

Q: Did that cause a flap in NATO?

Adm. M.: I don't think so. Also I've never quite understood why the Scandinavians apparently dislike Spain so much.

Q: Norway and Denmark?

Adm. M.: Yes. Why? I can understand why a Communist would. Maybe Franco was too much of a dictator. Maybe that's the reason. I don't know.

Q: I think it is.

Adm. M.: But, holy smoke, the Scandinavians come down there on a vacation in droves. I've never quite understood it but I've never really inquired because I guess I've never had sufficient interest to be concerned. But they are the objectors. Of course, NATO-wise you don't have Sweden anyway, you only have Norway and Denmark.

All in all, my tour of duty in SHAPE was highlighted by my ever-increasing respect for Norstad both as an individual and the way he ran his show and by the opportunity

McDonald #4 - 241

not only to get to visit all these countries but to get to know so many people from so many of these other countries and well enough to find out why they thought the way they did.

Q: It was great preparation for the ultimate top job in Washington, wasn't it?

Adm. M.: Yes, but, of course, I never expected anything like that at the time.

Q: Would you give me a picture of Norstad, as you knew him in Europe? How did he operate?

Adm. M.: He operated in a rather aloof manner. Some people think that he's sort of high hat, but I think the fellow's a little bit shy. He's very competent. He makes decisions easily. I thought he relied a great deal and put a great deal on his chief of staff, gave him a great deal of authority and kept his fingers out of the minutiae. He was setting policy and dealing with the people on his level or above, and very effectively. When people would come to the headquarters in groups, especially if they were influential people, he got up and made the presentations and told them what was going on. He operated the way I think the top man should operate. Let the underlings

McDonald #4 - 242

do most of the work, you make the decisions they can't make, and you set the policy.

Q: You said that when you first came with him, you had occasion to tell him that he wasn't very popular with the Navy. Why was that?

Adm. M.: No Air Force fellow was very popular with the Navy then, especially with naval aviators, especially those who had been promoted very rapidly. I guess we were jealous. I think we were sensitive. We naval aviators felt that we were just as good or better flyers than the Air Force. We'd done our job just as well or better, and they'd been promoted two or three ranks ahead of us. We were just sensitive. I was, and I know a lot of others were.

Q: Didn't that have something to do with the newness of the Air Force as an independent service?

Adm. M.: In a way, but this went back to the Army Air Corps. No, this was a philosophy of growth. The Air Force grew rapidly and they took the officers who were in the Army Air Corps and promoted them as the Air Force grew. The Navy didn't do that. The Navy said we are aviators at sea. We're naval officers first and we're aviators next, and our aviation is built primarily around aircraft carriers. To handle an aircraft carrier you've got to be a sailor as well as an aviator.

And as I have pointed out earlier, instead of rapid promotions of existing naval aviators we selected a certain number of senior commanders and junior captains and gave them a course in flying. These fellows were then designated naval aviators but although they never went into operational units they did command our carriers, carrier divisions and task forces.

Q: You're talking about men like Admiral King?

Adm. M.: King was earlier. I'm talking primarily about McCain, Gunther, Buckmaster, Fred Sherman, Chub Brown - there must have been twelve or fifteen of them. They skippered many of our carriers during World War II. Not all of them though. Buddy Weiber and Ralph Ofstie, who were my COs in the Essex were oldtime aviators.

But, you see, as the Navy's aeronautical organization grew, they brought outsiders in to fill many of the top billets, basically speaking. Whether that was right or wrong I don't know. Of course, we also promoted fast in war, but not like the Air Force.

McDonald #4 - 244

Q: And they needed top fellows, so they promoted them from the ranks?

Adm. M.: From within the Air Corps. So, I wouldn't say there's resentment or jealousy. I think sensitiveness would probably be the best word.

Q: When you were there was it not the practice to have an annual big meeting?

Adm. M.: Shape-ex, yes. SHAPE exercises.

Q: Was Montgomery still in the picture?

Adm. M.: Montgomery was there when I first got there and was there for about a year, I guess.

Q: Tell me about him. How did he go over with the rest of them?

Adm. M.: Oh, I don't think people paid much attention to him one way or the other. I didn't. He was odd, but I knew he was odd before I got there. I didn't have any particular dealings with him. I used to talk to the U.S. Army officer, who did most of the work for him, but I didn't pay any attention one way or the other to him.

Q: Was he effective? Was he up to date in his understanding of the technology?

Adm. M.: I can't answer that, because I really didn't have dealings with him. About the only time I saw him was when he put on his own little show at Shape-ex. What I watched at Shape-ex was the presentations, how well they did it. There were some people who stood up there who should have stayed at home. I was raised to believe that you don't make a speech without learning how to do it, and be impressive. Even if what you say doesn't mean anything, be impressive, because if you're got something worthwhile to say but you're not impressive, it's not going over worth a damn.

Q: So, so true.

Adm. M.: I must say that the most impressive guy at the Shape-ex was Lord Louis Mountbatten. He walked out there like a king, he looked like a king, and he talked like a king. You can say what you want, but when he stepped up to give his little talk, people kept quiet. I think he's one of the most impressive fellows I've ever seen.

Q: He has presence.

Adm. M.: He really does, and he doesn't get up and assume

that he must talk for half an hour. If what he has to say takes ten minutes, he gets up there and talks for ten minutes and he quits. I used to like to see him walk across that floor - he's a big fellow, you know -

Q: Big and handsome!

Adm. M.: Really impressive. Of course, I'm very fond of him personally and I've known him for some time.

Q: This was in the time when we heard a great deal about - I don't know whether it was a policy or whether it was a stated purpose in defense - massive retaliation. Did it have any repercussions in terms of the defense of western Europe?

Adm. M.: I don't really think so. I don't remember. The only thing that I seem to recall is discussions we used to have about the utilization of what is known as tactical nuclear weapons. Would you or would you not; if so, at what point, et cetera. That was one of the things one was always thinking about. We used to have a lot of chitchat about that.

The plans were pretty generally always being worked on. They were never finished. You were always going towards the objective but you really never got there!

Q: Thinking a little more of our pronouncements on that, on retaliation, did the western European countries more or less have an attitude that they would be protected by our atomic power?

Adm. M.: I think the military believed that, if necessary, we would use our atomic power to protect them. I believe the military felt that. How others felt, I don't really know. I mean I don't know how the citizenry felt nor do I know how the political leaders felt. The people with whom I worked were all military. Oh, we had a couple from our State Department, but 99 percent were uniformed personel and I think they felt if the chips were really down, we would use our nuclear weapons to protect them.

Q: Was there some setback in their thinking due to the Suez crisis?

Adm. M.: I don't know. I was in Op-55 when we had the Suez crisis, and if there'd been any change in thought that had taken place before I got there I wouldn't know, but I wouldn't think so. Of course, they're like us. They don't all think alike about the past, present or future. Even today, we've those who believe Truman was right and those who believe Truman was wrong in using the atomic bomb.

McDonald #4 - 248

Q: Yes, that hangs on as a controversial thing.

Adm. M.: And, I guess, just like anything else, you'll never get a unanimous opinion on anything that isn't definitive.

Q: What was the impact of Sputnik?

Adm. M.: I don't recall.

Q: It had a terrific impact in this country, a momentary one, at least. We felt that we were far behind the Russians.

Adm. M.: I don't really recall. Maybe they were like me. I never saw any reason to put a man on the moon in the first place. But, once again, we don't all think alike.

Q: Tell me a little about your personal travels about Western Europe at that time. This is a part of your story.

Adm. M.: I went almost everywhere I wanted to go. The only trip I tried to make and was thwarted, was to go to Banak. Banak is on the northeastern tip of Norway, right next to Russia. We built a little airfield up there with wooden logs like crossties.

Q: No marston mat?

Adm. M.: No. The Norwegian air boss at - golly, I've forgotten the name of the town now, but it is a few hundred miles north of Oslo, on the coast. Anyway, I had an invitation to come up. I went up to Oslo to look over the underground headquarters we had there, NATO headquarters, then I flew on up to this town and this officer was going to take me to Banak in an Otter, you know, one of these little British planes. I think he was a brigadier general. Anyway, he was the boss at this base. I arrived there and he and his wife were just simply lovely to me. I stayed there two days and you couldn't cut the fog with a knife, so I never got to Banak.

I went to Norway, though, several times. I don't believe my wife ever went with me to Norway. I visited Copenhagen numerous times, my wife with me. We visited throughout Holland. Arrangements were made for us to visit a town in what they called the Northwest Polder, where they had newly created land out of the Zuider Zee. This was the first time - and I guess the only time - that I had ever been able to view an area where 3,000 to 5,000 people were living, but it was laid out completely for about 40,000.

Q: You mean it's a planned community?

Adm. M.: Yes, really planned. Everything was already in, streets, et cetera. It was quite interesting.

We visited several unusual spots that people arranged for us. SacEur ran a little atomic course, a little nuclear course, down at Oberammergau which lasted about a week to which we would send NATO officers. General Schuyler said to me one day, "I want you to go down and take that course."

I said, "General, I don't want to go down there. I've been on the military liaison committee with the Atomic Energy Commission for two years. I know ten times what they tell these fellows down there."

"Well," he said, "look, we've got to keep sending a certain number of U.S. people down there or these people from the other countries will really think we're not telling them anything! Why don't you take a little vacation?"

Q: Well, it's a vacation spot!

Adm. M.: "Go on down there." So I said fine. My wife and I went to Munich then on to Salzburg, on to Berchtesgaden and then to Vienna. From Vienna we came back to Garmisch and we stayed in one of the Army hotels in Garmisch

McDonald #4 - 251

because the accommodations were practically nil in Oberammergau and it's only a short drive from Garmisch to Oberammergau. I had a car and driver furnished to pick me and a couple of others up and take us up to Oberammergau each day to go to school. Odd though it might seem the Army also assigned a car and driver to me to turn over to my wife and another fellow's wife to take them sightseeing every day. Then, when the course was over, we went up to Munich and, from there, we followed the old romance trail, a trip that had been planned for me by my boss, the German army Lieutenant General Foertsch, who'd lived in that area all his life. So he had plotted this little trip for us with places to stay and things to see that I don't think the average tourist even knows exist. This was one of the most delightful excursions, I think, that we had the whole time.

Q: Staying in old inns and so forth?

Adm. M.: Yes. And I think maybe I have mentioned earlier that we also took a couple of vacations down in Spain from Paris.

Q: Where did you go in Spain?

Adm. M.: Went to Sitges. Sitges is a little town twenty-

McDonald #4 - 252

five miles south of Barcelona. At that time it had a nine-hole golf course and it was almost the only golf course in that area then. Now they've a lot of them, of course.

Q: That's near to the area where the hydrogen bomb dropped, isn't it?

Adm. M.: Yes, not too far from there. And we went down to Switzerland a couple of times. I don't believe we got down into Italy by automobile. We flew down there.

It was all very pleasant, but I began to wonder about the future. I had been scheduled to get a carrier division at the end of a year and a half. Then, because of my little cardiac problem I didn't get it, so I wondered what was going to happen to me.

Q: Was it something that came on suddenly or what?

Adm. M.: I guess.

Q: Was it a fluttering of the heart?

Adm. M.: No. There was no warning of any type. I called the Air Force flight surgeon out at Orly and told him that I was flying over to Luxemburg that day but I thought I'd get back about four o'clock, and I said, "Doc, how about giving me my annual physical?"

He did, and when he got through about seven o'clock that night he said, "Everything's fine except I don't like the looks of this cardiogram."

I said, "what do you mean, Jerry?"

"It zigs when it should zag."

So I said, "Well, what do you suggest I do?"

He said, "I suggest you get to a hospital as quick as you can. Well, within twenty-four hours."

I said, "Where?"

"Well," he said, "I think you ought to go to Weisbaden. It's an Air Force hospital and I'm an Air Force flight surgeon."

I said, "Will you fix it?"

He said sure, so I said, "Okay, call them. I'll be out here at seven o'clock in the morning and we'll fly over there."

So I went over there and they put me on various machines. Then they called the Doc at Orly and said, "We think there's something wrong with your machine. We don't find anything wrong with him."

When I came back he put me on two different machines but they all zigged when they should have zagged. Well, my wife was scared to death. But the next morning (Saturday) I got up and about twelve of us, including some RAFers, flew to St. Andrews in accordance with plans we'd had in the hopper for 2 months. We played golf there Saturday after-

McDonald #4 - 254

noon and then took some Rolls Royce taxis to Gleneagles. We didn't stay up too late. We played the king's course the next morning, the queen's course that afternoon, drove back to St. Andrews and flew to Prestwick to clear customs. Arrived back in Paris about three o'clock in the morning. My wife said, "With that cardiogram and you aren't dead yet! But then I began to get concerned.

Q: But you had no feeling at all?

Adm. M.: Never had an ache or pain. But communications went back and forth to Washington, and finally I received a letter saying that I had been removed from flight status. Then I wrote a letter to Arleigh Burke and to a doctor at Bethesda saying that if I'm sick I want to know and I'll get out of the Navy. If I'm not I want to be restored to full active duty. No more of this monkeying around.

Then I guess Arleigh called Norstad and wanted to know when I could be spared for ten days to go to the Navy's cardiac center at Pensacola. Norstad said right away.

So I went to Pensacola and I spent a week there. I was looked over by ten different doctors and they tested me on about seven different machines. When they got through, Dr. Greybiel, who was one of President Eisenhower's heart doctors, said: "That lead goes down when it should go up but all the other tests are positive. This is the only negative aspect we can find. If you really have heart trouble, there should be some other indication. I don't believe you've had a heart attack. You've had some kind of an abnormality. I think that you ought to be careful and perhaps you ought to go on the heart man's diet."

I said, "What's that?"

He said, "Eat no animal fats, no dairy products, etc." this, that, and the other, "don't run up the stairs, walk up the stairs, if you get in a ditch don't try to push the car out by yourself. Stretch out and take a little snooze every day after lunch. Take a walk after dinner every night."

"Well," I said, "what's my status?"

"I'm restoring you to full active duty. I can't restore you to flying, that's not my bailiwick, but I'm going to recommend they put you back to flying. Just make sure to use oxygen if you go above 9,000 feet."

I went to Washington on my way back to Paris and I asked "what's the status of my carrier division." Well, we don't know whether we're going to give you this carrier division or not. We're going to see how you make out.

I went back to Paris and Norstad said, "Let me settle this." I said, "How will you settle it?"

"Keep you here another year and a half. You bring your pillow out here and take your rest every day after noon. If you get tired you go home. If you need some exercise instead of working, just take it. You do what you want to do. But stay right here with me. You'll get your CarDiv."

And that's exactly what I did. Furthermore, I stayed on that diet religiously for three years. I haven't had an ache or a pain yet. At the end of three years at Bethesda they said, "Okay, start eating anything you want. Just be careful. But watch that weight like a hawk."

To this day I get on the scales every morning and I write it down in a book. If it goes up about three pounds I do something about it.

Now there was one doctor who said, "If this had happened to you three years earlier, I would have been sure that that lead is affected by scar tissue." I can't say it since it waited so late to show up. In 1950 they went into my back, took a rib out, and went in and cut a growth off the diaphragm behind my heart, and I have a scar from my mid-front to my back. They still wonder about this abnormality. I was at Bethesda at eight o'clock yesterday morning for an annual physical and this one doctor said, "If you had some aches and pains and people who didn't know your background took a cardiogram, they'd really think you were going to die, but it's just that one lead." And it's still like that.

McDonald #4 - 257

Q: It's still like that? It hasn't changed?

Adm. M.: No except for normal, expected changes. But this scare was a Godsend. I never was fat, but I lost about fifteen pounds on this diet and then I leveled off. Otherwise, you know, over there in Paris where we went out a lot and were faced with all their fancy sauces and drinking all the wine - I'd have weighed a ton, if I hadn't avoided eating and doing these things.

Q: That takes the heart out of French cooking!

Adm. M.: But I think it was one of those fortunate things, and Norstad was right, I got my health back and I got the same carrier division, a year later. Are we ready to go into that?

Q: What was the attitude at SHAPE headquarters toward the countries behind the Iron Curtain? What was the real feeling about them?

Adm. M.: I don't really know. These things were, I guess you'd say, relatively insignificant to me at the time and since the time was a lot of years ago, I just don't really remember.

I remember one thing very disctinctly. I had a German

McDonald #4 - 258

Air Force colonel who at one time was one of several aides to Herman Goering. After the war this fellow became a lawyer. Then, when they began rebuilding the German armed forces, he came back in the Air Force. He was a colonel. He was a fine-looking fellow. Every morning he looked like he just came out of a band box. And in one of our sessions about tactics and nukes and this and that and the other, I'll never forget this German saying to me, "Admiral, don't ever let my people get that bomb."

But I don't really have any recollection of any comments for or against or feeling for people on the other side of the Iron Curtain.

Q: What about Sweden? Did you go to Sweden?

Adm. M.: I did not go to Sweden while I was in Paris. I went to Sweden when I was CNO, but I didn't go to Sweden while I was at NATO.

Q: Was there ever any interest, while you were there, in Sweden becoming a member of NATO?

Adm. M.: Not among those with whom I associated. Anything of that nature would be dealt with, I think, purely on a political basis. I mean, after all, that's just like

Spain.

Q: Since President Eisenhower was president at that time and had been instrumental in setting up this headquarters in Paris, did he continue to show any great interest?

Adm. M.: Yes. As a matter of fact, I think he visited us twice. I well remember one visit that he made to us there because it was the first time that I had ever seen this Army colonel, who was his interpreter, Walters, perform. The President made a talk in English with Walters standing right next to him. Without a note, when the President had finished Walters gave it in French and I don't think he missed a period or a comma. A most fantastic performance. I got to know Walters later real well. He was at one time the Army attache down in Italy and he visited me in the Sixth Fleet a couple of times.

General Norstad and President Eisenhower were close friends. When Norstad would come back to Washington he would go to see the President and there's no question but what the members of NATO felt that Norstad's actions had the complete backing of President Eisenhower. Rightly or wrongly, Norstad didn't bother with the Pentagon.

Q: So Eisenhower did maintain that direct relationship?

Adm. M.: No question in my mind whatsoever but what it was maintained while I was there.

Q: When he came to visit NATO headquarters, was his naval aide with him, Pete Aurand?

Adm. M.: I don't remember. I know Pete well. I've known Pete for years and years. I expect he was. Remember, I was so impressed with this performance of Walters, fantastic. Of course, he became quite famous later as an interpreter.

Q: How was your French?

Adm. M.: Poor, I regret to say. One year in prep school, three years at the Naval Academy, and three years in Paris and I still don't speak it well. Sorry. But when I come back in the next world I want to come back as a linguist! My wife, who'd never taken a word of French, could do quite well. She went to the Alliance Francaise's school in Paris for a while. But out at NATO, all those fellows wanted to speak English. I had about a half-hour French lesson twice a week, but I think to learn a language, you have to live with a family and speak nothing but French.

Q: Get down to the basic needs that you have?

Adm. M.: Yes, that's right. This young lady who was my instructor made some comment about my lack of progress and I said, "Look, Michelle, I'm not over here for the purpose of learning French." And also about the time I'd be progressing real good, I'd have to go away for a while.

Finally, I was ordered to take a command of Carrier Division 6.

Q: This was in the year - ?

Adm. M.: 1960, along about the 1st of October. I knew that after I came back to the United States, took one month's leave, took over Carrier Division 6 in Mayport, Florida, I would go immediately back by air to the Mediterranean, where I was to take command of the striking force of the Sixth Fleet, which at that time was composed of three aircraft carriers together with their escorts.

I also knew that I would stay over there for several months. My wife, of course, wanted to be over there with me, but she also wanted to be with me during the one month leave. She hadn't been back to the United States for three years. I communicated with the Navy Department, saying that when we came back and I took over Carrier Division 6, couldn't they arrange for her to have some

Navy air transportation back to the Mediterranean area. The answer was no. I don't know how General Norstad found out about this, but he did and he sent for me and said:

"I understand the Navy's not going to provide Tommie with any transportation back to the Med. She's been over here three years. You know I've invited her to go back to the States with me two or three times and she wouldn't go because she said she wasn't going back for just a few days because she could only see half the people she wanted to see."

I said: "I know that, General."

He said, "I think she deserves a return trip to the Med. I tell you what," and he handed me a piece of paper and said: "Here is the name of an officer in the Pentagon. When you leave Mayport to fly back to the Med, you put Tommie on a commercial plane or in an automobile and get her to Washington, D.C. and tell her to call this fellow. I will know what you're going to do. I will know when you're going to take over, when you're going out to sea, and when you're going to end up in Naples. If you will get her up to Washington, I'll have that girl in Naples by the time you get there."

By gosh, she went to Washington, she got on an Air Force airplane, they flew her to Orly Field in Paris, France, and she was met by a fellow who took her across

McDonald #4 - 263

the ramp and put her on another airplane and she went to Naples.

Q: The Air Force is less stuffy than the Navy about such things?

Adm. M.: Well, this thing the Navy did just doesn't make sense.

Q: Tell me about the striking force.

Adm. M.: Well, I came back to the States and took a month's leave, then took command of Carrier Division 6 in Mayport and then flew over to Nice. At that time, we had three aircraft carriers in the Mediterranean. I don't know just why we had three there but at various times tension would seem to build up and although we usually kept two, at times we'd build up to three. Maybe we had kept three from the time we had the Lebanon fracas in '58. We had three carrier divisions involved with the carriers in Atlantic and in the Mediterranean, and each carrier division was composed of two carriers. And since we kept two carriers in the Med all the time normally, we tried to rotate them on a one-in-three basis, and we'd have a carrier division commander in the Mediterranean. The other two carrier division commanders were back on the East Coast, one at

Norfolk and one down at Mayport, and they would be doing their administrative work, supervising the training of those units not deployed and serving on courts-martial, and things like that.

Q: During that time, were they under CinCLant?

Adm. M.: Yes, those located on the East Coast. But someone got the idea, somebody I don't know who, that two carrier division commanders on the East Coast weren't busy enough, and of course they just couldn't stand to think of somebody not working twenty-four hours a day. So they decided they'd have two carrier division commanders in the Mediterranean, two of the three. Well, you know, one of those wouldn't be doing anything, either.

Anyway, when I got over there the then carrier strike force commander (who had administrative command of one of the other two carrier divisions) was a couple of years junior to me, so I relieved him as striking force commander. This striking force was like a task force in World War II. Usually we'd conduct training exercises with two carriers and leave one carrier in port. But now and then we'd have all three of them out. Pretty generally, though when we had the three carriers, we'd have two of them at sea and one of them in port. And, of course, when I say two carriers I really mean two thirds of the entire striking force.

Q: That was under the Sixth Fleet?

Adm. M.: That was under the Sixth Fleet which was commanded at that time by Admiral Anderson, George Anderson. I believe I mentioned earlier that he and I had been together on many occasions. He had command of the Mindoro and, with one intervening officer, I commanded the Mindoro. He commanded Carrier Division 6 and, with one intervening officer, I then had Carrier Division 6.

Q: You had parallel careers?

Adm. M.: Yes, we did. One very interesting thing happened at this particular time. The skipper of the Saratoga, which was my flagship when I had the striking force, was the man who had been my executive officer when I had the Coral Sea.

The only unusual incidents that happened during these few months - I guess I must have gotten there in November and I came back around in March or April of the next year - we were going in to Athens, arriving on a Monday morning, with the Saratoga and several destroyers. About one or two o'clock in the morning we had a terrible fire in one of the firerooms. People say, well what are you supposed to have in a fireroom if you don't have a fire. Well, you only have a fire in the furnace and not in the fireroom itself.

There was a hot oil line under very high pressure that popped and the oil hit something and it flashed and the result was catastrophic. I think it was probably one of the most tense periods in my entire Navy career. This fire was so bad that the entire ship began to fill with smoke, everywhere. Nobody could stay in the control center on the hangar deck. We didn't know whether it was burning or smoking. There was smoke pouring out everywhere. Many were already asphyxiated, and many communications within the ship were cut off. Finally, I ordered destroyers to approach us, to come alongside. I felt we might have to abandon ship.

Q: What time of day was this?

Adm. M.: Early in the morning. This was a frightening situation; this happening on a ship full of gasoline and full of bombs. At one time the commanding officer said to me: "I think I'd better flood that fireroom." He was waiting for me to give him my opinion. I never opened my mouth. After a while he looked at me, and I said, "This is your ship, Roger."

Fortunately, within thirty minutes after that, we began to get the fire under control.

Q: Your silence might have indicated to him that you disapproved of that suggestion?

Adm. M.: Maybe. I brought the destroyers in, not alongside, but really ordered them in close. I didn't know just how bad the situation was because we on the bridges couldn't find out what was going on down below. No communication. It was pretty rough.

Q: There was so much smoke nobody could go down?

Adm. M.: I forget now how many people we lost. I know we lost a lot of them, including the best chaplain I've ever heard preach. Most chaplains aren't very good preachers but this man, who was a Lutheran, was marvelous. The executive officer came out of his room and fell in the passageway almost asphyxiated. Somebody stumbled on him or he'd have been dead. Stumbled on him and dragged him to the light. Happened to be a doctor there and he stuck a knife in his throat and put a tube in the hole. He's living today.

All was pretty well clear by daylight and I prepared

to carry out the planned schedule except we couldn't drop anchor until around noon instead of at 8 a.m..

I was scheduled to start making official calls at 8:30, and I'd set up a system where, instead of the people returning my calls as individuals, they would come out for lunch and we would give honors to the senior one. We'd all have lunch and then we'd give honors to the senior member of the party upon their departure. Helicopters in those days weren't too reliable, and we weren't supposed to go but 20 miles or so away from the ship. I obviously had to use a helicopter if I was to make my calls on time and yet we were quite a distance from Athens. So I sent some destroyers full speed ahead spaced three or four of them 10-15 miles apart. Then my aide and I embarked in a helicopter and flew over first one destroyer and then another on in to Athens. I made my calls and told everyone that there'd be some delay in the ship's arrival and that we would have lunch at one o'clock instead of twelve.

By the time we finished our official calls about 11:30 the ship came in and we went on back aboard. Believe it or not they'd cleaned it up pretty well. We had our official lunch. By this time all required communications with Washington had been completed and therefore I then explained to all of our guests just what had happened.

Quite an experience.

As a result of that fire, we had to lock one of the Saratoga's four shafts. We continued to operate for about two months on three shafts and came all the way home to Mayport on three shafts.

Q: What did that do to her speed?

Adm. M.: Cut it down. Therefore, our operations were then somewhat dependent on how much natural wind we had. If we couldn't get enough wind over the deck for certain planes, we wouldn't launch those planes or else you'd launch them light. After all, it wasn't war, you know, and we didn't have to put bombs on the planes if we didn't want to. But we never missed an operation after our week's stay in Athens. We just operated on three shafts.

That was the most interesting thing that happened while I was over there. I came on back to Mayport in March.

Q: You might tell me about the diplomatic responsibilities. You said you had to pay calls.

Adm. M.: They weren't too great at that time because most of the time I would be in port with the Commander of the Sixth Fleet and he would make the calls. Usually when the Sixth Fleet went east, took their eastern swing, so-called, part of the ships went to Beirut and part of them went to Istanbul and those that went to Istanbul would always go to Athens first. So in this particular instance, Admiral Anderson had gone with the group to Beirut, and then I was the senior one in Athens.

I didn't have to make as many calls then as I did with the Coral Sea, because with the Coral Sea I was more often the senior one in port, whereas this time I was often in port with the commander of the Sixth Fleet. Of course, once again, my NATO duty paid off because in nearly every one of these ports I'd go into there was somebody there that I'd either been with in SHAPE or if the fellow I was with was still at SHAPE, he would have written to his buddy about me. So we'd usually see old friends or meet mutual friends in these ports.

Q: These calls, at times, must have been rather burdensome, weren't they?

Adm. M.: Yes, particularly the language. As I said earlier, if I'm reincarnated I want to be a linguist because it's frustrating and unbelievably tiring to be unable to communicate with someone with whom you really want to talk. But most of the people I was with could speak pretty good English, especially the military men. The problem is not the official but the social affairs with the wives. They don't usually speak English. You go to a dinner party and you have a non-American on each side and you have to play charades. So many of the ladies over there simply haven't had the opportunities to learn English the way the men have; again I say especially the military men.

Q: Later on, when you became CNO, was there any feed in in this area? I mean the fact that there should be more emphasis of teaching languages? Did you do anything about that?

Adm. M.: No, not particularly. I've said for a long time we should emphasize languages a great deal, but, once again, it's what comes first. The general policy is: if and when we're going to send you to a foreign country we'll give you a course of language before you go, like they do our attaches. And I must admit, if there's a question of learning to fly or learning to speak French, you're going to learn to fly. But I still don't think we put enough emphasis on it.

You take our National War College, I'd rather study a language down there than strategy and tactics because you learn that when you're out at sea. Again, the Navy's different. We have our laboratories (ships) in peacetime but the Army doesn't.

Q: The striking force was under the Sixth Fleet, but SacLant also had a call on them - ?

Adm. M.: No, not SacLant. SacEur, the NATO Commander in Paris, but not SacLant. The NATO commander of the forces in the Mediterranean was sitting up in Paris. But he let Commander Sixth Fleet operate these forces the way he wanted to. I think Commander Sixth Fleet probably sent a schedule up to Paris and he showed to, I guess, the fellow who had the job I had, but all I did was just keep track of where they were.

Q: The striking force didn't necessarily engage in any different type of operations from the ordinary units of the Sixth Fleet?

Adm. M.: They were the ordinary units.

Q: Yes, but this was the other half?

Adm. M.: The striking force was composed of the carriers and the accompanying destroyers and a cruiser or cruisers. Then you had a submarine force. Then there was an airborne ASW force, headquartered in Naples (at that time we did not have an ASW carrier in the Med). So basically your carriers and destroyers and cruisers belonged to the striking force. Then you had your submarine force, then you had your ASW force, and you could bring them all together to conduct certain types of operations.

Q: that's what I was trying to say. There were no additional duties for the striking force over and above the activities required - ?

Adm. M.: No. It would have been all the same if you'd had two carriers and all the same if you'd had one carrier - just training operations in order better to prepare you to carry out wartime operations in case you had to.

Q: Then, why the special designation "striking force"?

Adm. M. Because that's almost the only force the Navy can strike with. You could project your power against either other ships or against land. I guess you could call a nuclear sub a part of a striking force, but I think they call that a strategic force. It's just military nomenclature.

When I came back to Mayport, the Saratoga, because of the fire, discharged her planes and went up to Norfolk to get repairs. The Shangri La, which was the other carrier in CarDiv 6 was in Mayport. I put my flag in her for a little while and then since they were going to do a lot of repair work on her, I put my flag ashore. My office really, but it is called your flag. I hadn't been ashore very long when Mr. Trujillo was shot. Then sombody in Washington got all excited and thought the Navy had better get a striking force, so-called, down in the area of the

Dominican Republic since they didn't know what was going to happen. So I was ordered to form a group with the Shangri La and some destroyers and head south. Gosh, we had to put our planes on the Shangri La with half the flight deck torn up. But they repaired it fast and away we went.

We spanned the water and the air off the Dominican Republic for several weeks. Nobody knew what we were supposed to do, so we just cruised around and showed the flag and tried to be prepared for any eventuality.

Q: And that let the people on the island know that you were out there?

Adm. M.: That's right. After a certain number of weeks we came back to Mayport. And then about that time, George Anderson went to relieve Arleigh. They called him back to relieve Arleigh without ordering a new Sixth Fleet commander. He left without being relieved but I was told that I was going over there but it was all a deep, dark secret. I took some people out to dinner on the Shangri La, it was Saturday night. One of them was a retired rear admiral. And I got a telephone call which said, "I've just come from the White House. You're going to be Commander, Sixth Fleet, unless somebody publicizes the fact within the next six hours. The President says he is damned tired of news getting out before he releases it."

"Well," I said, "How long have I got to wait?"

He said: "You can tell the people who are there now because he said it about five hours ago, so you can rest assured that you're going to be it.

So Monday morning an airplane arrived to take me to the Med. Oh yes, I spent Sunday selling my automobile and packing.

On Monday, I was relieved as Commander, Carrier Division 6, went down to the wardroom where my wife put three stars on me, and my wife, myself, a Filipino boy, my aide, his wife, their two small daughters, and their cat got on the airplane and away we went to Nice!

The next day, aboard the USS Springfield I took command of the Sixth Fleet by relieving the chief of staff who'd been acting.

Q: Before you go into that, a comment on the policy of secrecy in naming a man to command. I don't quite understand that, why it's necessary?

Adm. M.: Look, when I was in Ankara, Turkey in 1963 I was told by telephone at 1 a.m. Saturday to come back to Washington and be there at 7:30 Monday morning, they wouldn't even tell why, even though it was to inform me that I was to be CNO. It's just asinine, in my opinion.

Q: Was it a policy of BuPers, or what?

Adm. M.: I don't understand it. I never have. I don't know what was involved in my particular case. Once the President made the decision, you ought to let it go. I understand the reason for secrecy up until that point. In other words, if the chief of BuPers wants you to have this job and he comes in and recommends you to me and I'm CNO but you can't get that job until it's also approved by the Secretary of the Navy, the Secretary of Defense, and, maybe, the President then if the word gets out as soon as the nomination gets to me, some of the political animals might start getting their fingers into the pie.

Rear admirals are selected by selection boards and Secretaries or even the President can take names off that list but they can't add names. It's been said that they do add names. I know one case where a name was added, but the way the Secretary had it added was to change the precept under which the Selection Board was operating, that is, he issued a different directive to the selection board which, of course, is always made public. But neither the Secretary, nor anyone else can just willy-nilly add a name. But when you go from two stars to three stars and four stars, that's a different proposition. Those decisions are made as a result, pretty generally, of recommendations by the Chief of BuPers, who usually talks - when I was there - to the Vice Chief, and then the CNO and SecNav. That used to be the end, but now it goes on to the Secretary of Defense and probably go through his Deputy. And any one of them might have a couple of assistants they want to talk to, for all I know.

You can get too many people mixed up in this thing. The civilian hierarchy don't know our people very well. They've only seen them recently, generally speaking. That's not always true, but, generally speaking, they've only seen them a short time. Most probably they've only seen them in one assignment. They aren't as capable of judging military personnel as are their seniors in uniform. On the other hand, when he comes to business dealings, dealings with the Congress, this should be the civilian secretariat's long suit. That's where they should be a lot better than the military. In fact, I sometimes think that the military shouldn't be forced to have all these dealings with Congress.

Q: I would think that the Secretary would feel a little bit at a loss in invading a field - ?

Adm. M.: Ah, no, even though often a particular officer is the best they know, because they don't know anybody else. The Under Secretary tried to get me to have a particular captain over in Vietnam put on the command list because the Under Secretary thought this man was so good.

Well, within a month, he got court-martialed. He was in more skullduggery with the post exchange and Chinese women in Vietnam than you could shake a stick at. He made a wonderful impression and, he was energetic.

I told the Under Secretary that he'd better think about this because I didn't approve at all. And while he was thinking the rats came out of the woodwork and the fellow ended up with courts-martial all over the lot.

The Under Secretary came in later and said, "I'm not going to stick my nose in this personnel business any more."

I didn't know the officer personally but I told the Under Secretary that before they put people on the command

McDonald #4 - 279

list, a board of senior officers study years of records. Some say that it is helpful if someone on these selection boards knows you but you might also be adversely known and in that case it might hurt you instead of help you.

Anyway, to get back to where we were. In taking over the Sixth Fleet, I then acquired, attained, a spot that I had wanted for some time. I wanted to be commander of the Sixth Fleet.

Q: You'd wanted that ever since you were in Paris, hadn't you?

Adm. M.: Yes, or even before that. I'd been in the Pacific a lot but I thought that command of the Sixth Fleet was one of the finest jobs that a naval officer could get at sea.

Q: It was one of the active commands?

Adm. M.: Yes, very active, and when you weren't operating at sea your in port activities could be very pleasant and not the sameness that one might find in the Orient. There was as much difference, you know, between Istanbul and Marseilles, as there is between Marseilles and New York. Each country is different. We had no particular problems during my about twenty months with the Sixth Fleet. The world in general over there was stable. Very interestingly, the man who's been trying to get Lebanon back on a stable basis recently (1975) was the prime minister at that time, Rashid Karami. I got to know him reasonably well. Surprisingly, while in Lebanon I found that there was a Maronite Pope. I hadn't known that there was but one Pope. But the Maronite Pope lives over there and I had the opportunity of having lunch with him a couple of times.

Each time we visited Turkey, I always went over to Ankara. The ambassador there was a National War College classmate of mine, Ray Hare, and I think I mentioned that when I was skipper of the Coral Sea I had an opportunity to befriend the daughter of the mayor of Istanbul and there were some people there who still remembered that, and we enjoyed Istanbul.

Every time I went in to Athens, about the second day my wife and I would go out to the summer palace and have lunch with King Paul and Queen Frederika and the family. Just a quiet lunch with no one else there except the young Spaniard who was courting the older daughter, ultimately married her and is now (1976) the King of Spain.

Q: Juan Carlos?

Adm. M.: Yes. And I must say that the king and queen and their daughters and Constantine almost invariably accepted our invitation to come to the ship for luncheon during our stay in Athens. When we were first there, the prime minister was the man who is the head man now, Caramanlis.

Italy. I'd been to the Naval Academy graduation when I had the Coral Sea and I'd been down there once from Paris and I was there with the Sixth Fleet. So I've attended three graduations at the Italian Naval Academy in Livorno. I became friendly with the prefect there in Livorno at one time, and he later became the prefect in Naples. Of course, I visited La Spezia on several occasions since a NATO ASW school was established at La Spezia.

Q: You might tell me about the present Italian fleet?

Adm. M.: I can't, I don't have any idea.

Q: I mean the fleet as it was then.

Adm. M.: The fleet as it was then was very good. Generally, we had only destroyers operating with us even though they had some submarines.

Q: Did they have some cruisers?

McDonald #4 - 282

Adm. M.: Yes, but since a destroyer is both an escort and an ASW vessel, they were especially helpful.

Q: Were they their own build?

Adm. M.: I don't remember. I think so. One interesting thing was, of course, by the time I got the Sixth Fleet the French had withdrawn from NATO, but we had a lot of exercises with them.

Q: How did this come about?

Adm. M.: This came about because my ex-boss and longtime friend was the senior military man in Paris then, Andre Puget. Many of our exercises involved launching theoretical atomic strikes against the mainland and the French would like to practice defense against that. General Puget would send an air force brigadier to my flagship and with my operations officer they'd arrange operations and we just wouldn't communicate with Paris. That's all there was to it.

Q: Wouldn't this leak back to de Gaulle in some way?

Adm. M.: You know, people in high places reach the point often when they say "please don't ask me." There are things that they would like to see happen but they just can't afford to agree for them to happen. I didn't ask a lot of questions. Andre just communicated with me that he would send this man down and said make your arrangements. That's all there was to it. So we held numerous exercises. Mostly strategic strikes and they'd get defense practice.

Q: Yes, certainly advantageous to them.

Adm. M.: We didn't say anything to anybody. We might have had trouble if we had some crack-ups or collisions but it didn't happen.

Q: Do you know how long that kind of arrangement worked out?

Adm. M.: No, I really don't. It seems to me like we started this when I'd been down there about six months and maybe it's still going on. I don't really remember the details of it now because I just turned it over to Fred Bardshar, who was my operations officer, then I didn't pay any more attention to it. Because, you see, at this time, I wasn't the striking force commander. I was the Sixth Fleet commander. How my operations officer worked with the other people, I didn't pay much attention to.

That's one beauty of being lazy, you know, you don't

stick your nose in all the petty details. Let your helpers do it and if they get in trouble, then you get somebody else.

Q: This seems to have been a kind of reflection of what Norstad did?

Adm. M.: Yes, well, I guess. Remember I said earlier that when I was an ensign my division officer told me that the best officer in the Navy is the man who did the least and got the most done. I think when you're an ensign or a JG or two stripes, alongthere, you must operate in a certain way, but I think when you get a reasonable amount of rank, if you don't delegate you're in trouble. And if you try to look over the fellow's shoulder, to whom you delegated responsibility, sooner or later you're going to get in trouble.

Q: Let him -

Adm. M.: Sure. In other words, when the job gets too big for you to do it, then you must delegate, and when you delegate, for goodness sake, don't tell them how to do it. Tell them what you want done. So many times people tell you what to do and then try to tell you how to do it.

Q: While you were in command of the Sixth Fleet, several

McDonald #4 - 285

very important incidents happened over in this direction. First, there was the Bay of Pigs, then there was the Cuban missile crisis. What demands were made upon you and the Sixth Fleet in these emergencies?

Adm. M.: The Bay of Pigs actually happened just before I got over there.

Q: It did, indeed, yes.

Adm. M.: It happened while I was in Mayport with my carrier division staff ashore. One of the squadrons that belonged to my division was embarked in an aircraft carrier that did participate, or shall we say was prepared to participate in the Bay of Pigs, and because of that I got a good deal of information about the Bay of Pigs from the point of view of the pilots in the squadron who were prepared to do what they were never called upon to do.

While in the Sixth Fleet, however, the missile crisis did happen.

Q: I would like you to elaborate on that, the pilots who were called upon to do things that they were not prepared to do.

Adm. M.: They were not called upon to do what they were prepared to do.

Q: What, for instance?

Adm. M.: Well, they were prepared, of course, to give air support to the landings. Had they been permitted to do this, there's no question in my mind but that the situation would have turned out differently. I think it would have turned out that there would be no Castro today. Whether that would have been good, bad, or indifferent is anybody's guess, or whether they should have participated, I don't choose to say because I'm not familiar with the background. The fact is that when you send people out prepared to do a certain job, and they are expecting to be called upon to do it, if it's necessary, and then when it obviously becomes necessary and they aren't called upon, they wonder what's going on.

Q: Of course, they were not given much of a story, so they didn't know?

Adm. M.: No, I suppose not. I never really questioned it very much, but that's the way to really destroy morale, if you know what I mean. Maybe they were told later, but I don't think so. There's a difference of opinion there.

The missile crisis was a little different. This was rather interesting to me. I had a hernia that needed to be repaired. There was no urgency involved, but on one of our swings to what we called the Eastern Med (namely; going over to Athens and Istanbul and Beirut) we were conducting a lot of exercises en route, that is, from the Cote d'Azur, from southern France, to these other areas, with few exercises being scheduled on the return trip.

Anyway, this particular time, the flagship, which was the Springfield, a cruiser, was scheduled to go in to the Greek port of Saloniki, and when we left that port, the flagship and the Commander, Sixth Fleet, were not scheduled to participate in any exercises on the return trip. In other words, the ship was going from that port all the way back to Villefranche singly, and I selected that time to have my hernia repaired.

So, just prior to the departure of the ship from Saloniki, I took off in an airplane for Wiesbaden, Germany, and entered the Air Force hospital for a hernia operation. The flagship wasn't due back into Villefranche for a reasonable number of days, and, of course, I thought that I'd get over this and get down to the flagship without really being away from what was going on very long. But a few days after my operation I was listening to the radio in my room, on the 22nd of October, I believe it was, and I heard on the radio about the missile crisis.

Well, to make a long story short, the next morning I was wheeled out of that hospital into a car and into

McDonald #4 - 288

an aeroplane and flown to Nice, and picked up by helicopter at the airport and deposited on my flagship in Villefranche Harbor.

Q: This was at your own request, was it?

Adm. M.: Yes. I've been asked, what did you do after you returned to the flagship? We didn't do anything. I was asked from Washington what I proposed to do and I said nothing, because at that time we were operating on a schedule where approximately half of the Sixth Fleet was always at sea and the other half was in port, and the half that the flagship was with, namely the <u>Springfield</u> was in Villefranche and the carrier was in Genoa. I saw no reason to start running around like a madman in the middle of the ocean with every ship we had and nothing to do. So I proposed to sit there and take it easy except that, of course, we went on the alert. And that's what I had recommended in the Suez crisis when I was in the Pentagon, but I was overruled. Back then, we got everything that could float and sent it out in the middle of the ocean and I often thought, for what?

That portion of the Sixth Fleet which was in port just stayed in port and a lot of my staff laugh about this now. They say "everybody was running around, excited, except us." We never made a move that we wouldn't have made otherwise, except that those ships that were in port maintained a continuous four hour alert.

Q: I believe there were various merchant ships en route to Cuba. Were there not some from the Med area?

Adm. M.: I don't know whether there were or not. If there were, we in the Med didn't pay any attention to them one way or the other. In other words, this wasn't a Sixth Fleet problem.

Q: No, it wasn't.

Adm. M.: I felt that this was a problem where we should be ready to move if called upon to do so, but I saw no reason to start wearing out our equipment just to be out in the middle of the Med. Hell, you can't do any more in the middle of the Med than you could in port. I didn't think anybody was going to bomb us because we were sitting in port, just because of the Cuban crisis.

Q: I'm really surprised that you didn't get directives from the White House or the Secretary of Defense to do various things?

Adm. M.: I think they thought I was going to put all

elements to sea, but I didn't! And I feel the same way now. Before you move a lot of equipment and get a lot of people involved, you must decide what's your objective. There's no use running around in circles. That Cuban affair was pretty far removed from us. And, as I say, half of our force was already at sea.

I think that was the only thing of particular importance that happened during the time I had the Sixth Fleet. Really, at that time Commander, Sixth Fleet's work was about three-fourths diplomatic, showing the flag over there meant an awful lot, you know. That's one of the reasons we had the Sixth Fleet there, to convince the people that we were with them if anything should happen.

Q: And there are some mighty sensitive people there, aren't there?

Adm. M.: Very, and the way to convince them that you are with them is to be there. Of course, today things have changed. I didn't have to worry too much about the North African coast when I was there. Now things are quite different. The British were still welcome, or accepted if not welcome, along the African coast and were very definitely in charge at Malta. We were welcomed in there as a port of call.

Q: Was Mountbatten there at that time?

Adm. M.: No. I've forgotten his name now, a red-headed admiral that I had known before. No, Mountbatten wasn't there. I don't remember whether Mountbatten was the head of the Navy or the head of the Joint Chiefs then. I had called on him after I became boss of the Sixth Fleet. My real immediate peacetime boss was in London, CinCNelm, and I went up there to call on him and I also called upon Mountbatten because, as I think I stated earlier, I had known Admiral Mountbatten for quite some time.

Commander Sixth Fleet was a pleasant tour of duty. The one fringe benefit that I had which I think was worth its weight in gold was that my wife was authorized to ride in naval aircraft other than scheduled transports. The wives of certain four-star officers, and at that time the wives of two three-star officers in the Navy, one in the Sixth Fleet and one in the Seventh Fleet were authorized transportation in military aircraft provided that their husbands thought that their presence would help them carry out their duties, and there was no question about it in the Med. Consequently, let's say I was going out to sea for a week or ten days on an exercise and then go in to Naples. If we were going to arrive in Naples on the 5th, I'd send a message and say "pick up Commander, Sixth Fleet's party in Nice at ten o'clock on the morning of of the 3rd or the 4th for delivery to Naples." My wife would be at the airport. She never knew what kind of an airplane she was going to get in because she would fly in our logistic planes which were flying almost daily from Lisbon to Barcelona and all the way to Naples and Athens, hauling mail and personnel and things of that type. They would land at Nice and she'd get aboard. The type of planes she flew in most of the time were the little airplanes that they flew passengers aboard a carrier, those COD airplanes.

She would then go to Naples and we would rent a suite in a hotel, and most of the time there would be the wives of three or four of the officers either on my staff or on the flagship who would also "follow the fleet." They'd have to pay their own way, and they'd very seldom be the same wives, but, gosh, out of the sixty wives or seventy, there would always be three or four. They would join my wife and this was fantastic because in a lot of those areas local wives aren't usually invited out, but by golly, if our wives were there, then the wives of the foreigners would be invited. I just think it was worth its weight in gold. I really do.

One of the most unusual things happened in Casablanca. There were some businessmen (brothers) there named Septi, and every time the Commander Sixth Fleet went in there they always gave a diffa, which is a large native dinner, you know, where you sit practically on the floor. I'd been to a couple and never saw any women, except if you wanted to look up above, you could see some on a gallery or whatever it was called. No women at dinner, though, ever. But the last time we went to Casablanca my wife was there and the wives of, I think, three of my staff officers and one flagship officer and, believe it or not, they were invited to the dinner. We were playing golf at Rabat and my wife told me that they had been invited and I said, I don't believe it. Then I kind of jokingly said, "I guess that will change things, won't it?"

She said, "What do you mean?"

I said, "Well, normally, I would have been the guest of honor, but now you will be."

She said, "So what?"

I said, "So, now you can eat the eye of the sheep!"

Well, I'm telling you she didn't enjoy the rest of her golf game until she finally found out they didn't do that in that part of the Arab world!

Q: That was a mean thing to say!

Adm. M.: I tell you the presence of a few of these wives made all the difference in the world because the other wives would then come out.

I was paying for a place to live out of my own pocket,

not government-furnished, in Cap Ferrat all the time. I also had to pay hotel bills in all these ports out of my own pocket without any reimbursement, I couldn't very well have afforded the air transportation too, but by this being supplied it made things much more pleasant and, I think, more worthwhile for everyone.

Q: When you were called upon to entertain some of these people from on shore, were the entertainments always held on board your flagship? Or did you do it on land sometimes?

Adm. M.: Almost entirely on the flagship. On several occasions I held a rather large reception in Nice, at a hotel in Nice, because, you see, our flagship was home-ported in Villefranche, and practically all of our families lived there. We got to know a lot of the people and became somewhat obligated to many in the civilian community there. Additionally, some of our ships were always in Cannes, on the other side of Nice. Consequently there were quite a few individuals in that general area who were consistently helpful and kind to our people. So occasionally I'd give a large reception at a hotel in Nice. Generally, though, I'd entertain on the flagship.

I had a locker full of whiskey on my flagship that I'd replenish periodically in Gibraltar very inexpensively and I'd lock it up. Nobody touched it ever on the ship and it wasn't for sale. But let's say we were going in to a particular port and I wanted to have a dinner party aboard ship. I might well have a cocktail party in my hotel suite first. I would send my aide ashore to ask the customs if he could come ashore and bring so much whiskey and so many cigarettes for the cocktail party. Then we'd have the cocktail party in my hotel suite, and the dinner on board ship. That, of course, was for the size group that you could accommodate in your flag mess. Often we'd have a big reception on the fantail of the cruiser, with the awning and the flags and the band and what not, because many of the local people wanted to come aboard ship. They didn't want to go to a reception ashore.

I never served whiskey, wine, beer or champagne aboard ship. Some people tried to get me to write Washington and see if I could get a special dispensation so that I could have wine and champagne when I had official parties entertaining foreigners. I didn't agree with that at all. This idea that since the foreigners have wine at every dinner it will be an insult if you don't give them wine with their dinner on board ship, wasn't the way they thought at all. In fact, they rather seemed to enjoy this change. I did, however, buy periodically from England a non-alcoholic champagne. It fizzed just like champagne and we used it when proposing a toast. It was a conversation piece.

Everybody would laugh about it. Entertaining was a lot less expensive than it would have been if I'd had to furnish wines, real champagne, et cetera.

Q: Why I asked about the on shore entertainments was that I was thinking of Mrs. McDonald and the need for her to be so versatile and be hostess in various places.

Adm. M.: That posed no particular problem. She made friends everywhere. We became very friendly, I think, with Prince Ranier and Princess Grace in Monte Carlo. She was present when I took command of the Sixth Fleet. He was away from Monaco at that particular time. We were at the palace on more than one occasion and once she very nicely arranged for the Monte Carlo Symphony to give a performance on the hangar deck of one of our aircraft carriers. I played golf with him several times and my wife played with her. The four of us played a little four-handed gin rummy at the summer palace. We found them very delightful and she was a most gracious lady who had a hard job, a very, very difficult job, which I think she performed in an outstanding fashion. In a way, they lead sort of a lonesome life, you know. People in their category don't really know who their friends are. I rather felt that she welcomed an invitation from us now and then. I think one of the greatest compliments that's ever been paid to my wife was when I was CNO. About a week after President Kennedy was buried, Princess Grace came to the U.S. to put a wreath on the tomb. My wife got a call from Philadelphia saying that she was coming down to Washington and didn't want anybody to know about it. She was going to come down on the train, grab a cab and go right straight to Arlington, and could she, as quick as she did that, come to our house and have a bite of lunch with Tommie and then get a taxi back to the train. That's what happened, and people didn't know about it. But within thirty minutes after she left our house every newspaper photographer in Washington was there but it was too late.

These are the kind of friends we made that we'll always remember. Something a little bit different from the operational aspects.

Q: Indeed so. I recall back when Bernie Bieri was commander of the Sixth Fleet and I think he was just designated as that in those days, he had access to a villa in Naples, Villa Marguerita, I think it was, which was the home of Lady Hamilton. I wonder what happened to that.

Adm. M.: It's not Ville Marguerita now, it's Villa Nicki. We still have that. Wait a minute, let me backtrack. This belonged to the U. S. Navy and ultimately became the home of CinCSouth, which is a unified command - that and the Pacific and the Norfolk area - that the Navy holds. The Villa was maintained by the U. S. Navy. When I was in Paris, shortly after I arrived in Paris, I guess, Admiral Brown moved in there. Brown moved from the Sixth Fleet to CinCSouth.

Q: That's Admiral Cat Brown?

Adm. M.: Cat Brown. He lived there. He was there when he retired. When he retired, I had the great pleasure and privilege of giving him a retirement ceremony on a carrier. We invited many officers and their wives from his unified staff, international staff, many foreigners, along with Admiral Brown's wife, to embark in boats in Naples and come out to the carrier. Then we got under way. After we got out to sea, Admiral Brown was lifted in a helicopter and brought out. When he arrived over the carrier and looked down, the bluejackets had been placed in formation so that they spelled out, "Hi, Cat." He then came aboard and we had about an hour of very intensive air operations. Then we had a luncheon. Then we had a farewell ceremony on the hangar deck, and when that ceremony was over we had a red carpet going from the little rostrum on the hangar deck all the way out to the deck edge elevator, which was lowered. So, as Cat walked out the red carpet onto the elevator and it was being raised the band played Auld Lang Syne. He embarked in a helicopter, and, as he flew off, the formation of sailors spelled out "Bye, Cat." And then the carrier returned to port and let all the families off.

Cat was succeeded there by I believe Jim Russell, Jim, in turn, by Don Griffin. Somewhere along the line and I don't know just when or why, Villa Nicki was purchased or taken over by the Italian Navy. It is still lived in by CinCSouth, who was Rivero, following Griffin, and Means Johnson following Rivero and now Stan Turner. It's still occupied by CinCSouth, a U. S. naval officer, but I'm sure it now belongs to and is maintained by the Italian Navy. And I must say - I don't know what it cost but nobody could have entertained more graciously than Cat and Eleanor Brown. We had the good fortune of being their house guests on more than one occasion. Usually when we would go in to Naples they'd always ask us to stay out in this lovely villa. Very lovely, but like a lot of other things, maybe like Admiral's House was recently, it needs a lot of repair -

Q: But much older, because it dated back to Lady Hamilton!

Adm. M.: I didn't know that but I guess it's the same place. Mick Carney, I think, is the one who really got it for the Navy in the first place.

Q: I always associate in my mind with this particular subject and I wondered if you used it and how you used it, deception as a tool of command in fleet operations, deceiving the opposing units?

Adm. M.: Well, I don't think there's any question but what it is a real tool of command, very important, but I don't know - it's somewhat difficult, I think, to lay out specific deceptive practices in advance. The situation dictates it.

Q: Did you employ it in any sense in any particular operation that you can recall?

Adm. M.: I don't know that we did. You know, covert operations are a part of every operational plan. We don't always call it by that name but you usually have a cover plan.

Q: You avoid the obvious?

Adm. M.: Yes, it's the cover plan. That's what you're talking about. I don't remember any operation that didn't have a cover plan. Whether you put it into effect or not depends upon the circumstances. There's no question that at times you'd send a submarine off and have him surface and make signals and what not as though that's where something is that really isn't there.

Q: When you were in the Mediterranean, was there beginning to be any evidence of Russian activity?

Adm. M.: Not particularly. Let me change that. There was evidence all the time, but very little, a couple of their ships, always with us.

Q: You mean the trawler-type things?

Adm. M.: Yes, they were always around. You could see some, electronics vessel, whether it was a trawler or a fishing boat, it was there for the same purpose. Almost any time we had an exercise of any kind, you could be certain that no six-hour period would go by when you wouldn't see one. Nothing you can do about that.

Q: How would they have knowledge that you had an exercise scheduled or under way?

Adm. M.: Oh, Lord, that's no secret.

McDonald #4 - 302

Q: It's a published thing, is it?

Adm. M.: Sure. We published an operating schedule. That wasn't secret. Some might be, but generally no. Then, hell, you've got to let the ships' company know what you're going to do. If you try to keep that stuff secret, the media and our own personnel would damn you worse than the CIA is being damned today.

I've always had the view that unless there's something that you really shouldn't let anybody know and you can be pretty sure you can keep them from knowing, then let it out. This half-secret's no good.

Q: It arouses suspicion?

Adm. M.: Oh, it's no good. You can't act the part if you can't answer the questions. And I think that by generally releasing all information when you do slap a secret on something, people say, "Wait a minute, let's take a look." But if everything you do is hush-hush, why, it sort of becomes ridiculous.

Q: It becomes commonplace, doesn't it?

Adm. M.: That's correct. Oh, I think there were times when - our own people would growl at me or at others for not letting them know what port they were going into, or for saying, now look, your ships' going to Istanbul, but, for God's sake, don't tell your wife. The reason for that was that we hadn't gotten permission from the Turkish government, so you didn't want something coming out in the paper that this ship's going in to Istanbul when your request to the Turkish government hasn't even been cleared by that government. So sometimes there were delays like this and it was very awkward. My wife would say, "Look, I know where I'm going and you say don't tell anybody. It's silly." The people in the airplane know where they're going to take her. Things like that are just diplomatic niceties, but those things are hard to explain sometimes especially to Mamma and the children.

Q: And is it correct to observe that the diplomatic niceties don't always come as readily to Americans as they do to Europeans?

Adm. M.: That's right, and you see in our case, we never went from here directly to there. We would leave port and then we'd go out and have our exercises and at the end of the exercises we'd go into another port. So there was anywhere from one to two weeks' delay. Well, often you don't request entry into a port more than a week or ten days before you want to get there. Sometimes you leave a port and you know where you're going, unless something happens, but you haven't even asked for entry.

But, generally speaking, no attempt was made to keep our movements secret because had such an attempt been made it wouldn't have been successful.

Q: What do you imagine the Russians do with all the data they acquire through their trawlers and their electronic equipment? So much of it is just repetition.

Adm. M.: You know you shouldn't ask that after having walked through all the files we walked through getting to the office you and I are now in. We've got archives in this country up to here and we're getting intelligence information today from seemingly "40,000" sources, and I would venture to say that in many cases the same information is coming in to this government from two to six different sources. What do we do with it? We can't even process it all. It could be that they're as silly as we are. But I do think they learn a lot by watching us replenishing at sea, for instance, and various things like that. Our Navy isn't the most advanced Navy in the world in everything, but we are in an awful lot of things. And by watching everything we do, it's amazing the little things that they might pick up.

Q: Little techniques?

Adm. M.: That's right. Things that they might have picked up in other places but didn't impress them in the same way. And it doesn't cost them anything, practically speaking. If we had ships doing the same thing they'd probably cost ten times as much as the Russians and we'd have twice as many people on them. We don't do things simply and inexpensively. They've got these simple little ships and they sit there all the time.

We talked once, you know, about having small intelligence gathering ships, like the Pueblo - 200 of them, and look what happened in the case of the Pueblo. People raised hell because this thing wasn't capable of fighting itself out of a paper bag. These ships they've got aren't fighting ships either but they have a great many of them. What are you going to do to them? You're not going to blow them up.

Q: They don't expect us to do anything to them.

Adm. M.: No, of course not.

Q: Do they have women among the personnel aboard these ships?

Adm. M.: I can't answer that, Jack. I have seen Russian ships with women on them but whether they were on these little ships I don't really remember.

Q: I know they serve regularly on Russian merchant ships.

Adm. M.: Oh, yes. Not only Russian, but other merchant ships, too, I think.

Q: Since this is an age-old problem, did you run up against, or get in between, any of the Greek-Turk animosity?

Adm. M.: No, I really didn't, and I've been engaged in exercises where both Greeks and Turks participated and where we put Greeks on Turkish ships and vice versa, and the time was shortly before I left my flagship and had my hernia operation. The exercise was held not very far from Salonica.

Q: And they worked together?

Adm. M.: That's right.

Q: But these were naval people?

Adm. M.: That's right, and while assigned to NATO in Paris I'd invite Turkish naval officers and Greek naval officers over to the house to dinner together and they'd invite each other. As a naval officer, I'll do a lot of things with a lot of people that I don't do on an individual citizen basis. It's part of the job. If you can't afford to do that, then you'd better change jobs. And I believe many naval officers of other countries feel the same way.

Q: And then, too, it underscores the fact that the navies of the world form a kind of confraternity, don't they?

Adm. M.: Oh, yes. Without going into the whys and wherefores, it is a fact. And once again the Navy's different from some of the other services. And I want to repeat what I've said in an earlier session and that is that often I have said to bluejackets:

"Do you fellows realize what being in the Navy is like? A ship isn't just a factory or an office or a place where you work. A ship is a home away from home, and the man working next to you, right next to you, isn't just a fellow worker, a coworker, he's also a shipmate and, as such, you not only have to learn how to work with him but must also learn how to live with him. You'd better learn how to share his joys, his sorrows, his successes, and his failures, and you'd better conduct yourself in such a way that he will have complete confidence in you and you'd better learn to have confidence in him because you never know when you very life might depend upon how well he does his job."

It makes life in the Navy a little different and I wish people would preach this theme to our bluejackets. We shouldn't try to make life in the Navy like it is in the civilian world. We shouldn't permit Navy men to go around and dress like their civilian contemporaries do in town and act like they do. Because the Navy is jolly well different and unless one is careful the tendency toward democratizing the Navy may cause it to be less and less a military organization.

Q: Or are we?

Adm. M.: It seems to me that there has recently been great effort to make the Navy "Democratic" and it's no damned good. Some say that you can't get people into the Navy unless you let down the bars. Don't tell me you can't. I believe that there are a lot of young men today that are mixed up with street gangs that would give their right arm to get away from the street gang type of dressing and living if they could just do it. They used to think if they came in the military they could get away from it. Now they come in and do the same thing, that is, broadly speaking.

Once again, let's just lay it on the line, and if they don't like it - but they'll like it. I believe they will.

What started this dialogue, of course, is the fact that the Navy is a different way of life. So it is. A ship's company eat together, they sleep together, they work together, they play together, and while at sea they can't get away from each other. Somebody may say, well, you have to be a peculiar type of individual to do this. I'd prefer to say that you have to adapt yourself to an unusual way of life. That's the way I'd put it.

Q: Well, man is basically - we term him a social animal. He lives with others.

Adm. M.: Of course he is. If you don't like people, you might as well jump out the window to start with.

But referring again to this one particular NATO exercise - I think this was maybe the first time that we actually embarked Turkish soldiers in Greek transport, or vice versa (I've forgotten which) and put them ashore in a landing operation. We actually had the nationality of one embarked in the ships of another.

Q: That's quite an achievement.

Adm. M.: That's right.

Q: That leads me to a question about the Turkish bases. Did you, as Commander, Sixth Fleet, have anything to do with the Turkish bases that we have, or did have?

Adm. M.: No.

Q: This would be CinCSouth?

Adm. M.: Probably. I don't think, Jack (it's been so long now I may have forgotten) I don't think we had any Turkish naval bases that were of any particular importance to us.

Q: At this time, I think we had begun to help in a considerable fashion the build-up of the Turkish Navy, had we not?

Adm. M.: I don't remember whether we had or not.

Q: What about the Persian Gulf? Did you get over there at all?

Adm. M.: No.

Q: That was under your command, wasn't it?

Adm. M.: Only as CinCUSNavEur later, not as Commander Sixth Fleet. We didn't get outside of the Mediterranean at all.

Q: It was under your command when you became Commander in Chief, U. S. Naval Forces, in Europe.

Adm. M.: Yes. I think I'd like to make a couple of comments here for the record, more or less.

As the time drew near for the man in London's tour of duty to expire, which was normally a three-year tour, and as my tour of duty as Commander, Sixth Fleet, expired, (which had pretty generally been anywhere from a year to not more than two years) the question arose as to what the new moves were going to be. Pretty generally it was considered to be the custom for the man in London to go to Norfolk and become not only CinCLant Flt but SanLant.

Q: Had it happened once, or more frequently?

Adm. M.: I don't really recall now, but that seemed to be the chain, or maybe that was just in the minds of certain

McDonald #4 - 312

people. Anyway, it was in my mind and it was in the mind of the man in London, and it was in the mind of the Chief of Naval Operations, who happened to be Admiral Anderson. I had never wanted but two senior jobs in the Navy, really, the Sixth Fleet and I wanted to go to London. So, it seemed the natural thing that the man in London, who was three years senior to me -

Q: Who was that?

Adm. M.: Page Smith. He would have three years to go before retirement, so he should go to Norfolk and I should go to London. In three years he'd retire, then I'd go to Norfolk, and after three years I'd retire.

Well, we had word, via the daisy chain, the grape vine, or whatever you want to call it, that that looked like it was pretty much in the cards. Then, as Commander, Sixth Fleet, I got word that the Secretary of the Navy was coming over to visit us.

Q: And this was?

Adm. M.: Fred Korth, who had relieved Connally. And that they were quite interested in missiles. The Navy was having trouble with missiles. Well, it just so happened that about the day after he was scheduled to arrive, our regular monthly or quarterly operating schedule called for us to go out on a missile shoot. So I told my operations officer to pass the word that we weren't going to change a thing. We weren't going to put on any special show for the Secretary unless he asked for it. We'd go out and we'd conduct this exercise just the way we'd planned to conduct it before we knew he was coming over. If it worked, fine, if it didn't, fine. We weren't too sure it would work, anyway.

Well, they came over and we went out. I don't know why, but somebody up above must have been looking out for us. Everything went just like it was running in oil. The missiles worked the way they'd never worked before and the Secretary and his party began to think what in the world were they worried about in Washington; about these things not working. Then when they found out that we hadn't arranged this show for them, that we merely carried out the regular operating schedule which had been approved at least three months beforehand, they couldn't quite get over it.

But, the real point of my story is that as we went back into port the Secretary called me in for a couple of private conversations; in the afternoon or evening and again the next morning. He kept asking me who I thought should go to Norfolk and London. I made no bones. I thought Admiral Smith should go to Norfolk and I would go to London. He tried his best to get me to say that I didn't think Smith should go to Norfolk and that I should go to Norfolk, but I didn't agree with him. I told him I didn't. I said, "You don't give people jobs just because they're senior, but if they are senior and fully qualified you've got to bear that in mind." And I said that I thought Smith was more qualified for Norfolk than I was. He had been in London for two and a half years and knew all the British. He had worked with SacLant on all these NATO exercises in the Atlantic. I've been in Paris and down in the Med. He's perfect for the Norfolk job and he's senior to me.

Not long thereafter we got a message from the CNO telling me to get an airplane, with my wife, and fly to London where I was to join Admiral Smith and his wife and the four of us would come to Washington.

And the CNO wanted us to stay with him. We thought, gee, this is going to be fine, he's going to have a big dinner, and they're going to announce that Page is going to Norfolk and Mac's going to London.

Well, we got back and no decisions had been made of any kind. But we knew where the CNO stood.

Oh, I forgot,, the Secretary said to me before he left the Sixth Fleet, "Don't you think you're capable of handling that Norfolk job?" Of course, I kind of laughed at that, "I don't think it's very difficult.

I don't think that's the point. Sure, I can handle the job but that's not the point at all."

We were in Washington three or four days and nothing happened. We went back to London where we left Smith and his wife and my wife and I went on back to the Sixth Fleet.

Q: What kind of exposure did you have to the Secretary while there?

Adm. M.: None.

Q: Only to Anderson?

Adm. M.: Yes, I didn't know what this coming back to Washington was all about, and I don't know to this day.

Q: And still nothing happened.

Adm. M.: Well, finally the word came out - the orders came out. Smith was going to Norfolk. By that time I was in Athens, Greece. I got detached and I came back to the States for, I guess a week. Then I went back to London to relieve Admiral Smith.

Q: Was Smith aware of all this?

Adm. M.: Sure, we both were, but when I got back to

Washington as CNO, I found out that somebody (and I don't know who) for some reason didn't like Page Smith and simply wouldn't go along with Anderson's recommendation for Smith to go to Norfolk. Then ultimately Anderson did something where McNamara said he'd support it, so then the daisy chain started to move.

So I went to London and took over. And the very next day McNamara, Paul Nitze, George Brown, who was McNamara's aide - George was a colonel then, and several other people arrived and I went out to meet them on this first day of what I expected to be a three year tour. It was going to be just the way George Anderson and I had been talking about for quite a long time.

Going in to town, I rode with George Brown. The TFX problem was big news then. I'd heard about that when I was in Washington but I didn't pay any attention to it over in the Sixth Fleet but in Washington that was a hot subject. And on the way in to town - I'll never forget it even though it didn't register with me then, I said to George that the TFX subject seemed hotter than hell and George Brown said:

"You know that thing's hot. Some service chief is going to get his throat cut on this if he doesn't watch out."

This was in the morning. We got in to town about

ten o'clock or ten thirty and I went on about my business. About 4:30 I got a telephone call wanting to know if I could join this group at the ambassador's house that night, at the embassy, the ambassador's residence, for dinner. I said, yes, I'll come over.

So I went over and during the evening I talked to McNamara some and to Paul Nitze. There was quite a bit of conversation. After dinner McNamara wanted to wait up and see George Brown, the labor leader over there. It was late and I said, "I started early today and I'm going home if I may."

Then I spent about the next two weeks arranging an itinerary to go visit my domain; that is, the activities within my command.

Q: Which was pretty extensive.

Adm. M.: Yes. I was going to stop in Naples for gas only and then on to Turkey, going to spend a couple of days in Turkey, then to Teheran, then over to New Delhi, then down to Bahrein, and then up to Asmara. These were places where at least I had certain logistic support responsibilities. I hadn't been to Teheran, Bahrein, or Asmara, although I'd been to India.

I'd been in my London job just a month and off I went. I had a multiple hat there in London, so I had an Air Force officer with me, an Army man, my naval aide and my wife. We arrived in Ankara on a Thursday and we stayed with the Ambassador, who was Ray Hare. On Friday night we were given a delightful dinner by the Turkish CNO who also had as his guest the President of Turkey.

Q: Who was that, Menderes?

Adm. M.: No, this was in 1963. It was Gursel, I believe. Anyway, we had a fine dinner and very enjoyable dancing. And before the affair was over something happened that my wife will remember as long as she lives. When the President got ready to leave my wife was out dancing with somebody else and the President (who was crippled) got up and walked out to the middle of the dance floor where my wife was. As he walked out everybody just folded up and got out of the way and finally there was just the two of them saying good-bye.

The party broke up and when we got back to Ray Hare's house and started to go upstairs, Mrs. Hare said, "Look we really haven't had a chance to visit with you and you're going to leave in the morning. Let's have a night cap."

I was leaving the next morning for Teheran as was the chairman of their Joint Chiefs, General Sunay. I'd known General Sunay at certain SHAPE exercises. I'd met him in Paris two or three times and been with him. He was going over to Iran also and the Iranians were giving a big reception at six that night honoring me and Sunay jointly.

So we were sitting at the Hare's having a drink. It was after midnight and the telephone rang. I picked it up and it was a commander in Washington calling to tell me that the Secretary of the Navy wanted me to be in his office at 7:30 Monday morning. By that time it was one o'clock Saturday morning in Turkey. So I said why. "I can't tell you."

"What?"

"I can't tell you," he repeated.

"Well," I said, "You obviously know where I am. I hope you know what I'm doing. You know, we spend a lot of money to make friends in this part of the world and tonight in Iran they're giving a big reception honoring me and my very good friend General Sunay. I'd like to come in about Wednesday or Thursday. This will not interfere with tonight's reception in Tehran and then I can give the people advance notice in other places. But just to summarily cancel tonight's affair like this, not even giving them an explanation, not only will the Iranians be upset but I think General Sunay will have his nose out of joint and I think he's a pretty important fellow in this part of the world."

"Well, there's nothing I can do about it," said the Commander.

"Who can?" I asked.

"The Secretary of the Navy,"

I said, "Put him on."

"Well, Admiral, I can't. He's is San Juan."

I said, "If I contacted him, would it do any good?"

"Not a bit," he says.

I hung up the phone, and this is a very interesting thing. I hung up the phone and my wife said: "What was that?" I said, "They've fired George Anderson and, God dammit, I'm going to be CNO."

She said, "What?" and I said, "No. I was just kidding."

She and Ray Hare confirmed this later.

Max Morris was my aide, so Max got on the phone to London and got reservations on Pan Am for the two of us leaving Sunday.

We got on the plane the next morning and my Army and Air Force fellows were all in shorts. I said, "Where are you boys going?"

"Teheran. We thought it was going to be hot."

"No, you're going to London."

Well, we went to London. I talked from London to Washington, but still nobody would tell me a damned thing.

I got to New York and was changing planes when I saw a man sitting in the waiting room that I thought I recognized. I looked at him and he turned his back and walked away. Later he got on the same airplane to Washington and sat next to me. He was a naval officer that a friend of mine had sent up there to tell me what the hell was going on. He said:

"Certain people are over at the Observatory right now telling Admiral Anderson he's not going to be reappointed. You're going to be CNO but nobody will tell you until tomorrow morning." I had even been told not to talk to anybody on the phone at my wife's sister's house. Can you imagine that? But this officer later told me and the "powers that be" never did know that he came to New York and told me en route to Washington.

I walked into the Secretary of the Navy's office at 7:30 the next morning.

Q: Monday morning?

Adm. M.: Monday morning - into Korth's office. When he informed me about the CNO job I told him I was highly honored but I was also highly embarrassed. I was honored about the job but embarrassed to tell him I didn't want the job; never had wanted it, didn't want it then.

Q: What did he say to that?

Adm. M.: I explained a lot of reasons why. He said, "Will you tell Mr. McNamara that?"

I said, "I'll tell God Himself that."

He said, "Why don't you wait outside a little bit and we'll go down and see him."

Mr. McNamara wasn't there but his Deputy, Mr. Gilpatric was. Mr. Korth came out after a few minutes and said, "Let's go down and see Mr. Gilpatric."

We went down and went into his office but instead of me telling him he started talking. He started rebutting the things I'd said to Korth, so I said:

"I believe that Secretary Korth has already told you some of my feelings." Then, after a certain amount of additional conversation, I suddenly said, "We're wasting our time. I thought we were going to discuss whether or not I was to be appointed. From what you've just said, President Kennedy has already approved it and I'm going to be CNO, unless I just say I won't take the job."

And he said that's right. My reply then was, "Of course, I'm not that big a fool."

I'v always thought that was a hell of a way to appoint a Chief of Naval Operations? Never talking to you about it or discussing your views, et cetera.

Q: Never asking you how you feel?

Adm. M.: Never asking you your views. I guess they assume that every naval officer wants that job but, if they did, they were wrong in my case. I didn't want it, and I told Fred Korth I'd always wanted to be in London. That I had four stars and life was nice over there, I had been in the Navy a long time and I didn't have any desire to come back to the Pentagon. Over there I could do some of the things I wanted to do. In the Pentagon, you had a million and one people kibitzing.

I also said: "Look, Anderson has failed of reappointment because he doesn't agree with somebody on something. I don't know what it is. But he and I were raised in the same school and have operated together a lot. Generally speaking I think the same way he does. I don't want to get mixed up in a lot of arguments like he has apparently been in. It doesn't make any sense."

Interestingly enough, my friend in Turkey that I thought might be influential some day, within a year he was President and he was President for six years.

Q: Who's that?

Adm. M.: Sunay.

Q: Tell me about that end of it. How did you cancel

out on the Iranians?

Adm. M.: My aide just sent a message that the Admiral had received sudden orders to return immediately to Washington. He sincerely regrets. What the hell else could I say? It was just that plain.

Our ambassador, Hare, knew my side of the whole story. He knew that I'd tried to find out and couldn't find out, so I just assumed that he later explained as best he could. And, of course, later when I became CNO I had the Turkish CNO (who gave us the party the night before) as my guest in the United States for about two weeks.

Now, let me say this in support of their inability to delay my return. Why couldn't I come Wednesday or Thursday instead of Monday? The Secretary had some long-range plans which he had made to visit the Pacific and the Far East and those plans were all based upon a schedule that called for him to depart Washington Monday afternoon. Of course, it wouldn't have been as upsetting as mine. At least, they'd have some advance notice, but all of his plans, the dates and what not, would have had to be changed.

Q: But why was it necessary to do this within that given week, so to speak?

Adm. M.: Don't ask me.

Q: When did Anderson's term expire?

Adm. M.: One August. My sudden trip back was in April or early May and I didn't take over till the 1st of August. I stayed on in London nearly two more months. Then they sent over a very large Air Force tanker, that had been converted with bunks in it, and I put all my household gear in it and flew to Washington with my wife, and one steward. I couldn't take my aide. I picked up an aide in Washington. I spent the night in Washington and while my furniture was being unloaded the next morning, I went up to the Senate, to the Armed Forces Committee for confirmation. Then that afternoon I left for Alaska, Tokyo, Taipeh, Hong Kong —

Q: The whole circuit?

Adm. M.: Yes, I hadn't been out in the Pacific for a long time. I must have gotten back to Washington about the 10th of July or around the middle of July, and took over the 1st of August.

I have never understood many of these actions.

Q: How precipitate it was.

Adm. M.: Well, I wonder how precipitate it was. Because during my ten days in Washington before I went back to London, I had to call on the President, and I wondered what the hell I had to call on the President for.

Q: That was on order, request?

Adm. M.: I was told, by Mr. McNamara I believe, that I was to call on the President. I went over and called on President Kennedy, and there wasn't anybody in the room but the two of us. I guess we chit-chatted for fifteen or twenty minutes and when I got up and started to leave, he stuck out his hand and said, "You know, I'm real glad you came over because if I should ever hear your name in the future, at least I'll know what you look like," and then I left.

Q: Did you have any suspicion?

Adm. M.: No, I didn't. You see, we in the Navy all thought that Anderson was going to be reappointed as CNO and would later become Chairman of the Joint Chiefs.

Q: It was the Navy's turn, was it?

McDonald #4 - 327

Adm. M.: Well, it was somebody's turn besides the Army and the present chairman had a year or two to go.

Q: This was General Taylor?

Adm. M.: Yes. So you see, if George had stayed on for two more years, I'd have had about four years to go until I was 62 and so I wasn't coming into the CNO picture at all. Tom Moorer could come in at that time. He could be CNO and still have enough time left to be Chairman. I couldn't be. So I wasn't even thinking about the CNO job when I called on President Kennedy. I was planning on London and then going down to Norfolk. I didn't have any suspicion that George was running into a problem.

Now, later when George Brown told me over there about the TFX, I sort of did.

But let's go back a minute. I was told that after I'd called on the President to call on McNamara, and about all McNamara said was, "I'm not going to ask you now because you don't know, you haven't been there, but after you've been in London a while, I want you to explain to me why that job should have four stars."

I said, "Mr. Secretary, I can tell you that right now. I think the job can be done by a lieutenant commander, if you're talking about the actual work. But as long as the senior U. S. ambassador of the whole world is in London, then the senior U. S. military man in London should have four stars. Now, if you want him to be the Army or the Air Force, that's something else, but he should have four stars, for the same reason that the ambassador has to have that prestige. That's the way you do business with the British. It's just that simple. I don't have to go over there to find out."

Bob never asked me that again.

So I went on back to London, disappointed, very. I sincerely didn't want the job.

Q: How did your wife react to it?

Adm. M.: As badly as I did. I sincerely didn't want the job and the funny things, the strange things that had gone on, made me want it even less. I didn't want to be in that kind of atmosphere. Those few days had just sort of confirmed my suspicions in the first place.

Q: Something unhealthy about the whole thing?

Adm. M.: I had called my wife on the phone, told her I was going to be CNO and asked her to meet me at the airport in London.

Q: You left her in Turkey, didn't you?

Adm. M.: No, no, no. I left her in London. I called her on the phone and told her what happened and I said, "I'll be home tomorrow night. Meet me at London Airport." She did.

We had a flat in Grosvernor Square and a house out in the country but went to the flat for dinner and to spend the night because that's where the office was. And now I will tell you something which will show how little things can change one's way of life. I cleaned up a little bit and started to ask for a drink. I asked the Filipino boy to get it. I asked her what she wanted, "Martini, or Old Fashion?"

"I think I'll take a little sherry on the rocks."

I said, "What's the matter? Are you sick?" Even though she really drank very little she usually did have a cocktail before dinner.

She said, "No, but I've had about twenty-four hours to do an awful lot of thinking. When we go back with you in that job, we won't have dinner by ourselves more than one night a week, and when we go out, wherever we go, we'll have cocktails and wine and when entertaining at home we'll have cocktails and wine, and if I drink martinis before dinner and wine with dinner I'll look like I'm 100 within six months and I'm not going to do

McDonald #4 - 329

it. Sherry has alcohol in it, but it will blend with wine."

From that day to this, the only cocktail she has had is sherry on the rocks, usually with a little soda.

Q: That was quite a resolution!

Adm. M.: That's right, and she was right.

I hadn't been back in London but two days, or four days, when I got a long letter from Lord Louis Mountbatten. In it he said I understand you're going back as CNO. We'd hoped you'd be here two or three years but we understand you're going to be here only about six more weeks. Now, he wrote, I have listed in this letter all of the things that are going to take place within the next seven weeks that I think you and Tommie would like to see if you were going to stay here three years. Please let me know which of these events you want to attend.

Well, the first one was the Garter ceremony at Windsor Castle, and this was quite interesting. We went over and had seats in the front row, center, with our feet right where the Queen would practically walk on them. I was just dressed in civilian attire. I didn't wear uniform over there very much because the British don't. We could hear people almost whisper, "Wonder who they are. Why are they sitting there?"

When the ceremony started Lord Mountbatten was up in front, just ahead of the Queen.

Q: He was carrying the mace, wasn't he?

Adm. M.: Yes, and when he was about twenty feet away he looked over and winked at my wife. Then we could practically hear the people say, "Now we know why they're sitting there!" It was amusing. But he did make it possible for us to see a lot of things and it was something that we appreciated very, very much because we had looked forward to seeing them.

Of course, we already knew London quite well. I had been over a couple of times for the Farnborough Air Show when I was Op-55. Then, when I was in Paris, my wife usually went over with me when I attended this show. And, of course, since CinCNelm had been sort of my boss when I was in Paris and since they were friends of ours we'd visited them a couple of times. So we had some very definite ideas of the things we wanted to do and wanted to see. We were really going to enjoy life but the CNO assignment upset our applecart.

Q: The carpet was yanked out from under you!

McDonald #4 - 332

Adm. M.: Yes.

Q: And you didn't even have a chance to make a tour of your domain?

Adm. M.: No, I never did and never have been there since. Never have been too certain of those places. One particular place was Asmara. I later knew Prince Desta, who was the favorite grandson of Haile Sellasie. He was then head of the Ethiopian Navy and I had hoped to visit this area.

But listen to this strange story that Max Morris told me. Prince Desta and Max Morris were very good friends. I think Max knew him in college somewhere over here. And there was a very smart young lieutenant commander in the Ethiopian Navy that Prince Desta thought very highly of. When Max was at the Naval Academy Desta thought it would be good if Max could arrange for this lieutenant commander to come over and teach navigation at the U. S. Naval Academy. I think my subjects are correct. Max told me this. And Max made that arrangement and the lieutenant commander came over and taught at the Naval Academy for one or two years.

Several months ago I saw Max and I asked, "With all the uprising over in Ethiopia, did they get Desta?" "Yes," he said.

Q: They killed him?

Adm. M.: He got out at first and then he came back. And when he came back he was killed by the very same lieutenant commander that he had sent to our Naval Academy. How about that? I said, "That's playing rough."

But we came back and survived four years as CNO. If I had it to do over again, I don't know if I'd tell him I don't want the job. I might even go so far as not to take the job, but of course, if I'd done that I'd probably have been sent to Timbucktu.

Q: St. Helena!

McDonald #5 - 334

Interview No. 5 with Admiral David L. McDonald, U.S. Navy (Ret.)

Place: Quarters in the Washington Navy Yard

Date: Saturday morning, 24 January 1976

Subject: Biography

By: John T. Mason, Jr.

Q: Well, Sir, as usual, it's a great uplift to see you and I've been looking forward to this fifth chapter which will deal in a very great way with your years as chief of naval operations.

When we broke off last time, you had been to Washington, had been named as CNO, and had returned to London.

Adm. M.: Yes and one of the bitter disappointments was not being able to enjoy the lovely home out in the country between two 18-hole golf courses, with honorary membership in each being given to us.

Q: At Virginia Water?

Adm. M.: Yes, and our time was so short we couldn't start housekeeping out there really.

McDonald #4 - 335

Q: How much time did you actually have?

Adm. M.: I only had a total of about three months. I'd been there a month when I was notified I was going to have to come back as CNO. Then I had about two more months. During those latter two months we spent every weekend at Virginia Water, but, of course, we lived in town during the week because that was where my work was.

One rather amusing thing happened. When I returned from the Mediterranean as Commander, Carrier Division Six, I had a Volkswagen. Then, when I was ordered to go back as Commander, Sixth Fleet, I felt that although I would have an official car I certainly needed a private automobile to keep from using the official car at times when it shouldn't be used. So, I disposed of my Volkswagen while in the States and then when I got back over to Villefranche I wanted a car of some kind and I felt I should get as inexpensive a car as I could which would be satisfactory. So I got another Volkswagen. Then, of course, when I was ordered to London, I took the Volkswagen with me.

Q: This was a little beetle?

Adm. M.: Yes. Then, when I was ordered back as CNO, I found that the Navy would not transport my automobile, even on a space-available basis on a ship. Mr. McNamara had issued an edict that this wouldn't happen. I think the reason he did was probably because people were buying foreign cars and bringing them back and then selling them. I wrote a letter to the Secretary of the Navy and pointed out why I bought this car and that I was being moved on a permanent change of orders. No. Still no. Therefore, I made arrangements to ship my Volkswagen commercially at my personal expense. But just before this happened, a Coast Guard officer who happened to be on my staff came in one day and said:

"Admiral, I understand that the Navy won't ship your Volkswagen back on a ship and you're going to have to pay for it yourself?"

I said, "That's right, Bill."

"Well," he said, "if you can spare the Volkswagen maybe a couple of weeks before you leave, I'll take care of that."

I said, "What do you mean?"

He said, "Well, the Commandant of the Coast Guard is coming over and he's going to be in a C-130 and I'll put it aboard the airplane and they'll fly it right back to Andrews Field and put it in storage there."

I looked at him and he said, "You know, we of the Coast Guard don't belong to the Department of Defense!"

And that's what happened, and I later had the pleasure of telling Mr. McNamara that although he made it impossible to ship it back on a ship on space available, it was brought back by the government by air. That was one of the many things that looked a little bit silly to me.

Well, when the time came for me to be detached, a couple of weeks after I'd sent the Volkswagen back, they sent a large Air Force tanker to London. In that airplane they had rigged two or three bunks and they put most of my household furniture in it along with my wife, myself, and a Filipino boy. We three came to Washington, spent one night, and the next morning I went over to Capitol Hill and appeared before the Senate Armed Forces Committee for confirmation.

An interesting thing happened before the Senate Armed Services Committee. The chairman was Senator Russell, of Georgia. My father was born and raised in the country, just a few miles outside of a little town called Winder, which was Senator Russell's home town and my own parents had been living in Winder since, oh, I don't know, about 1933, I guess. So after a bit of questioning, Senator Russell made a little talk to the members of the Armed Services Committee in which he pointed out that he had known my family for a long time and he had known about me for a very long time and had known me for some time. And, of course, he said the usual very nice things. When he finished, Senator Saltonstall of Massachusetts turned to him and said, in effect:

"Mr. Chairman, I don't know the Admiral, of course, the way you do, but from what you've said I'm sure that he will make a fine chief of naval operations."

Senator Russell said: "Well, Senator Saltonstall, I think he will. I know you don't know him and, to be frank with you, he didn't go to Harvard but he was graduated from a little Georgia high school, which is really the equivalent."

Of course, that created a great deal of laughter and then I left and they all voted.

Our first stop was Alaska, where I talked mostly with the U. S. Air Force there. Then Japan, where I spent some time not only with U. S. Navy personnel but a good deal of time with the Japanese Navy personnel.

Q: You had Mrs. McDonald with you?

Adm. M.: Yes.

I must tell you an interesting story about what happened in Japan. In the winter or spring of 1928, the Japanese midshipmen's training squadron visited Annapolis. They were doing then what our Naval Academy used to do, namely, the seniors, upon completing their course of instruction at their Naval Academy, had to make a cruise as passed midshipmen before being commissioned. So on this midshipmen's cruise to Annapolis were the midshipmen from the Japanese Naval Academy, including, of course, the passed midshipmen. I was a senior at the Naval Academy, a first classman, and just before their arrival I was made the chairman of a reception committee of about forty midshipmen, to meet, be with and escort the Japanese midshipmen. The senior

Japanese midshipman - I think he actually was the senior, at least he was the one in charge, my counterpart you might say - was a young man named Tanaka. They were there for quite a few days and along toward the latter part of their visit I made arrangements for Tanaka to spend two days and nights in the typical midshipman's room. You know, there is or was, I guess there still is today, in Bancroft Hall a place they call "a typical midshipman's room," so visitiors, particularly fathers and mothers, can come in and see just how the rooms their sons live in are arranged. This fellow lived there for a couple of days.

In subsequent years, for five, six, or seven years, Tanaka and I corresponded with each other, off and on. He would usually send me a bunch of picture postcards about Japan every Christmas. Along in the latter part of the thirties, before the war, I lost contact with him. After the war, when I was out there, (I was in Japan a little bit after the war) I tried to find out something about this fellow and had no success whatsoever.

Well, on this makee-learn CNO trip, if you want to call it that, the Japanese CNO gave a very delightful dinner party for my wife and me one evening at a hotel in Tokyo and there were quite a few senior Japanese naval officers present. Of course, their CNO was the senior one, but there was another one junior to him but was a classmate of his, it turned out. During the course of the evening, I related this story to them. Of course, they had been on that trip and they said that they knew Murata and thought they knew where he was. But I said his name was not Murata it was Tanaka. Oh, no, Murata. Well, I learned something then that I certainly didn't know before. In Japan, it's not unusual for a man who has brothers to marry a Japanese girl who has no brothers and the man adopts his wife's family name to perpetuate her family name. This fellow had done just that.

In tracing this one down, he had left the Japanese Navy at the end of the war and had gone to work for the United States Navy at the U. S. Navy shipyard in Yokosuka and had become the man in charge of their design section. But at that particular time he had some illness - I think it was something like hepatitis, thinking back, and he was in the U. S. Navy Hospital at Yokosuka. I was going out there the next day, so I said, "All right. I'll have arrangements made for me and my wife to visit this fellow in his room about 1:30, but don't let him know about it."

We went to the hospital, the next day and up to his room. You can imagine the look on this Japanese man's face when we arrived. He'd been told he was going to have visitors just before we got up there but not who they were and he was in his robe. We stopped at the door and he suddenly saw a lady and a U.S. naval officer in white uniform and with four stars. I guess he must have wondered whether I was there to tell him he was going to be court-martialed for something he did in World War II. But we just stopped and without an introduction, I looked at him and I said:

"You don't know who I am, do you?"

"No." It had been a little over thirty-five years since we'd seen each other.

I said, "Do you remember that as a passed midshipman you came to the Naval Academy at Annapolis?"

"Yes."

I went right on down describing things we had done and stopped now and then to say "You don't know." No. I said, "You remember when you stayed in the typical midshipman's room?"

"Yes."

"Don't you remember that I'm the man who arranged that." All at once, his eyes sparkled. "Ah, so, ah so." You've never seen anything like that in your life, and after this happened, some photographers came. When we started to leave, after about fifteen minutes, he said that he was going down to the car with me and I said"

"No, you can't go down. You're sick." He was on the second floor.

"I was sick, but I am no longer sick," he replied and he walked down the stairs with us, walked out to the car.

Well, the next day, of course, there were big headlines in the Japanese papers and I think I was sort of a hero. Later, he recovered from his illness and I believe about 1965 I received a letter from our commandant saying that the time had come - I presume at 60 years of age - when Mr. Murata was going to retire and he had never gotten over our visit out there. Anyway, I wrote a personal letter to him expressing the U. S. Navy's appreciation for the contributions he had made to our Navy, and that was read at his retirement ceremony.

Q: What a lovely story.

Adm. M.: I received a very nice letter from him after that, a letter of thanks, but of course I haven't heard from him since.

We completed our trip without incident. It was very interesting to me, a very worthwhile trip. I think we were gone about three weeks.

Q: Nothing like seeing with your own eyes.

Adm. M.: That's right.

We came back and stopped in California.

Q: It must have been pretty strenuous.

Adm. M.: It was strenuous except that I had no immediate responsibilities. We stayed in Honolulu I think for three or four days on our return trip and then when we got to California I released the large airplane. At that time, my daughter and her husband were living in Covina and so we spent two or three days with them, and then came on back to Washington by other means of transportation.

Q: You were with the Felts in Hawaii, were you? Don Felt was there still.

Adm. M.: No, I stayed down in a little cottage at Fort de Roussey, down at Waikiki. If you stay with the Commander-in-Chief you don't get the rest that you're after. You're still involved in a bunch of parties, dinner parties and small-talk chit-chat, and that's a little more tiring sometimes than work. So if you want to really rest up, you have to get away, and we stayed down at Fort de Roussey.

We came on back to Washington and moved into an apartment. I presume that with all the investigations going on today, they would have called it conflict of interest because this apartment was owned by Aerojet General, or General Tire. Why was I in it? Because when I was aide to Dan Kimball, who was a former president of Aerojet General, I had rented this apartment for Dan in the Westchester. He still had it at this time but he wasn't living in it, so he simply said, "Why don't you and your wife go up there and stay in this apartment? You're familiar with it. After all, you rented it and you put the stuff in there for me. You know all about it."

So we did, we went there, and stayed maybe a couple of weeks.

Q: There's something to be said for those days when people weren't snooping around under every chair!

Adm. M.: I agree.

I felt then and I feel now that if I can't be trusted I shouldn't be put in the job. I realize that a lot of people are put in jobs they shouldn't be, but I think you can go to extremes.

Q: During your trip to the Far East and thereabouts, you must have had some time to think about the job you were stepping into and you must have, knowing you, had some objectives that you wanted to achieve when you were chief of naval operations. What sort of objectives?

Adm. M.: Jack, I'm glad you asked me this. I believe the answer you would get to a question like this would be different from every CNO. Your objectives depend a great deal upon the time and the existing circumstances. I thought we had a pretty good Navy. I had grown up in a Navy that everybody, I think, thought was the best in the world. It was a Navy that participated in one of the greatest wars, certainly, we'd ever had and I thought the Navy did itself proud in World War II. Here I was, the son of a country preacher in Georgia and the existing system made it possible for me to become head of this Navy.

So I saw no compelling reasons to try to turn this Navy upside down. I thought it was pretty good. Maybe the thing to do instead of trying to change the direction, and as I said turn it upside down, maybe we ought to just see what we can do to make the existing system more efficient.

Part of this thinking, of course, was conditioned by the fact that I came in under unusual circumstances. Let's face it, my predecessor had been fired, in that he wasn't reappointed. Mr. McNamara and some of his people were bound and determined, (at least many in the Navy thought this and I had no reason to think otherwise or to change my mind later) that among other things, they were going to reduce the number of carriers, if they never did anything else. And there was no real communication between many in the Department of Defense and many in the Department of the Navy. If there wasn't a sort of underlying mistrust there was certainly no cooperation. So it was obvious to me that my main job was to pour oil on the troubled waters. Certainly not try to upset anything. Things were upset enough. Let's calm down. Let's communicate with the people in OSD. Let's don't downgrade the Whiz Kids. Let's find out how we can work with them.

The first thing I set out to do was to keep from reducing the number of carriers. Some may say, well, that's because he's an aviator. That's not true. Carriers are the very backbone of task forces.

Q: We learned that in World War II.

Adm. M.: And if you reduce the carriers, you reduce task forces and that means all the other ships that comprise the task forces, all the way back to the tankers and the supply ships.

Maybe I didn't accomplish many things. But I'll tell you one thing. As long as I was there, the carrier force was not reduced, not even by one ship, and the day I walked in there as CNO I believe nine out of every ten naval officers in the Pentagon would have bet you ten to one that there was going to be a reduction and it was just a question of how big it was going to be.

You can say, well, Vietnam came along. Yes, Vietnam came along, but we didn't put troops in Vietnam till I'd been CNO for two years.

So, if, in past years, I had had ideas about how the Navy should be changed, I think I would have hesitated to put them in effect at this time. And, as I said I think in another transcript, I never aspired to be CNO in the first place. But, having reached that point, sure there were things that I thought should be changed. One of the things at that time that I felt should be done and I never was able to do it, was I felt we were deploying ships overseas at a ridiculous tempo, and I haven't changed my mind. I saw no reason to send ships to the Mediterranean for six months, bring them back for three, and send them back for six again, in time of peace. Why, it's asinine. Why couldn't we change it? Well, I guess, politically. But really we had adopted a system which basically justified the total number of ships we needed by the number we keep deployed. For every one we kept deployed we had to have three. If we wanted fifteen aircraft carriers, we were going to have to keep five of them deployed all the time. That's not the way it should be done but it was the way it was being done.

The number you need should be determined by the number required to fight the kind of war you think you might have to fight, but figures like that are very hard to prove. However, you can make a pretty good case on three for one, and that's one of the reasons we kept deploying them. That always sort of irked me. But that seemed to be the surest way to maintain the force level and strength we needed. But I thought it was basically wrong then and I think it's basically wrong now.

Polaris submarines? Keeping twenty-one deployed all the time? Asinine. Why do we brag about that? Why don't we say we've got thirty or whatever it is and don't let anybody know the number deployed. Maybe tomorrow we will have three, maybe next week we've all thirty. But, no, we took great pride in saying that we were keeping all these deployed ninety days at a time. Well, why? That was the great deterrent, and we indicated that in order to keep all these deployed we had to have a certain total number. A lot of people won't agree with what I'm saying, but it's true.

Q: This involved, too, the fact that the Congress has to know?

Adm. M.: Of course, you have to go before the Congress to argue for what you need. Sometimes, of course, the State Department enters this picture and perhaps quite rightly. The State Department wants you to keep a certain number of ships deployed in various areas for geopolitical reasons. But let's take the linen off the table and say that maybe sometimes we in the Navy have gone to the State Department and said: "Look, fellows, won't you ask us to send one more ship over there so we can make a little better case."

It isn't that the brass wants to just build up the Navy. It's because the so-called brass sincerely believes that these are the numbers that we should have if we're going to be prepared adequately to face what is foreseeable.

Q: After all, we face that yearly accounting in Jane's Fighting Ships, don't we, and so we have to be listed?

Adm. M.: That's right, and really I guess if there were some way to get the Armed Services Committee or the Congress to agree that they would fund our Navy based upon what Jane's puts out, I expect our Navy would be real happy.

This is a long way of answering your question by saying that I felt it was going to be so very difficult to maintain the status quo, or to return to what had been the status quo, that I just didn't feel that innovations, if that's the proper term, were really in order. And, looking back on it now, I think the same way. Now, had I come along let's say at Zumwalt's time I think that I would have instituted many changes although I don't think I'd have done some of the things that he did. I think the lack of cooperation in the Pentagon between the Navy and other people in the Department of Defense didn't exist any more in Zumwalt's time and he felt that both the time and conditions were right for some changes.

Now look at the present. Admiral Holloway is doing a

little bit different from Zumwalt. In other words, Zumwalt went to great extremes. But Jimmy Holloway isn't saying that everything Zumwalt did was wrong or right but he's saying some of the things he did were wrong and he's letting it settle back down, but again, without trying to reverse course 180 degrees.

So I think every CNO, regardless of what his objectives might have been over the years, what he might have said that he would do if he ever became CNO, when he gets there he simply must be guided by the conditions that exist at that particular time.

Q: He's got to be realistic?

Adm. M.: That's right. I know people have said of me, "He didn't make any changes, he didn't do this, that, and the other." Well, no, but I did what I thought was proper at the time and -- of course -- under the existing circumstances.

Q: When you came in, the Navy was really pretty sore, wasn't it, at losing Anderson and Denfeld?

Adm. M.: Sore?

Q: Yes.

Adm. M.: Yes, they were upset, and, of course, I even made the statement that I didn't know what Anderson had done or hadn't done, but I knew enough about him to know that if they brought me in there to do some things he hadn't done, they were bringing the wrong man in because he and I thought pretty much alike. We'd been together a lot, we'd served together in Seattle and Alaska, we'd both skippered the same little carrier, we both had commanded the same carrier division, we both had commanded the same fleet, we'd been personal friends for years, we were only one year apart, and our thinking was pretty much alike. I didn't quite understand why Admiral Anderson was not reappointed. I never have quite understood, but I never really inquired too much because I felt that I probably never could get the right answers anyway.

Q: Did you know McNamara very well before this time? Did you know what you were dealing with?

Adm. M.: No. I had met him just the once before I went to London. I think I said in an earlier interview that he arrived in London the day after I took over and, later that afternoon, I was invited to join him at the ambassador's residence for dinner. I expect I must have asked questions of and talked to various and sundry people that evening but, of course, what I was doing was mostly listening because I didn't know and didn't have any background as to what their business was. I also talked to him for a while.

But I did not know Mr. McNamara. I think I talked at an earlier time about Mr. Korth's visit to the Sixth Fleet.

Adm. M.: That was the only time I'd ever seen him. I've always had the feeling that maybe the fact that Senator Russell and I were from the same area in Georgia and he was so powerful, they might have thought that I would use my personal friendship with him. If they did, they were disappointed because they learned later that I never contacted Senator Russell on a personal basis, never, but one time and that was to keep Vice President Humphrey from getting the CNO's house and, by God, it worked. That's the only time I ever communicated with Dick Russell on a personal basis. I don't believe in doing things like that. But I've often wondered if that wasn't the reason. I don't know. I never asked. I had been told by Admiral Anderson that I was on top of the list to relieve him, but I think the thinking at that time was that he would move up as Chairman of the Joint Chiefs and that I would relieve him then.

Q: Well, Sir, you came into office and what were some of the first problems you dealt with?

Adm. M.: The first problem, of course, was saving the carriers.

Q: How did you go about doing this?

Adm. M.: I don't really know.

Q: What did you discover was the truth about the attitude in the Department of Defense?

McDonald #5 - 352

Adm. M.: One of the first things that happened was before I became CNO, about two days before I became CNO. It happened when I was over in the Pentagon in what they called the visiting flag officer's office. The head of the Whiz Kids around there was named Alain Enthoven, and Alain's wife had a baby and he was passing out cigars. Somebody, I don't know who to this day, but somebody suggested to Alain that he come around and present a cigar to the man who was going to be the Chief of Naval Operations within a couple of days. So this stranger came in to where I was. I had heard about him, and he came in and said, "I'm Alain Enthoven and my wife's had a baby, have a cigar." He didn't know that I knew who he was, I guess. I said, "Thank you very much. I don't smoke but I sure do talk. Have a seat." We had a very nice conversation.

Then, right after I got the job, I made it a point very shortly thereafter to invite this fellow to come up and have lunch with me in my office. I did that with several of the people down in the Department of Defense and said, in effect, you know a lot of people round here think you fellows have got horns. "Look, we've got to work together. We can't go our own separate ways." So our good relations developed that way.

Another interesting thing. About two weeks later, several of us were down having some discussions in Mr. McNamara's dining room, around his table, his dining table. We hadn't started the discussions, we had just arrived to have the discussions. Among others who appeared was Enthoven, standing next to McNamara, and I

McDonald #5 - 353

said, "Hello, Alain, how's the boy?" And, jiminy, Mr. McNamara's face turned red as fire. Many people had been referring to the Whiz Kids as a bunch of kids or boys and he thought I was referring to Alain himself as the boy. I saw Mr. McNamara's face turn red and I turned and I said, "Bob, I'm speaking of Alain's young baby boy."

Q: It was a bad atmosphere?

Adm. M.: Yes, but it all worked out. I'm sure there's another side to this picture. I'm sure the people in the Department of Defense didn't like this lack of communication, as I choose to call it, and here was a new pilot at the helm, and I think they also went out of their way to pour oil on the troubled waters. So it wasn't my doing any more or maybe as much as their doing that enabled us to get together and have more rapport.

Q: Your personality certainly fit into a situation like that, I would think, a necessary element?

Adm. M.: I was supported by Mr. McNamara rather early in the game on a couple of decisions, which I thought were vital to the morale of the Navy. He supported me when I couldn't get support from others, including, I regret to say, the Commandant of the Marine Corps. However, these things made me sort of obligated to Mr. McNamara.

McDonald #5 - 354

Q: What were they?

Adm. M.: I don't think I should mention specific instances, Jack, but one was very important, I thought, to the Navy. There are people, so I've been told, in the Marine Corps who think that I didn't support the Marines the way I should have supported them. My answer is that I always supported the Marines but there were times when I didn't support their Commandant, but the reason I didn't was that I was abiding by the rule that he laid down.

Early in the year 1964 the question of the relief for Don Felt, as C-in-C Pac, was hot on the burner. Most people in the Navy believed that the Army and the Air Force would get together and try to remove the Navy from this position which the Navy had always held. I knew that many in the Navy were looking to see if I had enough support to prevent this from happening. Remember, many in the Navy were still seething over the unexplained departure of Admiral Anderson and I felt that the naming of the new C-in-CPac would be indicative--in the eyes of many of the Seniors in the navy--of just how influential I was in the job.

As the time approached, I believed that the Army and Air Force would agree on one individual; that the Navy and Marines would agree on one and hopefully that the Chairman of the Joint Staff, who was an Army officer, would not vote. Then with a two and two vote perhaps I could get Mr. McNamara to support me. When the time came for us to vote on this matter imagine my surprise when the Commandant of the Marine Corps voted against me. I couldn't believe it. After the meeting I called him on the telephone and asked if he knew how very important this was to the Navy and, of course, I said a few other things also. His reaction was that he proposed to call them as he saw them. My answer was that henceforth I would abide by his rules although I regretted that the two of us found ourselves in this position.

I proceeded forthwith to see Mr. McNamara and told him what had happened, told him before the report from the JCS reached him. I pointed out to him the importance of this appointment to the Navy and, incidentally, to my position as CNO. Although Mr. McNamara didn't commit himself I felt that he was most understanding. Later, of course, he did support me and sent Oley Sharp to the job. Even though I had made no 'deal' so to speak with the SecDef I did feel obligated to him for this support. It was too bad that this had happened between the Commandant and me but you always have some disagreement and family arguments.

And, of course the Commandant, like all Marine Commandants are rightly interested primarily in amphibious ships, and sometimes I felt that he thought I wasn't giving a high enough priority to amphibious ships. In one of our many heated discussions where there were quite a few people present, including the Secretary of the Navy, I simply had to point my finger at the Commandant of the Marine Corps and point out in a very forceful way that I was obligated to see that we had the right number of destroyers, submarines, carriers, cruisers, et cetera, as well as amphibious ships, whereas his primary responsibility as far as ships was concerned was to try to get enough amphibious ships. Consequently, I was going to determine what ships we got and not he. I don't know whether certain people appreciated that or not.

Q: How did you begin to get across your philosophy, your ideas, about carriers?

Adm. M.: I don't know, Jack. I really can't answer that, other than to say that I continued to support them by using what I have already called the "wrong" philosophy, namely, for every one that we had to keep deployed we needed three, and you keep making us deploy five. I got a great deal of support on this from a fellow in the State Department. Some of my colleagues in the other services at one time said to me, "Is Admiral Johnson coming over today?" meaning U. Alexis Johnson!

But I was CNO at a time when we had very few squabbles among the Joint Chiefs, really. Later on, with Vietnam we were all so out of sympathy with Mr. McNamara's ideas that we sort of stuck together, but it didn't really do any good.

Q: In connection with carriers, you were there when the decision was made against a nuclear carrier, were you not?

Adm. M.: Yes. I was there when the decision was made not to put nuclear power in the Kennedy.

McDonald #5 - 357

Q: When was that?

Adm. M.: I don't know, 1964, I guess.

Q: Yes.

Adm. M.: Anyway, we wanted nuclear power and I went for nuclear power, but later I agreed to have the ship without nuclear power because we needed decks and we needed them badly. After all, some of our carriers went back to the Essex. I was convinced that we were not going to get one the next year, but I had reason to believe that if we stayed off nuclear power we could get that carrier. So I went for it. And by agreeing to go off nuclear power at that time I got at least partial support from McNamara. I think everybody agreed with me, except Admiral Rickover, maybe, but I think Rick saw my point.

I can express my views best by telling you of an incident in Senator Pastore's office. He was a member of the atomic energy committee on the Hill and they are the atomic extremists, if you want to put it that way.

Q: You mean the joint committee - ?

Adm. M.: That's right, Senator Jackson, Senator Pastore -

Q: Chet Holafield?

Adm. M.: Yes. Well, in the middle of this argument, a few of us went into Senator Pastore's office one day for a discussion. He began to scream as only an Italian can. Of course when he does that he doesn't really mean it.

I'll never forget. He jumped up from behind his desk and, pounding on the desk, he pointed his finger at me and he said, "Admiral, here we are trying to get you to go for a loaf of bread and you're willing to sell out for a slice."

I looked at him and I said, "Senator, we're awful hungry." And that ended the conversation! And that's just the way I felt about it. I don't think Senator Pastore ever forgot that, and we became very good friends. I just thought we couldn't get it the other way, and we were hungry, we needed a deck badly.

Q: What was the determined opposition to a nuclear carrier?

Adm. M.: Money.

Q: Just money?

Adm. M.: Money. Rickover can tell you it's just as cheap. Well, I can't say it is.

Even if you could make the argument that over a period of ten years it would be just as cheap it wouldn't be as cheap during the construction years and that is the time that incumbent Senators, Representatives and even Secretaries of Defense are interested in.

You see, you don't go to the Hill and get appropriations for five or six years at a time. So, even if you could prove, and, of course, they never quite convinced me - nobody ever said it's cheaper _now_, they would point out the fuel that you'd save over a period of time. Of course you get a lot of flexibility, that's not cheaper but it is efficiency. You have to stretch the money out over a period of time to even try to prove it's as cheap, but you're not voting funds over a period of time, you're voting them now. So that's very, very serious when you have a limitation on funds.

I never would call anybody a liar, but I never agreed with Mr. McNamara when he said there was no budgetary limit, we are a rich nation and we can get whatever we need. He always said that. He never admitted that there was a ceiling on the budget. I said to him one day, "Bob, you might be right, but the higher the budget gets, it's obvious the less the "need" in your opinion. Prior to McNamara (I don't know whether they've gone back to it or not) I used to like the three-level budget; that is, if we're going to get this much money, this is what we should get; if we're going to get another amount, this is what we should buy, etc.

The way we were working when I was CNO, we asked for what we thought we needed and when the budget was cut back, who cut the detailed purchases back? Not we fellows in the Navy, but the Whizz Kids in McNamara's office. They decided what we could get along without, instead of us deciding. However, before I left, we were having some cooperation with them on that. But to go all out and say there's no ceiling, well, anybody with one-half of an ounce of sense knows better than that. We all knew that the White House had an input into our Budget and we felt that such should have been admitted.

Q: Congress does, too, doesn't it?

Adm. M.: Of course. I don't know why people don't admit it, but some people won't admit certain things. They whack it off without proper explanation and that's basically wrong. You ought to come back to the people who are going to have to fight with these things and let them have more of a say-so. I think they're doing that now, but I'm not sure.

Q: What was the philosophy back of their taking the action without recourse to the Navy itself?

Adm. M.: Because they felt they were smart! I felt there was a feeling - well, let's put it this way. Often, if I expressed a view based upon my experience, it was looked upon as a parochial view. In the eyes of some the only thing experience had done for me in the Navy was to make me parochial. And I learned pretty soon not to raise the issue of experience before certain individuals because you were shot down, that just made you parochial.

Q: That was especially true of Secretary Nitze, was it not?

Adm. M.: No, I don't think so. That was more true of Mr. McNamara but especially true of the Whizz Kids. I don't want to use this term "Whizz Kids" in a derogatory fashion, like a lot of people do. I think they were smart and I think they did more good than harm ultimately. But they did have an inferiority complex from the point of view of experience.

Q: They didn't have it?

Adm. M.: That's right. You see, if you started arguing figures, slide rules, and all this kind of stuff, efficiency, they could really argue you down because they were brilliant in that area. But they didn't want to talk about experience because they didn't have it. So they would resort to the fact that all that experience gives you is simply a parochial point of view. On one occasion, I think it was McNamara who made the statement, "Oh, let's quit doing it John Paul Jones's way. Can't you have an original thought for a change?" Well, I guess if I was in his position I might think that, too, because we do go by custom in the Navy. And we do a lot of things John Paul Jones way because we've found that they're still good. A smart but inexperienced individual, when talking about Vietnam one day said, in effect, "I know you military fellows have always been taught to get in there with both feet and get it over with, but this is a different kind of war. We don't have to upset the whole country, we can win this little war with both hands tied behind our backs."

I later had some personnel problems with respect to numbers

of naval aviators. When we started fighting in Vietnam and were being shot at I said that we were short of aviators and should increase our training program. The analytical people in the Office of the Secretary of Defense came up with long lists of naval aviators and said, "You aren't using your aviators efficiently. Look, you've got Joe Blow over here behind a desk, you've got this fellow over here in BuAir, you've got this fellow out at Point Mugu. Why don't you have them out there fighting?"

Well, it took a long process of education in explaining why we were utilizing our aviators this way and I'm not sure I ever did get it across. My point was, look, we don't have an aviation corps in the Navy. We decided years ago that we not only wouldn't join the Air Force we wouldn't have a separate aviation corps in the Navy. Our aviators are naval officers, as well as aviators. Consequently, they're spread throughout the Navy. That was the decision we made back in the thirties and forties. Instead of joining the Air Force or instead of just setting up a naval aviation corps, it was felt that the Navy and the country would be better off if naval aviation was completely integrated within the Navy. As a result, we do have aviators behind this desk and that desk, we have an aviator commanding a tanker and various other things. I said that if SecDef was now going to tell me that we've got to pull all these aviators out of their present assignments and have them do nothing but fly airplanes in combat, then we would have to restructure the whole Navy personnel system. Those in the office of the SecDef didn't really realize that. This was one of the big issues that I raised and literally pounded my fist about at the ranch before President Johnson - that our pilots flying out there were flying too many sorties and that we must increase our pilot production rate. He agreed and after that we got more people in our flight training program.

But you see, Jack, I didn't get mad, if you want to put it that way at the Whizz Kids, so-called, to use that expression again, because they came up with that. They didn't know, and you can't criticize a man for doing something based upon the information he has, provided that when he gets other information he'll also take that into consideration. They never did go along with my line of reasoning completely, but almost. We had one rear admiral in the Pentagon by the name of Gerry Miller that our Under Secretary, Bob Baldwin, was very fond of and so was Alain Enthoven. Between the two of us we got pretty good ultimate results from Alain. He never came around completely to our way of thinking but he was quite helpful. That was one of the battles, if you want to put it that way, I had in the latter part of my tour as CNO. But it turned out pretty well.

Q: Various men have told me that the Secretary himself would say pointedly, "Well, if you're doing it this way, it must be wrong. Let's do it some other way." Does that tie in with some of your experiences?

Adm. M.: Who told you that? I don't agree that was that difficult.

I think I mentioned that Mr. McNamara would never admit that there was a budgetary ceiling. He insisted that we were a wealthy country and we could get anything we needed. Of course, it was very odd to me that the higher the budget got the less we seemed to need the things we then asked for!

McNamara had another - and I'm not being critical when I say this, I think, characteristic in that he would never admit that his recommendations had been overridden by the President. What I mean by that is simply this. We Chiefs and the Secretary might have all been unanimous in agreeing on a particular operation and he would go to the White House with the plan. Then later that day or the next day he would call us down and issue an order that was contrary to what we had agreed upon. He would simply indicate that he had changed his mind and would never, under any circumstances, admit that the President had ordered him to make this change. He said that he felt that any order he issued should come from him as his order and that he was not going to hide behind the President's skirts, as it were.

One day, in discussing this particular thing, I said that I met with my vice chiefs, my deputies, rather, every Thursday morning and I had on more than one occasion told them that either the Secretary of the Navy or the Secretary of Defense had issued a certain order, which I disagreed with completely, but that I had made my case and the order had been issued. Now, by golly, we'll carry it out. I didn't feel that by so doing

McDonald #5 - 365

I was hiding behind anybody's skirts or being disloyal. At least my deputies knew my thinking, and it's a little bit difficult when every order you issue indicates that it's your thinking when, in some cases, it's not and it's sort of hard for us to know just what your thinking is. In some cases, it makes it a little bit difficult to work with you.

Q: How did he react to an argument like that?

Adm. M.: All right. You could argue, but the outcome was always the same. It wasn't a question of him getting mad and getting up and throwing you out. You could express yourself forcefully and disagree.

On one particular occasion discussions were being held about a large ship that would carry a lot of equipment for soldiers and the idea was that the ship could take all the equipment and the troops could be flown in great big airplanes and land and marry up with their equipment - FDLs, I believe they called the ships. I felt at the time that Mr. McNamara was trying to find some way to reduce the number of troops we had in Europe without upsetting our NATO allies in Europe, and this seemed to be one way. Of course, I never could see how we could guarantee that there'd be a landing field anywhere near where the ship would anchor or tie-up and furthermore that it would be completely out of enemy range. But, of course, the Army liked this.

Since it was a ship, Mr. McNamara thought that I should

carry the ball, so to speak, before the Congress. I told him that I didn't think I could do this because I simply didn't believe in this kind of strategic thinking. He said, well, if I felt that way, there wasn't any use in going through with it.

"Oh," I said, "no, you can go through with it, if you want to. I just don't want to carry the ball. But if the others want it and I can't support it, I'll keep my mouth shut, as I have done in a lot of cases."

He didn't quite know how that could happen, but said that would be all right. So we went before the House Armed Services Committee - we being those representing the Army, the Navy, the Air Force and the Marine Corps. I was on the far end of the group.

After the others had testified, Mr. Rivers asked me for my comment and I said:

"Mr. Chairman, I don't think I can add anything to what has already been said."

The chairman hit his gavel, no questions were asked. They didn't realize that I had, prior to that meeting, told Mr. Rivers what my reply would be and said, "Please, without asking me why, don't let anybody ask me questions."

The odd thing about this is that that ship went all the way through until it was ultimately killed by Senator Russell personally. It's never been built yet. I believe that Mr. McNamara probably thinks to this day that I went to see my fellow Georgian

Senator Russell. I never did. At the Alfalfa dinner in 1968, about five months after I'd retired, Senator Russell came by me at the table and said, "Look, if you aren't otherwise obligated, how about coming up to my room after dinner."

I went up to Senator Russell's room and I guess we talked for two or three hours, over a little bourbon here and there, and it was really interesting when we got around to the FDL and Senator Russell said that a lot of people wondered if he was right about this and he said, "What do you think?" When I told him the story, he said, "Now I feel better." That's the first and only time I ever talked to Dick Russell about the FDL ship, and it hasn't been built yet.

Q: What reasons had he given for killing it at the time he did so?

Adm. M.: The same reason I did. He didn't think it made sense. I thought, and of course I could never prove this, the only reason this thing was dreamed up was to try to take U. S. troops out of Europe and convince our allies that we could get them back over there in a hurry.

This kind of thing doesn't make any sense, if you're going to do it in a hurry. But that was the theory. We were going to marry the equipment up with all these troops who were going to be flown over in I think a C-5A - that was before they got the bigger ones.

Here was where I had what some might call a serious disagreement with Mr. McNamara but it was pleasant, and the same thing with Mr. Nitze. I never got into real hot water with Mr. Nitze.

Q: He came in shortly after you?

Adm. M.: Very shortly. Mr. Korth went out and that must have been along in November.

I think Mr. Nitze and I both realized that we were very opposite in nature. He's an intellectual and I'm not, far from it. But we both, I think, said to ourselves and on occasion we said to each other, there's one thing we're not going to do. We're not going to fight each other, and we didn't.

I had some problems with the Under Secretary for a while, Bob Baldwin, in front of Mr. Nitze on occasion, so much so one time that the next morning, which was Friday, I was called in by the Secretary and he said, "I wish you hadn't said what you said yesterday because I've just had a telephone call from Bob and he's leaving and going back to Wall Street."

I said, "He should never have come here in the first place."

Then the next morning, Saturday morning, I came to work about 7:30, as usual, and about 8:00 the Secretary called me again and said, "Mr. Baldwin would like to come in and talk to you." I said sure, so he came in. He didn't do the talking. I did the talking, I guess for two hours. When I got through,

McDonald #5 - 369

he got up and shook my hand and walked out. When I retired, Baldwin was still under secretary but was acting secretary. He had learned though that he was not going to be appointed secretary.

Q: He hadn't returned to Wall Street!

Adm. M.: No. And I was able to shake his hand and say: "Bob, you know how I hated your guts for a while but the way you acted after we'd had our long talk, I can look you in the eye and say 'I'm sorry that they aren't going to make you Secretary of the Navy.'"

Q: What was the issue?

Adm. M.: There were many issues.

Q: But the one that provoked you so?

Adm. M.: I don't remember the exact one. But in general, I think Mr. Baldwin was led to believe by those who talked him into coming to Washington, that the Navy was so messed up "they need somebody down there to really straighten it out." And he came down with the idea of straightening it out. Instead of coming down with the idea that he was to help us, he didn't come down to help us, he came down to straighten us out and he ran in all directions. As I told him in my talk to him that morning:

"Look, fellow, you were a great athlete at Princeton but you haven't been a team player since you left there. But here you simply must listen to others and give their views careful consideration before you make a decision. I don't make a major decision around here without calling my deputies in. They don't make it for me, but let me tell you, if the majority of them don't agree with me, I think pretty long and loud before I do it. You go off half-cocked around here in half a dozen directions. For instance, you're trying to change the uniform of the sailors. You haven't even talked to me about it. You just came back from the West where you visited a bunch of ships and you came back here saying the ships were so damned crowded they're sleeping on cots in the passageways. When we build a ship, do you know we allow a certain number of cubic feet for a Marine to stow his equipment in, a certain number of cubic feet for a Chief, and a certain number of cubic feet for an enlisted man. My God, if you change the uniform so that every bluejacket has to have the same storage space as a Marine or a Chief, where are you going to put the people?"

He said, "I hadn't thought about that."

"That's my point, Bob. You run off as though you know it all. Don't do that. Seek advice first."

It was just one thing after the other and the thing that teed us off, teed me off, was that he brought an advertising man or personnel man down from New York to handle some personnel problems and he should have been an Assistant to the Under Secretary. But the fellow wanted a bigger title than that, so they decided they'd make him Deputy to the Under Secretary. There wasn't an authorized billet for such a title. I went in to Nitze and I raised hell about it, but then we found out that Baldwin had written this thing up and had taken it down and it had already been approved by the Deputy Secretary of Defense. That was in the morning.

That day, our chaplain was having a luncheon for a group of preachers and chaplains over at the Marriott Motel and asked me if I'd come over. Well, I went over and was standing in the receiving line. After about half a dozen came through, here came this new fellow who'd just arrived from New York, and the chaplain said, "Oh, Mr. Secretary," and put him right up at the head of the line.

I never stood on protocol very much, but I was teed off at that. I went in that afternoon and we really had it with Mr. Nitze up one side and down the other and I shook my finger at the then Under Secretary and said:

"If what the Secretary tells me is true and I don't doubt but what it is, you railroaded that through. You knew damned well I wouldn't approve it and you knew he wouldn't approve it and you wrote it up because you wanted that fellow. You went down and you got it approved in the Department of Defense, in that office. If you think I'm going to work with anybody like that, you've just got another thought coming."

But, as I say, after our Saturday morning talk he became extremely cooperative. It's too bad somebody didn't really lay it on the line the day he got down there. He's president of Morgan Stanley now and when he was elected to that Presidency I wrote him a letter and got a nice letter from him. He's a great guy, smart as a whip, a real patriot and loved the Navy.

Q: He's the one who established Orlando, the training center, isn't he?

Adm. M.: Yes, they've got a lake down there named for him. Getting Orlando going was very interesting.

Q: Tell me about it.

Adm. M.: It was simply this. We had some hepatitis scares in our training commands that pointed up the crowded conditions that existed and we felt that we just had to have a third training station. Bainbridge wasn't really any good. So we decided we'd go down to Orlando with a small training establishment, knowing full well - or at least some of us thought - that ultimately it was going to be one of the biggest because just from a climatological point of view it just makes sense. Although many of us were involved, Bob carried the ball and did a real good job.

Q: But with your backing?

Adm. M.: Well, I don't think he could have done it without my backing plus the backing of others but he really was the "action officer" so to speak. But please note that even Baldwin and I didn't fight in public but in the Secretary's office. Bob did a world of good, but we did have a lot of arguments. But from that Saturday morning on, we never had an argument, and I've always felt that we lost a great asset when we lost Bob Baldwin. Tom Gates had him tagged right, he just had the wrong idea when he came down.

I think maybe Bob might have rubbed McNamara a little bit wrong towards the last, but you see he could outsmart them. He was quick on the trigger, too, and would do his homework on a lot of these projects which were to be discussed with the SecDef's helpers. I wouldn't do much of this. Why should I sit down and spend days trying to prove mathematically the correctness of things that I'd lived with all my life. I just wasn't going to do it. It wasn't worth arguing about because you pretty well knew what the answer was going to be anyway.

But Nitze and I got along, at least, as well as any CNO and Secretary have for a long time. He, like all secretaries, got more and more into the detailing of personnel. I think that's the wrong job for a Secretary. And even Bob Baldwin tried to get into this.

Secretaries too often evaluate a service officer with

very little knowledge of his background. As CNO I had every three-star and every four-star officer write me a personal letter every six months and in that letter they would put down about six people that they thought should be promoted to three stars. The four-star people, in their letters, would put down the number they thought should be promoted to three and to four. Each of them would also put in there those who had three stars who they thought should be demoted to two.

You see, I could get information in these letters that I couldn't get from a fitness report. We were discussing an officer one day, Mr. Nitze and I, I think it was for three stars, and I was objecting. I brought up some information and he said, "How do you know that?" So I told him about these letters that I got.

"Oh," he said, "gee, I'd love to see them."

I said, "Paul, I wouldn't show you one of those letters for love nor money. This is a personal matter. Now, if you want to write these admirals and ask them to write you the same kind of a letter I'm sure they'd do so, but I don't know whether they'd tell you the same things or not. You can do that, but I'm not about to show you any of these."

And he agreed. I used to say to some of our civilian bosses: "Look, fellows, we know our people. You might be better businessmen, you might be a better systems analyst, and all this, but you can't possibly know our people the way we do because in addition to fitness reports, officers have what we call service reputations. You don't know about this. You just see a fellow once and you make up your mind. Then you come and tell me to put stars on him (Here I'm only referring to those being promoted to either three or four stars). But don't forget I've known them or known about them for years and years."

I might be repeating here something I've said previously but anyway - on any flag officer, whether he was a rear admiral or a vice admiral or a four-star, any proposed orders were sent to the Secretary. I thought that was wrong. Back when I was aide to Dan Kimball only the three and four-stars came in. But when I was CNO the two stars were coming in, and one day the Secretary, Mr. Nitze, told me that he'd been talking to the Under Secretary, about some of our personnel matters and he would appreciate it if I would route the recommended assignment of flag officers through him, and I said, "I won't do it. I m not going to let him kibitz my recommendations. It's none of his business. I'm going to send them in here, Mr. Secretary. When I send them in here to you, you can call in a janitor, if you want to, and have him review them, but I'm not going to send my flag officer recommendations through the Under Secretary; in fact, I think the assignment of flag officers is already out of hand. You don't know half of these people, and just to have some other civilian who's never heard of them except maybe he's got some pet, and that's not the way we do this."

Mr. Nitze agreed. Whether or not in the subsequent time period he discussed any of these with Baldwin I don't know, but Mr. Nitze agreed with me and said, "I understand."

I think that one of the mistakes being made is too much civilian control over flag officer assignments. Sometimes I think the Congress interferes, but if they interfere they express their views to the civilian secretariat and not to the men in uniform. They put it to the civilians.

I have been told that within the last couple of years there have been officers who were told by the Secretary that they were going to be promoted and where they were going, when, as a matter of fact, it never happened. Somebody else was promoted.

Q: Got selected?

Adm. M.: Got selected by an individual and I think as a result of pressure on the Hill. The real selection board, of course, selects rear admirals, but the way they made the three and four star admirals when I was there was the Chief of the Bureau of Naval Personnel made up his list of who he thought should be promoted to three and four stars. Then he took his list to the Vice Chief of Naval Operations and they discussed it. Then the Vice Chief would bring it to me and we discussed it. We not only discussed the list, we discussed any variation that there might be on that list from what the Chief of BuPers had recommended and why. And then I would take the list with my recommendations and send it in to the Secretary and he would okay it if he wanted to. Usually he would call me in and we could discuss it back and forth.

Q: Why would civilian Secretaries and Under Secretaries presume to interject themselves into an ongoing system of promotions when they were so, in a way, temporary? As Secretaries they're only there for a limited period of time?

Adm. M.: You'd have to ask them that. That's a question that I have often wondered about and the only answer I can give you is we all want power and if you can control people and money you've got all the power, yet it doesn't really make sense.

Q: Because, in truth, they admired the system, did they not?

Adm. M.: Well, let's be fair. While I was there, unless my memory fails me, there was only one man who got stars that I did not approve of. I ultimately approved of it because I said to the Secretary, "I'll be damned if I'm going to have this go down to the Joint Chiefs with the Secretary recommending one thing and the Chief of Naval Operations not supporting it, because if it does my JCS conferees in uniform are going to support me. Then SecDef might support you. Anyway either you or I or both of us would look silly. I'm not going to do it."

To the best of my knowledge, that's the only time in four years that a man got a star that I didn't approve of. And as far as I know, the Secretary disagreed with my recommendations on just one occasion. Not the same man, this was a different case, where I wanted to put another star on a man that he didn't agree with. In both cases the Secretary won - or, in both cases, I gave in. If they'd been other people, maybe I wouldn't have given in. He had good reasons in both cases. I thought I had, but our differences weren't great. I think if I hadn't agreed, it would have been just a question of being stubborn and didn't make any sense. Besides, if the Chiefs agreed with me, McNamara would agree with him. You couldn't win in that game. He was too close to Mr. McNamara. So there are some things; you know about the fellow who says, "I'd rather be right than be President," he never was president.

My job, I thought, was to do everything I could honorably do to acquire for our country the kind of Navy I thought we ought to have. If that required me to grovel every now and then, so be it, as long as I could look in the mirror and shave without cutting my throat. But this idea of just saying I'm right when you know you're not only going to lose this argument but the chances are you're going to lose the next one too, isn't any good. By giving in to something I knew was going to happen anyway, made it easier for Paul to give in to me on something else. That's the sort of way we worked for the whole four years and I can't help but think the Navy benefitted.

Q: It's a sensible approach, certainly.

Going into this field, I know that you had some firm ideas

about the merchant marine. What were you able to do in that area?

Adm. M.: Nothing. I do have some firm ideas about the merchant marine. I'm pro merchant marine but in some ways I'm so anti the unions that man the merchant ships that one sort of offsets the other. How are you going to have ships that work on an hourly schedule, like you do ashore? None of the rest of the world does it. They're going to cut their throats. Unless we change I'm convinced the Russian merchant marine will run us off the seas. You simply can't let people who go to sea live like they do ashore. It's a different kind of a life, and when you try to make their life out there the same as it is here, you price yourself out of the market.

This bothers me today but I don't really know how you're going to lick it.

Q: The Russians seem to have a workable system in that their merchant marine is really an arm of their navy, isn't it?

Adm. M.: I don't really know, Jack. Everything is really an arm of their benevolent dictatorship, if that's what it is. The controlling element in it is dictated. It's run that way. They don't worry about whether this poor fellow over here is making $4,000 a year when somebody next to him is making $8,000 or whether he lives in a dachau like a member of -

Q: An elite?

Adm. M.: Yes. We're so anxious to carry out what Huey Long said he believed in, namely every man a king, that what we're going to do is have every man a peon. The leveling process, I believe, from time immeorial has resulted in everybody going down to the lowest common denominator. Of course, that's getting into something entirely different from being CNO. I might get back, though and say I think one reason that I didn't want to be CNO was that although I was born and raised a Democrat I wanted no part of the New Deal, socialistic, new frontier ideas. Mr. Johnson called it something else but it was still what I believed to be a socialistic approach with which I do not agree.

Q: The Great Society.

Adm. M.: Yes. I just didn't believe in that kind of thing, but as a naval officer I guess I wasn't supposed to concern myself with it. But I think I would have enjoyed working on this higher level if I'd agreed with more of the policies of the federal government. I didn't agree with it from welfarism to Vietnamism, so it made it a little bit difficult.

Q: Going back to the merchant marine, I saw some statement of yours somewhere to the effect that the merchant marine should be an arm of our intersts in an international sense, reaching out, they should combine the economic and the political interests of the country.

Adm. M.: I think that is right, not only for it to be beneficial in peacetime, but in time of war if we have any more overseas wars, different though they will be from any in the past, we still need a lot of logistic support, and never, in my opinion, will we build enough navy auxiliaries to provide that. You must lean and lean heavily upon the merchant marine, and the better it is, the more efficient it is, and the more people that are interested in doing their job, instead of working an hour for ten bucks, then the better off, I think, we'll be. But I don't think we're making an awful lot of progress in that respect.

Like during World War II, why should you pay those of the merchant marine all this hazardous-duty pay when they're in an area with a bunch of sailors who weren't getting it? Why not draft them all? Let everybody play the same game.

I guess the merchant marine today would say, "We are going to play the same game because all the military people are going to be unionized, too." But that's not for me to worry about. I think we'd better get back on track.

I think I've talked enough about promotions and other things, except Vietnam. Basically on Vietnam, as I remember it and I don't think my memory fails me, before we went into

Vietnam - I mean landed Marines there - the Chiefs felt that if we didn't intervene militarily, South Vietnam would fall. At the same time, I think we felt, I certainly felt, that it wasn't the business of the military to decide whether or not South Vietnam should fall. That was a political decision, not a military decision. But once the decision was made that we would intervene, the military men felt that we should go in to win it quickly, and I well remember upon one occasion and I think it was in May or thereabouts of 1965, in the White House, when it was suggested that we mobilize, call up the reserves, and go for a supplemental because I - and I think the record would show that I as an individual was asked how much - and I said in the neighborhood of 12 billion dollars. I believe it was Mr. McNamara who said, oh, that's way off base.

But of course the decision was made not to mobilize, not to call up the reserves, and not to ask for a supplemental.

Q: What was the basis of that decision?

Adm. M.: I'd be glad to tell you what I think the basis was because it made some sense not calling up the reserves, etc. Reserves are civilians, they're businessmen and they're in the process of providing for their families, and although they have entered into an obligation to be called up, nevertheless when you do call them up it really is upsetting throughout the country. Certain reserves had been called up in the

Cuban missile crisis.

Q: As well as the Berlin crisis.

Adm. M.: And they were not needed, not even used in the Cuban crisis, and it was said, Mr. President, if you call up the reserves again and they aren't needed, you'll really look like a fool, and I don't think they'll be needed. We can take the people that we now have in uniform and by moving those that are east to the west, by the proper adjustment of their location, we can win this thing. It's not going to last very long. And as for mobilizing, oh, Lord, you'll upset the whole world. It's not going to last long. And as for the supplemental, let's postpone that. We don't need that. We've got a lot of reserve material in our reserve stock-pile. We've got enough there, this thing will be over before we use all that up, and then we can replace that gradually with just a little additional money in the budget each year, instead of going for the whole pot now.

Q: This was the Secretary of Defense?

Adm. M.: Yes, and others, but basically SecDef. That sort of made sense, and, of course, that's the kind of a thing that the President wanted to hear. As far as we in uniform were concerned, we looked at it from another angle. If we're going to

McDonald #5 - 384

have a war, get in there with both feet and get it over with. But many thought this was such a different kind of war that we didn't have to follow the normally accepted ways to fight a war and win.

That was the thinking and it's what happened. And, as things went along, little by little -

Q: Deeper and deeper! You were there at Tonkin Gulf?

Adm. M.: Yes.

Q: Tell me about that.

Adm. M.: I don't know any more than what you read in the papers. The first attack was an out and out attack and the second one was always questioned.

Oh, and the statement was made to the President that if you go to Congress for this supplemental and they give you that, it will show you they're really behind you. But, the rebuttal to that was, wait a minute, what do you mean "behind?" Good Lord, it hasn't been a year since we had the Tonkin Gulf resolution and the whole Senate with, I think, one or two exceptions, supported it. How much more support do you want? That was the line of reasoning even though I'm not inferring that they are exact quotes. Only one non-military fellow stood steadfast all the time, don't do it. George Ball never wavered. Don't get in under any circumstances.

Q: You mean on the land.

Adm. M.: Yes. He didn't want to get in it anywhere. He might have under some other conditions, but basically he thought this whole thing was wrong.

There were many interesting sidelights. Once it was reported that we didn't have the right kind of bombs. I was called down to the Secretary of Defense's office. "What do you mean you don't have enough bombs?" Some of his analysts asked and they showed me certain figures. It was really interesting. Their figures showed that in the area we were talking about, we had more of the bombs we were talking about than I even knew we had. The trouble was they had counted bomb bodies but there weren't enough tails. These smart analysts, with no experience, didn't know that you made certain bombs with bodies and tails separately and you had to marry them up and if you didn't have tails to go on the bomb bodies the bombs weren't any good. Ridiculous, but it happened.

We also had occasions where, in order to support statements that were made, bombs were sent from the East Coast to the West Coast. This got so bad at one time that I was told to come before Senator Stennis' Committee alone.

Q: What do you mean "alone"?

Adm. M.: Well, there was a Defense Department edict saying that no service chief would go before committees of Congress without the service Secretary with them. So when I was asked to come alone the word went back to them from the grapevine that they'd have to be more positive than that or my Secretary would be with me. How much more positive do we need to be, they asked. You've got to state emphatically that you do not want the Secretary or the Secretary will be there. I went up alone.

Q: They did state that?

Adm. M.: Yes.

Q: Was this a closed meeting of the committee?

Adm. M.: Yes. I went up and when the minutes were written up they were sent to the Navy Department for me to correct. I did and sent them back via the Secretary of the Navy and the Secretary of Defense. The SecDef didn't like certain things in the minutes and wanted me to change them. I wouldn't make the changes. I said, "You can change it, if you want to." Oh, there were some mistakes that I corrected but not the sum and substance.

Q: How could he retract what you'd said to the committee? Simply by changing the text?

Adm. M.: Yes, or deleting.

Q: Yes, but you'd already spoken to the committee?

Adm. M.: Oh, yes. Anyway, after about two weeks I agreed to an addendum in which I said, "Subsequent to my testimony, the following corrective measures have been taken." They had been taken by the time I got the script and he wanted me to change the script to indicate that these conditions didn't exist when I testified.

But you can't be too critical of SecDef's decisions because I still don't know what decisions Mr. McNamara made or what things he did that somebody else told him to do. And, of course, as the war went on, those in the combat areas would recommend target lists and we Chiefs would look them over and make recommendations, and give them to the Secretary of Defense. He'd go to the White House, and often you wouldn't even recognize the list after it had been approved. Odd though it might seem, on many occasions we would have to do such things as estimate how many civilians might be killed if we executed certain bombing missions.

It all throttles down to what I hope we've learned, as a country, but I doubt it because we don't seem to learn anything from the past. One thing is, don't ever commit our country to a shooting war without agreement by the Congress.

Second, once you get in a shooting war, the civilian secretaries better keep their fingers out of military operations,

McDonald #5 - 388

otherwise you're in trouble.

Q: This is a practice that has grown up. It wasn't only peculiar to the Vietnam mess but it was also involved in the Cuban missile crisis.

Adm. M.: This has come about for two reasons. First of all, the atomic bomb.

Q: Yes.

Adm. M.: But primarily because of rapid means of communication.

Q: Why is this an excuse for civilians to make decisions on bombing missions and that sort of thing?

Adm. M.: I don't know. But during the Vietnam "Fracas" I, for one, felt completely frustrated because of such decision-making. A lot of people have heard me say, maybe you have, that on more than one occasion I said to my right hand man, Ike Kidd, and my wife, "I think I'll just turn in my suit. I just don't think I can do this any longer." My wife never said anything but Ike Kidd on more than one occasion said, "Look, if you did, you'd simply be replaced by another naval officer who'd been trained the same way you have, probably thinks the same way you do, and will not be able to benefit from the one or two or three years'

McDonald #5 - 389

experience that you have had.

I think Paul Nitze would probably remember than when he came to me along in the spring, about the same time we went into Vietnam, I think, of 1965 and said:

"Well, I think it's about time for us to send your name over to the White House to be nominated for two more years."

I said, "Paul, I think there are certain things you ought to know." One of them was my little heart problem I had in Paris. Then I said, "I wish you would do this. I wish you would make sure the powers that be, and you'll have to figure out who they are, if they do nominate me, I want them to know that they shouldn't be surprised if I request retirement after I've served one year of my second two-year tour. There are some things I have in the hopper that I believe I can accomplish in another year, and that's the only reason I'm really willing to stay on for another year."

He might have reported this to the higher-ups, but I doubt it.

Getting the next carrier was one of the things I wanted to do and I believe I did this at the next meeting at the ranch -

Q: This was down at Johnson's ranch?

Adm. M.: Yes. We argued our case in the morning.

Q: For a carrier?

Adm. M.: Yes, among other things. We had lunch and after lunch, we service Chiefs were flying back to Washington, but there were some other people down there, the Secretary of Commerce or State or CIA had come down and were to hold their session in the afternoon, and Mr. McNamara was to stay. As we got up from the table, someone said, "Well, let's go in and say good-bye to the President." We all shook hands. I was at the tail end of the line and as I shook hands I said that I had enjoyed the trip down and thanked the President for the nice lunch. Then President Johnson put his arm around my shoulder and whispered in my ear, "Don't you worry too much about that carrier, Boy."

I walked out of there with a great big smile and Johnny Johnson said, "What's the matter with you?"

I said, "I won it!"

"What do you mean?"

I said, "The president told me not to worry about that carrier."

But I sometimes wonder even now if I should or should not have requested retirement early. If you're on the team you must carry out the plays even though the quarterback doesn't call the plays you agree to, but if he keeps on calling plays you don't agree with there comes a time when maybe you should leave the team.

Maybe we military men were all weak. Maybe we should have stood up and pounded the table. But I don't really think it would have done any good. They'd have just gotten somebody else, because they weren't really being guided by our advice anyway.

Q: It was a different kind of a - ?

Adm. M.: They really didn't need ours. If they were going to be smart, they'd do what the fellows in the field recommended. When the target list came through us all we'd do was dress it up a little bit so we could hopefully get a better list approved than would have been approved had we just sent it in the way it was. Oley Sharp used to say, "Why do you fellows in JCS change some of our target requests?"

Our answer was that we had a pretty good idea of what would happen to their recommendations if they went over the way they came to us. So what we were really trying to do was to get the best that we thought we could get or come as near getting for them what they asked for.

Q: Oley Sharp says that he felt like a messenger boy.

Adm. M.: Well, we were of some help in supporting him, in getting support, seeing that he got the material, seeing that we had the proper training, but not much help as far as "fighting" the war was concerned.

Q: What was their overriding purpose in fighting a war without the aide and advice of the military?

Adm. M.: They honestly believed - I think they honestly believed, that they could get this thing over with both hands tied behind their backs. And they honestly believed that by escalating incrementally we could win without the expenditure of any more men, money or material than was necessary.

Q: But it soon became apparent that it wasn't!

Adm. M.: It never did. Finally, we blockaded Haiphong Harbor and bombed Hanoi.

Once, when there was talk about what China might do, what Russia might do, I expressed the view: "Look, why don't we just figure out what we should do and quit worrying about what somebody else might do?"

I saw the time, before we embarked upon one particular mission when London was even communicated with by telephone before we took action.

Q: For a mission?

Adm. M.: Before, to let them know what we were doing, and to get their reaction.

It was just unbelievable. Of course, when you talk like

this, Jack, today people just say, "Well, you know, that's a bunch of sour grapes." It's not sour grapes. I'm not proud of what was done because I was a part of it and I'm sort of ashamed of myself, too. At times, I wonder, "why did I go along with this kind of stuff?" It's a hard question to answer.

Q: Even considering the two points you made as to the reason for this process of decisions going from the White House on military operations, in your own mind is there any justification for it, having gone that far?

Adm. M.: No. I think the way the thing was conducted was wrong. If we ever went in again, I don't think it ought to be done that way.

Q: Was it done that way because we had a group of personalities at that moment who -?

Adm. M.: I can't answer the question. I think part of it was that President Johnson was a Franklin Roosevelt New Dealer from the word "go." And I think in his many years in political office he said to himself, "If I ever get to a point where I can do it, there are certain things I'm going to do for my country." And then when he became President he found that he was fenced in by a war that he didn't want, and what was uppermost in his mind was let's get this thing over with without

McDonald #5 - 394

upsetting my Great Society plans any more than actually necessary. And he was led to believe by some of his advisers that this could be done the war we went about it, and he ended up by losing both the war and his Great Society and it broke his heart.

I really think the reason some of this was permitted to go on was his great desire to do these other things (many of which I personally didn't approve of) which he felt were for the good of the country. If he went all out to win the war he probably wouldn't be able to do these other things since his time in the White House, like everybody else's, was limited. He wanted to do them both and he had people who believed he could do both, I guess, at least they convinced him that he could.

Q: Yes, people who were all sold on the Great Society.

Adm. M.: So I can be extremely critical of what was done without criticizing Mr. McNamara or the President, because there's no question in my mind but what they did what they thought was right. I don't think there was anything two-faced about it. I think they did what they thought was right. Of course, I must say this. I think a lot of things Mr. Nixon did which were terribly wrong were done because he thought he was right, too.

Q: You mentioned Mr. McNamara some time back as basically a pacifist?

Adm. M.: Well, that's just my opinion. He's an intellectual; has an extremely alert mind, is really conscientious and energetic.

Both he and Paul Nitze were nice to me. For instance, one of the things that used to irk me was to see all of my ships christened by the wives of people who didn't have a close relationship with the Navy. Representative Joe Blow's wife, for instance, and he might not even be on the Armed Forces Committee; or a mayor's wife.

Q: Just a nice thing for her to do it!

Adm. M.: So I got a policy approved by the Secretary - and I'm sure Bob McNamara agreed - which says that the wife of every naval officer who attains the rank of three stars or more will christen a United States Navy ship and we made it retroactive about a year. I couldn't thank them enough because that was something that you could say was just one of the little quirks I had had in mind for years and years that I was able to carry out. I don't know that that helped the Navy. But it at least helped morale among the senior people. I believe very strongly that morale starts at the top. I don't care how many perquisites you give to the seaman first, if he is aboard ship where his captain and the commander are the navigator are, to use a sort of a foul expression, "sore-assed," he's not going to be aboard a happy ship. I don't mean by that that you're supposed to look out for the vice admirals and pay no attention to the bluejackets, but these people that make it a point of showing interest only in the "common man" and in so doing completely neglect the others are doing wrong in a military organization. I'm not sure they're not doing wrong anywhere. I think it's just as bad to do that as it is to look out for the brass only and say to hell with the enlisted people.

I think you've got to look at the whole problem. Support flows up as well as down, but so-called morale doesn't. The man on top is the man who's got to build the morale, I think. And I think among the many things that were done within the last few years, some of them, completely shot the morale of certain layers of personnel, at one time the chief petty officers.

Some of these things I guess we all have different feelings about, different ideas. I guess the one thing that I regret the most is having to say that I don't believe I ever looked forward to anything more than I looked forward to the day I retired. I think that was most unfortunate. I think that a man who's Chief of Naval Operations should be in a position where he feels he is doing so much good that he just hates to leave. But during about the last year, maybe year and a half, I felt completely frustrated. I was supporting so many things that my heart really wasn't in. I was just waiting for the day and it was a real happy moment when I could say "I'm out of there after having been able to stick with it till the very end of my appointed term."

Q: I'd wager that some of your peers felt pretty much the same way, on the Joint Chiefs, didn't they?

Adm. M.: I can't answer that, Jack. My personal belief is that they did because we had some pretty good conversations. It's been rumored that there were times - and a particular time - when the Joint Chiefs threatened to quit. If there was, it wasn't during my time or I certainly wasn't aware of it. Somebody writing a book wrote me about that and said that they'd heard about it. Somebody might have said facetiously, "Why don't we just turn in our suits boys, and see what happens." But as far as getting together and saying, "It won't do any good, Joe, if you quit or I quit. Why don't we just all?" No, I don't remember that ever being suggested during the time I was there.

No record of my tour as CNO would be complete without a reference to my Vice Chief. When I became CNO I inherited Admiral Anderson's Vice Chief who was Claud Ricketts whom I had known and respected for many years; the two or us being only a year apart at the Naval Academy. However, within the year he died suddenly of a heart attack. But several months earlier I had brought from Norfolk one Horatio Rivero with whom I had worked in Hawaii while on the Staff of Admirals Radford and Stump. Rivero was promoted to three stars and put in charge of a very important element within the office of CNO. After Ricketts' death I was asked to name two or three who would be acceptable to me as my Vice Chief. But as far as I was concerned there was only one man and that was Rivero. Fortunately for me - and certainly for the Navy - I was able to get the required support. He had been in the Pentagon long enough to become known and appreciated by my civilian bosses. There's just not enough nice things that I can say about his helpful assistance to me. And, of course, after I retired he served as the boss of the NATO Allied Command at Naples and then as U. S. Ambassador to Spain. One of the last things I said to Paul Nitze before I left was please take care of Rivero.

McDonald #6 - 399

Interview No. 6 with Admiral David L. McDonald, U.S. Navy (Retired)

Place: The Naval Institute, Annapolis, Maryland

Date: Tuesday afternoon, 1 June 1976

Subject: Biography

By: John T. Mason, Jr.

Q: Admiral, at the outset, I must tell you that I was so truly pleased with your last interview. I was pleased because it sets you forth as the person you are, the man of great integrity and decisiveness and honesty. All of these characteristics of yours stand forth in that last interview, as I reviewed it this morning. And, above all, you are portrayed there for what you are again, a very warm-hearted, human person, a person with a sense of humor and all the rest. As a result, this self-portrait, I think, is a very laudable one and I'm very grateful to you for giving it to me, even though you didn't realize you were doing it.

Adm. M: Thank you, Jack. I feel that being truthful and forthright is probably something that was taught to me from childhood. And another thing that I think has helped me along similar lines is some advice that I believe I've related previously, which I received from a senior of mine who was a commander at the time I first got to know him real well. Later on, he became a rear admiral and the first time I met him after he became a rear admiral, he indicated that he thought maybe I was surprised that he was a rear admiral and he said that he was sort of surprised himself. And maybe he wouldn't have been a flag officer if it hadn't been for the war. Then he chuckled and said:

"You know, there are a lot of people who think that I'm the most stupid rear admiral in the Navy. Perhaps I am but, if I am, maybe it isn't my fault. Maybe I was born that way. But there's another thing. I'm the most polite rear admiral in the Navy, and even a dumbbell can be polite," and he pointed his finger at me and added, "and don't you ever forget it." I hope I never have!

Q: I think you haven't! I think you demonstrate it all the time, not only in your relationship with people around here but in what you said last time.

Well, Sir, I think perhaps today we should start by dealing with a few of the subjects you mentioned in that previous interview and perhaps elaborating upon them. You said that one of your objectives when you became CNO was to communicate with the people in OSD. Now, as we understand the set-up, OSD was a creature of the Secretary and it was a kind of an organization that was almost parallel with the CNO organization, wasn't it, in some senses?

Adm. M.: Jack, OSD was created by a law; i.e., the Unification Act. However, the operation of the office of the Secretary of Defense was somewhat similar to SecNav-CNO organization.

Q: Yes?

Adm. M.: Certain members of SecDef's staff did, of course, offer him advice and make organizational recommendations which otherwise he might have sought from the various service personnel. So there was some parallelism, but these people I presume he felt were a little closer to him. Sometimes we in the service felt that maybe they kibitzed our recommendations a little too much before they got to the Secretary, but that was the Secretary's prerogative, to accept those that he wanted. But there was some parallelism, yes.

Q: What was the virtue in setting up OPA?

Adm. M.: OPA (Office of Program Appraisal) was a creature of the Secretary of the Navy. This office of program appraisal, so-called, was composed of a small number of people who would appraise Navy programs for the Secretary of the Navy. I thought this completely unnecessary. After all the entire Navy Department was under the Secretary of the Navy and programs which reached the SecNav had already been appraised all the way up from the man who initiated them right on up, through the deputies, right on up through the Vice Chief, right on up to CNO. When they finally went to the Secretary, why should he have a couple of lieutenant commanders and a captain, for instance, kibitz them again? It didn't make sense to me then and it doesn't make sense to me now.

Q: What was the reasoning back of it? Do you know?

Adm. M.: I don't really know, except I think the reasoning back of it probably was perhaps the Secretary of the Navy thought that there was another side to each program that he hadn't heard about. In other words, perhaps a program had been argued through and it had come up through me and maybe I had made a decision which was contrary to the recommendations of various people on the way up. And he hadn't been able to hear their side of it.

Well, I thought he ought to trust me. If, however, he wanted to hear the other side of it, as the Secretary of the Navy, he could sit in on any meeting we had any time he wanted to. If you really want to know why SecNav created OPA, you'd have to ask him. I wanted no part of it, and at times it was sort of a thorn in my side. Kaufman, I believe, had it when I first got there.

Q: Was Kaufman the first to head OPA?

Adm. M.: I believe so. And then, when Draper came over to the Naval Academy, I believe Tom Davies took it.

Q: That's right.

Adm. M.: Some people thought - I don't say I did, I don't say I didn't - that Davies tried to use this to try to put his own ideas across to the Secretary, ideas that he wasn't able to put across to the CNO.

Q: I suppose that was a temptation?

Adm. M.: Of course, it is. It's human nature. It's no criticism of Tom. But I felt, well, it's just not the way to run a railroad.

Q: Rivero pointed out one area where it was useful, at least to the Marines. He said that if some decision came out of that organization pertaining to the Marines, they were much more ready to accept it than if it came out of the CNO's office!

Adm. M.: I guess so, and, of course, you can't say that it did no good because any set-up like that is bound to do some good over a period of time. But, once again, Jack, it's a question of -- well, I hate to use one of the terms that Mr. McNamera's whiz kids used to use, cost-effectiveness, but it certainly wasn't cost-effective. It was superfluous.

Speaking of Rivero, but do you want to talk about this OPA some more?

Q: Yes.

Adm. M.: I don't think there is much to say about it.

Q: There isn't much more to say, unless you can give me some illustrations?

Adm. M.: It's hard for me to do that, Jack, because, as I have mentioned on more than one occasion during our talks, since I never kept a diary of any kind and I've been away for, lo, these many years and have purposely put bygones behind me, I don't remember very many of the details. I do believe, though, that

Tom Davies, if my memory serves me right, was a proponent of the gas-turbine-driven frigate, destroyer, or whatever you want to call it, perhaps more so than others. I seem to remember that those who were not too favorably disposed thought that the OPA group wanted to go too fast on it. Years ago, if the Navy wanted to buy airplanes, they'd buy a couple and try them out before they'd ever go to production. Then along came Mr. McNamara and we started buying them a little bit differently. Some of us felt that on the gas-turbine ship we should develop just a couple and really try them out before we went on to a good-sized program.

I might be wrong about this, but I believe that OPA was more gung-ho on the gas turbine than was the office of CNO, and, of course, this brings up a rather interesting point. Why should the Secretary on one side have the office of CNO, which is the Chief of Naval Operations plus all of his deputies and most of the Navy Department, and on the other side have three or four naval officers headed up by a captain? It didn't make sense.

Q: You might complete the discussion on the gas turbines because I understand that you vetoed them?

Adm. M.: I don't really think I can, Jack, because as far as I was concerned this wasn't going to happen on my watch. It's just like we were not going to put a helicopter on the stern of a real small ship during my watch. I didn't think it was worthwhile. Not that I was against helicopters aboard ships but I thought there was a size of ship below which you couldn't go and make the helicopter operation effective. Likewise I wasn't against gas turbines but I wanted a slow approach to determine their effectiveness before going to production.

Q: At one point you made a statement last time that might invite some comment. You said, "Don't downgrade the whiz kids."

Adm. M.: Yes. As a matter of fact, there's never been any doubt in my mind that the people they called the whiz kids were very bright and very competent and did a lot of good. Unfortunately, they were inexperienced in military matters and I think they felt a certain inferiority complex because of this. Then, of course, we who had spent, I won't say "our lives" but let's say many years in uniform sometimes became a little irritated when we felt that the Secretary of Defense had made his decision based upon the recommendations of the whiz kids which were contrary to the recommendations that we made. Naturally, this created some friction. I felt, at the time and I feel now, that I got along with those fellows pretty good, particularly Enthoven. I didn't always agree with him, but I believe that there were times when I was able to get Alain to change his mind, simply by presenting to him some information that he hadn't had.

What I tried to do instead of locking horns with them, when there was some disagreement, I tried to bring up certain facts that had been used in making recommendations to me that I felt they simply didn't have. It was a sort of touchy thing sometimes because to indicate their lack of military experience was almost like rubbing salt in a fresh wound.

Q: That would be the wrong thing.

Adm. M.: That would indeed be the wrong thing. I think I said in one of our other conversations that on more than one occasion when I indicated that I knew certain things because of past experience they simply indicated that all that experience had done was make me biased in favor of the Navy.

Q: Parochial!

Adm. M.: There's no question but what my experience made me parochial, but I think not in a narrow way.

I think there was some relationship between OPA and another outfit that was exceedingly worthwhile, and that was the Office of Program Planning.

Q: That was Rivero's set-up. Strategic planning, program planning?

Adm. M.: I thought that office was very worthwhile.

Q: Were you not responsible in large measure for setting this up?

Adm. M.: I wouldn't say that. The thing I do want to take credit for, though, is bringing to that office one of the most competent naval officers I've ever known, and that is one Horatio Rivero.

Q: He, in this office of program planning, had to work with the whiz kids, did he not? Was this not an office that had to do with all these studies that were set up?

Adm. M.: I think so, Jack. I have to be wishy-washy on that. I just don't remember. But I do know that he had a lot of dealings with them. Just how that office operated I don't remember. I guess one reason is that when I gave Rivero a job, I forgot about it. I didn't put my finger in it any more. He would run it and I knew it, and I could devote my time to something else. As a result, pretty generally speaking, any time that Rivets and I worked together and he had a particular responsibility, I wouldn't know too much about that because I could forget it. This is one of the nice things about having an individual like that. You don't have to feel that you must keep your finger on that particular tab all the time.

Q: Indeed, yes. And at that time CNO had gotten new responsibilities which were in large measure concerned with the Joint Chiefs of Staff, had he not? And the Vice CNO had to be concerned more and more with the day-to-day operations of the Navy?

Adm. M.: That's right. But of course the Navy was still my responsibility and that's one reason my job was a little bit hard. However, I couldn't get too interested in the Joint Chiefs of Staff. I didn't see they were really doing very much.

McDonald #6 - 408

Q: Well, you were there at a time of great frustration for the JCS?

Adm. M.: Hindsight's hindsight, but you know that whole OSD set-up, the whole unification set-up, just kept growing and growing and growing. I didn't feel that during my time the Chiefs as a group drew much water, really.

Q: With that feeling and that experience, this turned you back in some sense to the day-to-day affairs of the Navy Department, did it not? You got involved in more details?

Adm. M.: Yes, and I felt that our Secretary, Mr. Paul Nitze, had far more influence directly with the Secretary of Defense, Mr. McNamara, than I did through the JCS. I could probably come nearer getting my point across by selling it to our Secretary and having him sell it to Mr. McNamara, than I could down through the JCS.

Q: So, seeing that, that's what you did?

Adm. M.: Pretty generally. There were times, of course, when the Chiefs accomplished things as a group. I was fortunate being a member of the Joint Chiefs during a period when there were very few disagreements among the Chiefs. There have been times when certain ones of the Chiefs almost called others names. But I can't recall a single instance, really, when I shook my fist at the Army or the Air Force or the Chairman, or had them in turn shake theirs. We disagreed, but they were pretty generally friendly disagreements. No personal rancor ever, even when LeMay was there. I say "even" because a lot of people think that LeMay is hard to get along with.

Q: He was more controversial than many!

Adm. M.: Yes, but I didn't find LeMay difficult. I thought it was very easy to tell when Curt had made up his mind. Once he'd made up his mind there wasn't any use wasting time talking to him about it. You could talk forever and a day, he wouldn't change it. Others weren't necessarily like that. You could tell. They'd make up their minds but they were still open. But I really didn't feel too much was accomplished down in the Joint Chiefs even though we got along real well.

Q: The Secretary of Defense began to overshadow the JCS?

Adm. M.: Yes, and as time went on the Secretary of Defense met with us - instead of saying "less frequently" I'd say he spent less time with us. Sometimes it seemed that he came down because he was just supposed to show his face. I had the feeling sometimes, that he didn't expect to accomplish anything at our meeting.

Q: That certainly would down-grade your role in the JCS, didn't it?

Adm. M.: I think I said earlier, when President Johnson first became President we Chiefs used to go and have lunch with him a lot. As time went on, we got to where we saw him less and less and less, then practically no one from the JCS saw him, except for the Chairman. The Secretary of Defense similarly spent less time with us. With respect to Vietnam, as time went on, it didn't make much difference what we recommended. It was going to be hacked to pieces, anyway, by somebody higher up. I wouldn't be able today to tell you who.

Q: Going back, Sir, to the point you made about working through the Secretary of the Navy in order to put forth some idea or something that you were desirous of, can you give me any illustration of this sort of thing, of this technique?

Adm. M.: No.

Q: Convincing the Secretary of the Navy of something?

Adm. M.: No, I can't in particular, Jack. I think that on the nuclear carrier he helped us a great deal with Mr. McNamara, although I have reason to believe that the final decision was made at the Ranch. When we got into some problems of not having enough pilots for Vietnam - in other words, our pilots were flying too many missions and our input to Pensacola was too restricted, we ultimately got that raised. But once again, that was discussed at the Ranch. Gerry Miller was very helpful in this also with his close relationship with Alain Enthoven, but I think Mr. Nitze agreed with us, honestly, sincerely agreed with us, and was effective in discussing it with Mr. McNamara. So it was all of us together.

The nuclear carrier and increased pilot inputs are two things we had quite a hard time getting approved. Increasing the pilot flow was certainly more important than the nuclear carrier at the time.

Q: Was this an area where you were able to work and maintain the level of carriers, number of carriers?

Adm. M.: No, we'd already settled that pretty well. It was a question of a new carrier and whether it would be nuclear or whether it wouldn't. We had given in right after I got there, really, that first year, on the Kennedy as non-nuclear, but we wanted the next one to be nuclear.

I might say a couple of things about Nitze, the Secretary. I think I said before that he and I were two different types of individuals. He's quite an intellectual and maybe not too practical. I would say that I'm certainly not an intellectual but I think somewhat practical. But in spite of these personality differences I didn't go away with a bad taste in my mouth about Paul Nitze. I believe I said at my change-of-command ceremony that I wanted to take that opportunity to salute him publicly.

Even though we had many disagreements, I think Paul would lean over backwards to agree with me and I with him. The only thing over the whole four years that I thought he was doing and shouldn't have been doing was paying too much attention to the assignment of flag officers. But that is not a criticism of Paul

Nitze as an individual. That custom had grown up prior to his time and had become sort of the prerogative of the Secretary.

Q: Yes. Isn't it true, Sir, that the selection of men by a board for rear admiral is a professional thing. This is based on the man's record as a -

Adm. M.: That is right and it's done that way, and the Secretary or even the President cannot add anybody to that list. They can change the precept, the order under which the selection board operates and in that way practically assure the selection of an individual. But, basically they can take anybody off, but they can't add on. And I think that's as it should be, but I would go one step further and say furthermore, the assignment of those rear admirals should be the prerogative of the CNO. My fear is that as the Secretary gets more and more into the assignment of rear admirals, the next thing you know he'll want to dictate who's going to command carriers or destroyers.

Q: That's stepping into a professional area?

Adm. M.: Yes, and I just don't believe this is an area that they should get into because - well, let's face it - the more the civilians get into the assignment of people, the more politics are in it. Now, of course, some will say "Well, you're CNO, you pick your pet." "That's military politics, what's the difference?"

McDonald #6 - 413

There's a good deal of difference.

Q: Yes, I can see that.

Adm. M.: There's a good deal of difference because generally speaking the performance of a man that the Secretary picks does not affect the Secretary's reputation. But the man I pick, he's working for me and believe you me we're both still in uniform, and how he operates jolly well affects my reputation and thus I'm going to be certain of his competence as well as his personality.

Q: Going back to Mr. Nitze, Rivero told me that he thought that Nitze, as he got settled into the job of Secretary, began to be more and more interested in getting control of everything. He was ambitious in that sense, and he finally began to get involved in operational things because he just felt that this was the destined role of the Secretary of the Navy.

Adm. M.: Jack, it's my belief that this is what most of the Secretaries do. After all, there aren't many people in a military organization who are content to limit themselves to logistics. You've a few of them. Most people want to operate, and a civilian Secretary is no different than anyone else. They don't want to go up on the Hill and argue or try to figure out how many of this and that we need - they want to operate. They want to be strategists, I guess. That's the nature of an individual and, unless he's unusual he won't curtail his activities in this area. Let's get back to Dan Kimball.

Dan didn't do that. He was willing to let the professionals run the professional part of the Navy. But I don't think that's true of many of them. I think you're going to find that a lot of CNOs and the Secretaries have problems because of this. I don't know whether you've interviewed Tom Moorer yet. My guess is that Tom Moorer and Mr. Chafee clashed a lot. I'm not sure of that. I haven't talked to Tom about it, but that would be my guess. I don't think I would have gotten along very well with Chafee either.

Even though Paul Nitze did try to get into operations a bit I still would be very hesitant to voice much criticism of the way Paul Nitze dealt with me.

Q: I suppose it's inherent in the man who serves as Secretary of the Navy, he being usually a man from the industrial world or the business world who is an executive, and if he's put in charge of something, he's going to learn it.

Adm. M.: You see, Paul had been in on a lot of the policy planning and all that kind of stuff. He was sort of a semi-pro. He'd been on the government payroll for years and years, doing first one thing and then another. He certainly has a good head on him and he doesn't want to stay confined. He's desirous of reaching out and he was there about four years. A lot of them don't stay that long.

Q: I wonder if you would say more about the problem that confronted the Navy when we began to get heavily involved in Vietnam - the problem of rendering all sorts of services to the Marines in transporting them and so forth, and the fact that there seemed to be a thought prevailing in the Navy that perhaps it was getting in too deep without adequate resources for carrying out the commitments it was asked to make?

Adm. M.: Well, it had been a long time, Jack, since the Marines were put in the position of operating like an Army. I don't believe they did that during World War II. I don't believe they did that during Korea. The Marines were an expeditionary force, basically, and that's what they were supposed to be when they went into Vietnam. But some people didn't like the term "expeditionary force," so they called it an amphibious force. I think that's what they called it. Of course, if I'd been smart I would have objected to that because the Marines were not the amphibious force. An amphibious force has ships, sometimes with Marines embarked. The Marines aren't the amphibious force. Marines are the landing element of the amphibious force. But they called them that because it didn't seem desirable to use the term "expeditionary" for various political reasons, I assume.

As more and more Marines were put into Vietnam they became

basically tied down like the Army.

Q: Like land troops?

Adm. M.: That's right. However, I don't know that they suffered for lack of anything any more than the striking forces at sea. In other words, we all were a little short of various types of bombs and so forth every now and then. There's no question but what the plans prior to Vietnam were based upon the Marines doing what Marines have always done; going ashore, securing the situation, being relieved by the Army. And when they went in and just grew and grew and stayed and stayed, the problem that confronted all of us from a logistic point of view was different from the one that had been planned. Whether it was right or whether it was wrong is basically immaterial. It was different from what either the Navy or the Marines had planned. I think, however, they were taken care of pretty good. I'm not sure that they lacked anything which, had they had it, would have permitted them to do any better.

Q: Isn't it a correct assumption, that the Navy was concerned about whether or not it could fulfill the demands the Marines made upon it?

Adm. M.: I don't believe any more than the demands being made upon various other elements of the Navy. Sure, we had trouble getting certain things to them, but we had trouble getting the right things for our striking forces at times, too.

Q: And pilots, too.

Adm. M.: Yes. I presume there were times, Jack, but I can't recall any particular times. The Marines would probably say something different and would undoubtedly be more accurate in what they would say, but it wasn't so serious that I remember it, anyway!

Q: I wonder if you would say something more about Rivero and your working with him?

Adm. M.: I think I've said about all I can, Jack. He's just a great fellow and his actions as Vice Chief, didn't change my mind one way or the other. I wasn't particularly high in my praise because I expected it. I knew that he would be simply fantastic in every way possible. I believe that almost my exact words to Mr. Nitze when I got ready to leave were, "Don't forget the little fellow."

I had reason to believe, and I think some others did too, that Rivero would be the Navy's best bet to relieve Oley Sharp. I didn't have any promises or anything like that, don't get me wrong, but I had every reason to believe that he would be the best bet we had. Then, not too long after I had been retired,

I learned that this was not to be. Then I heard - I hate for people to say "I heard" and not give the source -

Q: A high authority!

Adm. M.: Yes. But I did hear that Rivero wanted to go and be CinCPacFlt, if he couldn't get CinCPac.

Q: As a non-aviator?

Adm. M.: That didn't make any difference. There'd been non-aviators before, I think. I think it was before I left Washington which was about the 7th or 8th of December 1967, I talked to Rivero again, and I had the feeling that he would probably be going to Naples. I wasn't too sure about this but I said:

"Look, fellow, I think that you and Hazel will love every day of it in Naples, but most of all I think you can do a world of good there."

Q: You had some inkling of his diplomatic ability?

Adm. M.: Of course. I know Rivets, know him well. I think that Rivets would say today that he's glad he went there. My wife and I had the good fortune of visiting him there. We stayed with them several days. They loved the people down there the way those people loved them, I know they're glad they went.

Q: It was a step to Spain, wasn't it?

Adm. M.: Oh, yes. I really felt that Rivero should have been CinCPac and if he didn't get that I wasn't sure how he would feel about being CinCPacFlt. You know, Rivets doesn't expose his thoughts very much but, once again, we're all human and I think he felt that he was deserving of the CinCPac job and if he didn't get it being right out there next to it he might not have been happy as CinCPacFlt. At least, that was the way I felt, but I never discussed that angle with him.

Of course, he went to Naples and did a wonderful job, then went on to Spain and did a wonderful job. I just hope that he and Hazel are now enjoying life the way they deserve it. I hope you notice I don't say "Rivero" on these jobs, I say "he and Hazel" because when you get in those kind of jobs you must give the wife full credit. There's not a question about it in my mind. I've said many a time that I climbed the ladder of success on the shoulders of my juniors, but I really climbed the ladder on the shoulders of two women, my mother and my wife. There's no question about that. I know myself, I know what I did and what I didn't do, what my inclinations were, and some of the things that I probably would have done had I not had the one I had to guide me along the proper route. I think women are important from the very beginning, they steer you. After you get a lot of rank they might quit steering you but they then share the burden, there's no question about it.

Q: That's a fine tribute.

Adm. M.: That's the reason I say "Rivets and Hazel." They're a wonderful combination.

I had another combination while I was CNO that was perhaps the world's best, Kidd and Zumwalt.

Q: Yes, I was going to ask you about that. I mean they were sort of the kitchen cabinet.

Adm. M.: For three of the four years that I was CNO, Ike Kidd was my right-hand man, Zumwalt was Secretary Nitze's right-hand man. I hardly went to the bathroom without Ike knowing it. There was absolutely nothing that he wasn't privy to, as far as I was concerned. I think the same situation existed between Zumwalt and Nitze and, as a result, Zumwalt and Kidd deserve an awful lot of credit for the good relationship that existed between me and Mr. Nitze. I think they put a lot of fires out that we might not know about.

Q: I understand that they all met every day, practically?

Adm. M.: Oh, yes, and I don't know how many times. I would say to Ike, "Be sure and talk to Bud about this" and vice versa. Zumwalt, as aide to the Secretary, had to be loyal to his civilian boss. But here I was, the senior uniformed man, and he couldn't cross me either, and he walked that fine line in perfect style. While Zumwalt was aide to Nitze and a little bit thereafter, I found him to be one of the best I'd ever worked with. And I'm the guy that said that we ought to create our own ops analysis and then brought him back for the job after he'd had his flag command not very long. I brought him back to set that up, with Nitze's concurrence. Nitze concurred provided I would agree that I would leave it up to Bud, which I did, and he came back.

It was because of the work he did in that job that he got tapped to go to Vietnam and, of course, from there to CNO.

Q: There was a junior member of that kitchen cabinet, too. That was Gerry Miller, who was close to Rivero?

Adm. M.: Wasn't he Rivero's right-hand man?

Q: Yes, he was.

Adm. M.: I don't remember. Not that I've forgotten Gerry. I remember Gerry well and most favorably. He had a particularly fine rapport with Under Secretary of the Navy Bob Baldwin. Baldwin thought Gerry Miller was something special and Gerry's a fine guy. He'd get along with the devil himself. I just didn't remember whether or not he was Rivets' right-hand man.

Q: Yes, he was, and he told me that the three of them, the juniors, Zumwalt, Kidd, and he had a get-together every day.

Adm. M.: I knew that Rivets was cut in on everything but I didn't remember through whom. Gerry was also the man who really worked on the increased pilot program, sold it to Baldwin, first, then helped sell it to Enthoven. Those were three very fine individuals. All of them different. Zumwalt's probably more intellectual, without down-grading his other fortes. Kidd works very long and hard, without down-grading any of his other qualities. Gerry Miller's a well-met, slap-you-on-the-back type of fellow that everybody likes at first meeting, not to down-grade his other qualities. I would think that Zumwalt's intellect, Ike's hard work, and Gerry's -

Q: Out goingness!

Adm. M.: Yes, he's a good-fellow type. That combination is pretty hard to beat.

Q: Yes. It's a matter of personalities and it just happened that they all came together.

Adm. M.: That's the word I want - Gerry was Mr. Personality.

McDonald #6 - 423

Not that the others weren't. They were fine, too, but Gerry - a lot of people, you know, you aren't really attracted to them when you first meet them but the more you know them the better you liked them. Gerry is attractive immediately.

Q: I wanted to ask you about Op-05. I know that Rivero got heavily involved in Op-05 and there was some question as to whether it should be abolished or whether it should be reorganized and given a broader base. Also, there were a number of new planes coming on stream.

I wonder if you got involved and if you would talk about that area?

Adm. M.: I got involved a little bit, but not too much. But first let's look at why Op-05 was created. There are many reasons, but basically this was the only element within the Navy that had competition. Nobody else in the United States had battleships, nobody else had destroyers, nobody else had submarines, but the aviation part of the Navy had head-to-head collisions for some time with the Air Force. I think it is pretty well known that many in the Air Force hoped that the aviators in the Navy would take naval aviation into the Air Force. It has been rumored many times, probably without foundation, that it was indicated to Radford that he might be chief of staff of the Air Force if he would bring naval aviation in with the Army Air Corps to form the Air Force. Of course, this wasn't done and as a result the competition was quite strong.

In order to compete, if you want to put it that way, on somewhat equal terms we had to have aviation within the Navy concentrated so that you could talk with one voice, as it were.

Q: And strong enough to withstand?

Adm. M.: That is correct. Now, should it be continued? That is Op-05?

In 1955-1957 I was a rear admiral Op-55. Vice Admiral Bill Davis was Op-05. Rear Admiral Jim Russell was Chief of the Bureau of Aeronautics. I went to Bill Davis one day and I said:

"Bill, we've gotten to the point where we've put a lot of aviation down in 03 and 04 and by so doing we have diluted the concentration we once had in Op-05. I think that's wrong. Some people don't know who is speaking for naval aviation now, you or the Chief of the Bureau of Aeronautics." This situation existed in Personnel in 1948. I know, because I was aide to John Nicholas Brown, who had Personnel. Admiral Fechteler was DCNO Pers. Admiral Sprague was Chief of BuPers, and no one knew who was speaking for personnel.

I heard Admiral Sprague say more than once, "By golly, I'm Chief of BuPers." But Fechteler was DCNO Pers. Then along came Admiral Holloway, and what happened? Holloway was made Chief of BuPers and DCNO Pers and he delegated his DCNO Pers responsibility to a rear admiral who sat over in the Pentagon, while Holloway stayed over in the Bureau of Personnel. But there was no question in anybody's mind about who was running Personnel in the Navy in uniform. It was Holloway.

"Why don't you do a similar thing? Why don't we create a Chief of Naval Aviation, with the subtitle Chief of BuAer? You've got the three stars and you can have a rear admiral over in BuAer running that office. Then there'll be no doubt in anybody's mind who's speaking for naval aviation."

That might have happened had anybody been Chief of BuAer except Jim Russell, because Jim was not only likeable but so competent and everything else, this would have been sort of like hitting Jim in the face with a wet rag. Maybe if it had been time for Jim to leave, they could have picked someone three or four years junior and it might have happened. But I thought then that unless this was done that 05 would be dissolved. And I wasn't sure at that time, Jack, that that would be in the best interests of the Navy. But I was just as sure as I'm sitting here that unless they did that, by golly, 05 was going out of the picture.

I think probably when Rivets was there he thought that the concentration had been so diluted that perhaps it wasn't necessary any more. I don't really remember getting into any serious discussions about wiping it out. I really don't. Of course, now we see what's happened. Holy smoke, they've got a three-star fellow in charge of each facet of the Navy. In addition to 05 they've got a surface man, they've got a submarine man, etc. Far be it from me to criticize because I'm not there, but instead of wiping one out, it's sort of developed like the Department of Defense. We unified but instead of unifying what we did was expand. That's what's happened in the office of the CNO.

I don't remember too much about the new airplanes.

Q: I can call some of them, the A-6.

Adm. M.: I remember some, i.e. the A-6, the E-6, the E-6B.

Q: The F-4?

Adm. M.: The F-4 had come out a bit before that. I do remember that we were extremely anxious to acquire planes that could do almost anything in almost any kind of weather. Nobody had airplanes like that, short of SAC.

Q: That sounds like the ideal!

Adm. M.: Maybe the E-6 was the first one that could do a little bit of everything in most any kind of weather, but honestly I don't remember these numbers now. Of course, at that time there was a big dog fight, if you want to call it that, over the TFX.

Q: Do you want to talk about that? It didn't come to a climax in your time.

Adm. M.: I don't know whether I talked about this before or not. Well, there was a feeling - on the part of some people - that the TFX problem was one of the things that had something to do with my predecessor not being reappointed. I don't know whether that's true or not. I never asked him or anybody else. But there was a feeling that it was so. When I got there I said, "This is something I'm not going to get in a dog fight about." It didn't take me very long to realize that this was the Secretary of Defense's pet. If he had made the decision, we were going to have to accept it. I like to argue loud and long until the final decision is made, but once your boss makes a decision, if I've had my say, I think my job is to carry out the orders. Although I hadn't had my say, the people before I arrived, the Navy, had had its say long and loud and the decision had been made, so my position was let's quit arguing about why this thing is not going to work. Let's see how we can make it work.

After I arrived there Mr. McNamara created a TFX committee with Mr. Nitze at the head of it. They met I think about once a week, but I wasn't on that committee. I don't remember whether I was asked to be on it or not. Anyway I don't want to be on it because I am not a technical man, never was and this was more a technical question, will this work or will it not work?

McDonald #6 - 428

Q: Aeronautical engineers?

Adm. M.: I had, however, been in military requirements as a captain in 1947 in BuAer. I had been the head of Air Warfare which was the head of Requirements as a rear admiral in 1955. And there was no question in my mind but what this plane was no good for the Navy. But had I been asked "Why" this plane was no good for the Navy I would have had to say: "from my experience, etc." and giminy, that would have been just like waving a red flag. If I could have taken a couple of slide rules and some aeronautical engineering manuals and what not and proved it, then the powers that be, mostly Mr. McNamara and his technical people, might have listened. But I couldn't do that. So I never attended a committee meeting. I did, however, have a pretty good idea of what was going on.

Q: The committee was set up to verify this, was it?

Adm. M.: No, the committee was set up primarily to reduce weight and what not in order to make it operable from carriers.

I did go to Mr. Nitze one day and say I thought one of the best aeronautical engineers that I knew was a young rear admiral named Bill Sweeney who was on duty over in Paris. I apologized to Bill later for getting him back, but he was brought back and put to work on this thing. They tried to reduce the weight, they tried to do a little bit of everything.

Well, as luck would have it, we had already planned to beef up the elevators on the carriers. We did not beef them up solely for the TFX. We would have had to, but we were going to do it, anyway. Basically, in my testimony before the Armed Services Committee - I would say:

"Mr. Chairman, this is a technical problem. I am not a technical man. My technical people have told me this thing will work and I have no reason not to believe them." That was a sort of wishy-washy response, but that was the way I felt because I didn't think it was cost-effective. Sure, it would work. You could fly it but, holy smoke, it wasn't any good. But there really wasn't any percentage in arguing, so I really kept my mouth shut. In retrospect, maybe I shouldn't have.

But in retrospect, I wish I'd done several things. I wish I'd just walked out on some of the Vietnam decisions and said I'd just had a stomachful. But I guess if I was in the same situation in the same set of circumstances today I'd probably do the same thing. Hindsight, you know, is pretty good.

I'll tell you one thing in reference to the TFX that's real interesting. After I retired - I retired on August 1st 1967 and moved to Florida in early December. If my memory serves me correctly, it was early the next year that I got a telephone call -

Q: 1968?

Adm. M.: Yes. I got a phone call saying that Senator McClellan "wonders if you come up to Washington now and then and, if you do, he would like very much to sit down and have a long talk with you about the TFX." Well, it so happened that I was going to come to Washington not long thereafter. Anyway, I came up and I want over to Senator McClellan's office and the senator and I had a long talk, I guess for two or three hours. No one else was present. Without going into what was said, I'll never forget that when I got up to shake his hand and leave, he said: "You know what, Admiral? Nobody feels any worse about what's happened about this plane than I do. But this would never have happened if one individual had been just a little bit humble."

I thought it was very well put!

Q: I take it your long conversation was focused on the TFX?

Adm. M.: Oh, yes, and I told him very frankly that my views were based almost entirely on the experience I had had in the past. I said, "You should never buy an airplane that doesn't have great growth factors. Look at the P-2. They've hung everything on the P-2, including jet engines or pods. As a result we used it many years. When an airplane first comes out, people can say 'we're going to buy this plane and we're never going to make a change.' If you have technical advances which can be accommodated in that plane, of course, you're going to make a change or you're going to spend yourself silly building a new plane."

So, I said, it just stood to reason if we were having to trim everything off the TFX to get it to operate when it was brand new we shouldn't buy it. However, that didn't mean it can't operate. He said: "Why didn't you say that?"

And I said, "You saw what I said. I said this was a technical problem and I supported what my technical people told me." But the technical people weren't asked, is this the kind of plane that should be bought? They were asked "can you make this airplane operable?" Well, making it operable and making it the type of plane that should be purchased, of course, were two different things.

I did say, however, that I did not believe that Mr. McNamara's original thinking was necessarily wrong, namely, that you can build an airplane which can be used by all services. I think you can. It won't be perfect for any one of them, and if you're going to do that, then you're going to have to put down the specs for each of the services, and then go through and see which is the most critical. I said in this case the most critical factor was weight to operate from a carrier. And if you'd started from there, it would have been something else. But basically what was built was the airplane that the Air Force wanted, and then they tried to knock things off and adapt it to naval operations on the carriers. It was just too bad.

Q: You say, Admiral, that you're sure a plane could be built that would be serviceable in the Air Force and the Navy - ?

Adm. M.: Look at the F-4.

Q: But what about the cost-effectiveness?

Adm. M.: Look at the F-4. The F-4 is the best fighter the Navy, the Air Force, the Marines have ever had. I think they'd all admit it. I think the Air Force would admit it. So it can be done. Now, a man who wanted to argue against it could perhaps find a feature that wasn't optimum for the Marines or the Air Force or what not, but overall it's excellent without a doubt.

I think the F-4 has proven rather conclusively that certain types of planes can be built very cost-effectively for all the services, and this is what Mr. McNamara had in mind.

I guess they got caught, Jack, on the theory that this plane would be the optimum when it came off the line and they would never have to make modifications. That's what they said. This is going to be the optimum, so you don't have to prepare for growth. That's a fallacy.

Q: That's flying in the face of experience!

Adm. M.: Of course, it is. But worse things happen. Look, today the Navy is having to put storage space on ships for the average sailor's chief petty officer type uniforms and for civilian clothes for them, when we've been fighting tooth and nail to get enough sleeping space with all the power generating equipment we need with the increase in electronics. Mr. McNamara and his whizz kids didn't have a corner on asininity, in my opinion.

Q: I was just thinking, to plagiarize on that title "A Man for All Seasons," what you were anticipating was a plane for all seasons!

Adm. M.: Not me but someone else. Well, it was too bad. It cost a lot of money, a lot of man hours. I think Bill Sweeney's reputation was hurt a little bit, and mine. There are a lot of people who don't know why we didn't just come out and say it's no good. But, you know, it's the same old story - the man who had rather be right than President - well he never was President.

When I was CNO there were certain things I thought the Navy ought to have and I saw no reason to conduct myself in such a manner that I'd make sure we did not get them!

Q: I wonder if you'd talk about the subject of training in the Navy, particularly aviation training?

Adm. M.: I presume, Jack, you're talking about the training command as it exists today?

Q: Yes.

Adm. M.: Let's go back to when I was CNO and even prior to that. The only particular part of the Navy, I guess, that had a training command was aviation which had the aviation training command, and I believe that it was pretty generally recognized that the aviation part of the Navy had better control of/its training than any other part of the Navy. For instance, the surface training wasn't knitted together tightly.

Q: It grew like Topsy!

Adm. M.: It sort of did. Submarines were fairly tight, of course, but I do believe that everyone in the Navy, whether they were in aviation or submarines, destroyers, amphibs, or what, I think they all really appreciated the way the naval aviation training command operated. On more than one occasion the question arose: "Why can't we set it up so all Navy training will be like this?" As I say, I guess it's been talked about for many years, I know it was discussed a lot during the time that I was there, the time I was CNO, and I presume it continued because subsequent to that time they have established on all inclusive training command.

Q: I suppose it came to the fore - you told me that you were instrumental in transferring the training to Orlando, and I suppose it came to the fore then?

Adm. M.: No, that's a different thing. That was primarily boot training, at least in the beginning. Orlando started out as a third boot camp. Other training which came to Orlando existed, I believe, at Bainbridge, but it was operating directly under BuPers. I think that today all navy training is under the training command boss in Pensacola. Although Pensacola was the headquarters of the aviation training command, that is now the headquarters of "the" training command.

Q: Cagle made it so?

Adm. M.: Yes, I believe he started it, that is, he was the first Commander, a non-aviator by the name of Wilson is there now. I don't know how it's working. The discussion used to be, "Well, we might get it too big, and when it becomes too large maybe we can't make it operate as efficiently. Maybe we can't have the hand on it like we now have on the aviation training command. Maybe we should create a separate training command for other than air."

I'm inclined to think that what they did is the right way, or was the right way. How it's worked out, I have no way of knowing, but you know, if they'd left the aviation training command as it was and created another training command, then they'd have had to put somebody else on top of two of them, other than BuPers. You just keep pyramiding these things. I would be anxious to know, really, how the new training set-up has panned out, but I don't. It's my fault, I guess, because since I've retired I've interested myself in other things.

You mentioned something about seaplanes, and I guess we did decommission some during my time as CNO but that was only happenstance because the decision to eliminate seaplanes had been made several years before. I believe it was between 1955 and 1957, somewhere along in there.

Q: When Bob Pirie was in it?

Adm. M.: If so, it was subsequent to that time. When I was there Bill Davis was DCNO, Air. Maybe it was subsequent to that that the decision was made to phase out seaplanes. Of course, when was just a matter of time depending a great deal upon when you could no longer cannibalize airplanes to get parts to make the others - once again, the old whizz kid term - cost-effective. The squadrons, I think, were decommissioned while I was CNO.

Helicopters, of course, were coming into their own, primarily because of Vietnam. But the Navy was using helicopters an awful lot before Vietnam.

Q: Oh yes, and the Coast Guard before the Navy.

Adm. M.: The Coast Guard before the Navy. Then we got to where we were using them a good deal not just for personnel transfer but in connection with some of our replenishment operations at sea. Then when Vietnam came along, the helicopter business really exploded. It really did. I don't know how it is today.

Q: I understand that Vietnam also proved how vulnerable they are to ground defenses?

Adm. M.: Yes. I don't know that I d like to be doing close air support or observation in one of them over an active enemy line. I think you'd be pretty vulnerable!

Q: Going back to seaplanes for just a moment, I understand that there are experiments going on with seaplanes. The Russians have begun to use them in a different sense and quite effectively, that is, almost a vertical-rising seaplane type that they're experimenting with.

Adm. M.: Well, I wouldn't know. But I think I mentioned in one of our previous conversations, where the Martin Company proposed a plan whereby a seaplane would land and put down a sonarbuoy and listen for a sub and if there wasn't one present would take off and fly a reasonably distance, land and do the same thing again. They would operate sort of like a pogo stick dumping a sonarbuoy here and there. It's another one of these things, Jack, that are nice and useful to a degree but one must ask oneself, is there anything else that would be nicer. You can't have everything. That's what we're continually confronted with.

And that's what CNO is often faced with in making his decisions. I don't agree with some of one of the former CNO's statements that fraternities within the Navy fight each other, the aviators, the submariners, and the surface people. I really think that it's a difference of opinion as to what is the most important. I believe that, generally speaking, a man in submarines can see greater advantages that the submarines offer than can a destroyer man. Maybe a man who's been flying for a long time can see certain advantages that aviation offers that maybe the submarine expert can't see. So I don't think it's a question of being narrow-minded or parochial or beating the drum for "my specialty," as much as it is getting the experts' advice in their own field and then making a decision as to what's best for the Navy. That's what the CNO's for.

Q: More intimate knowledge.

Adm. M.: He should be equally interested in all, and just because he happens to be an aviator, I don't think he necessarily sides with the aviators. I don't think Arleigh Burke, just because he was a destroyerman necessarily sided with the destroyer people. I don't think that's true at all. If the CNO is that narrow-minded, somebody made a mistake in putting him in there! At times, it might appear that he is, but I just don't believe it's true.

Q: Maybe Assistants are intended to give a man a much broader spectrum?

Adm. M.: Certainly. I know that the Marines often felt that maybe I didn't support them, and the amphibious people that I didn't support amphibious vessels quite enough. Maybe I didn't but at the time I thought that either a destroyer or a submarine or a carrier or something was needed a little bit more. That's the reason you have project officers, etc., to advocate certain specialties. Then you have people on top of them that help you make your decision. Pretty generally, decisions aren't made by the CNO operating in a vacuum. They're made by the CNO and the Secretary who listens to these presentations, too. Although the Secretary is not as familiar with these professional matters as is the CNO. If the CNO is being obviously biased, I think that the Secretary could see to it.

I think that's about all I have, Jack.

But I would like to say again that because of the lapse of time, some of the things that I have said might not be letter perfect, but, to the best of my knowledge, what I have said is accurate, and although I was very pleased when my tour of duty expired because of my disagreements with some of the ways in which the Vietnam War was being conducted, I did not leave with a bad taste in my mouth. I did not and do not believe that I was treated unfairly by anyone. I'm not critical, other than through disagreements and I still say that my good fortune in getting to the job, which I did not want, was due to some good luck and primarily to the kind of support and I guess you'd say direction I got from my wife. And I'd also like to add that I regret that it hasn't been practical to mention the names of the many loyal aides and supporters who have been so helpful to me throughout my career and especially during my Flag Officer years.

Q: Again, that's a fine tribute. I am deeply grateful to you for this very, very useful document. Thank you.

Index

to series of interviews

with

ADMIRAL DAVID L. McDONALD

USN (Retired)

A-4: p. 211

AIRCRAFT CARRIER TRAINING UNIT: NAOTC sets up (1942) unit at
    Glenview, Illinois, p. 89.

AIRCRAFT CARRIERS: McDonald's determination to maintain the
    level of carriers when he came to office of CNO,
    p. 351-2; p. 356; decision to use conventional
    power for the carrier John F. KENNEDY, p. 356-7;
    story of Senator Pastore and a nuclear carrier,
    p. 357-8;

AIR WARFARE DIVISION - Chief of Naval Operations (Op. 55);
    McDonald becomes Director, p. 206; concern with
    aircraft requirements and readiness, p. 206-7;
    resultant F-4 and P-3 (Orion), p. 206-210;
    aircraft carriers, p. 215-6; McDonald's comments
    on the super carrier, p. 217-8; contacts between
    military and manufacturers - how they work in
    tandem on new designs, p. 221;

ANDERSON, Adm. George: succeeds Burke as CNO, p. 274; p. 312;
    p. 314-5; p. 320-1; p. 323; p. 325; p. 349-50;

AVIATION CADET PROGRAM (1935), p. 56-7.

AVIATION MILITARY REQUIREMENTS (Navy Department); McDonald takes
    over task of drawing up specs for planes and carriers
    (1947), p. 127-131.

AWARDS: McDonald gives his views on awards, p. 106-7;

BAKER, Richard D, Jr.: p. 92; p. 115; p. 125-6.

BALDWIN, The Hon. Robert: Under Secretary of the Navy, p. 363;
    his disagreements with McDonald, p. 368 ff; over
    clothing for bluejackets, p. 370; over a new billet
    - Deputy to the Under Secretary, p. 371-2; his role
    in establishing the training center at Orlando
    Florida, p. 372-3; p. 375; p. 421.

BALL, The Hon. George: his opposition to involvement in Vietnam,
    p. 384-5;

BAY OF PIGS: p. 285-6.

BROWN, Adm. Charles (Cat): his retirement ceremony in the
    Mediterranean, p. 298-9;

BROWN, General George: aide to McNamara as a colonel, p. 316 ff.

BROWN, John Nicholas: McDonald becomes aide to Secretary Brown,
    p. 133-6;

BURKE, Admiral Arleigh A.: p. 254; p. 274.

CAR DIV 6: McDonald takes command in October 1960, p. 261; p. 263-4; Striking Force of the 6th Fleet, p. 261; p. 263-4; p. 272-3; fire on the SARATOGA, p. 265-8; diplomatic responsibilities, p. 269-271.

CARRERO BLANCO, Admiral (Spanish): p. 198-9;

CASSADY, Adm. John H.: p. 82; p. 84; p. 119.

CHAFEE, The Hon. John H.: p. 414

CHURCHILL, The Rt. Hon. Winston: visit as Prime Minister to Bermuda (Dec. 1941), p. 79-81; p. 85.

CINC NAV EUR: McDonald is named to replace Adm. Page Smith in London, 313 ff; McDonald's prospective tour of his command (1963) p. 317 ff; McDonald's answer to MacNamara on need for full admiral in job, p. 327-8; p. 331-2.

CINC NELM: p. 227; p. 233-5;

CINC PAC FLT: McDonald becomes Operations Officer on staff, p. 170 ff; preparations for the Korean trip of President-elect Eisenhower (Dec. 1952), p. 175-6; discussion of the Joint Command as it functioned under Adm. Radford and Adm. Stump, p. 184-6;

CNO (Chief of Naval Operations): McDonald's remarks on scope of his authority as CNO, p. 139; McDonald named suddenly to replace Adm. Anderson, p. 318 ff; Mrs. McDonald's reactions, p. 328; problems with transfer of personal belongings from London, p. 335 ff; confirmation in the Senate, p. 337; McDonald's trip to the Far East, p. 338-343; McDonald's objectives as he came to job as CNO, p. 344 ff; task of maintaining level of carriers, p. 351-2; budgetary matters, p. 358-9; McDonald's frankness in carrying out an order when he didn't agree, p. 365-6; McDonald's temptation to turn in his suit, p. 388-9; his reservations about a re-appointment as CNO, p. 389; the President's promise of a new carrier, p. 389-90; McDonald's disapproval of proposals for a gas turbine-driven frigate, p. 404-5; p. 438-9.

USS COLORADO: McDonald assigned to her - difficulties on board, p. 37-8.

CONNOLLY, The Hon. John: as a senior lieutenant on carrier ESSEX in Pacific, p. 115.

COOK, Vice Admiral Arthur Byron: McDonald called to be his aide and flag secretary, p. 76-77; a crisis in relationship, p. 78; Force Commander (Nov. 1941) for six U. S. transports with British troops, p. 79; takes McDonald with him to new command at Jacksonville, Florida, p. 82 ff; p. 98; Cook becomes Vice Admiral and goes to San Juan (1943), p. 98; Admiral McFall takes over from him, p. 97; p. 100; p. 121.

USS CORAL SEA: McDonald takes command (1954), p. 183-4; p. 188 ff; p. 197-9; McDonald's remarks on precision and discipline and teamwork as practised on an aircraft carrier, p. 200-3; McDonald's comments on the CORAL SEA vs the ESSEX, p. 204-5;

CROMMELIN, Captain John: p. 43-5.

CUBAN MISSILE CRISIS: p. 286-7; McDonald's operation for hernia and how it complicated his situation with the Sixth Fleet, p. 287-8;

DAVIS, Vice Admiral Wm. V. Jr.: head of Op-05; p. 424;

DE GAULLE, General Charles: his policy for France, p. 237-8;

USS DETROIT: C.O. asks McDonald to come aboard and qualify as top watch stander, p. 48-49; p. 52.

EISENHOWER, The Hon. Dwight David: his Korean trip (Dec. 1952) p. 175-6; p. 226; his friendship with Gen. Norstad, p. 259-60;

ENTHOVEN, Dr. Alain: McDonald's first meeting with him, p. 352-3; p. 363; p. 405;

USS ESSEX: p. 22; McDonald assigned duty on her, p. 99; air officer on staff of Ralph Ofstie, p. 108-9; Pacific operations, p. 109-110 ff.

ESSEX Class Carrier: compared with the CORAL SEA, p. 204-5; p. 215.

F-4: see entry under Air Warfare Division, CNO.

FELT, Adm. C.D.: p. 219; p. 225-6; p. 228.

GARDNER, Adm. Matthias B.: skipper of fighter training squadron at Pensacola, p. 52.

GENERAL ELECTRIC COMPANY: their research on an atomic powered airplane, p. 220; p. 223

GILPATRIC, Hon. Roswell L.: Deputy Secretary of Defense, meets with McDonald over his appointment as CNO, p. 322.

GREEN BOWLERS: p. 43-5;

GROS, Robert: Public Relations man for Pacific Gas and Electric, p. 171-2;

HARE, The Hon. Raymond Arthur: Ambassador to Turkey (1963) - entertains McDonald as CincNavEur, p. 318; p. 320; p. 324;

HELICOPTERS: p. 211-212;

HOLLOWAY, Admiral James L. Jr.: p. 348-9;

ISTANBUL: The CORAL SEA pays a visit, p. 190-1;

JCS (Joint Chiefs of Staff): status in the time of President Johnson and Secretary McNamara, p. 408-9;

JOHNSON, The Hon. Lyndon: his agreement on pilot training, p. 363; p. 364; p. 383; his promise of approval for a new carrier, p. 389-90; p. 409;

JOHNSON, The Hon. U. Alexis: p. 356.

KENNEDY, The Hon. John F.: p. 322; p. 326.

KIDD, Adm. Isaac C.: persuades CNO to stay on job, p. 388-9; as aide to McDonald, p. 420; p. 422.

KIMBALL, The Hon. Dan: Assistant Secretary for Air (March, 1949), p. 134; p. 137; becomes Under Secretary of the Navy, p. 138; McDonald serves as his aide, p. 139-140; p. 142-4; his divorce and remarriage - his death, p. 145-6; p. 149; stories of Kimball as speaker, p. 149-151; p. 222. p. 414.

KODIAC: p. 65; p. 67

KORTH, The Hon. Fred: Secretary of the Navy - his visit to the 6th Fleet, p. 312 ff; the missile shoot, p. 313; his aide telephones McDonald in Turkey and calls him back to Washington at once for meeting, p. 318-23;

LeMAY, General Curtis: p. 409.

LOENING, Grover: p. 46-7.

LIQUOR ON SHIPBOARD: McDonald's comments, p. 294-6;

MacARTHUR, Gen. Douglas: p. 158;

MacDONALD, Sir Malcolm: p. 172-3;

U. S. MARINE CORPS: McDonald felt let down by the vote of
         the Commandant in the JCS on a successor to Adm.
         Felt as CincPac, p. 354-5; disagreement of McDonald
         and the Commandant over priorities for amphibious
         ships, p. 355; value of OPA to them, p. 403; the
         Marines as an expeditionary force, p. 415-6;

McCLELLAN, The Hon. John L. - U. S. Senator: on the TFX,
         p. 429-30;

McDONALD, Adm. David L.: personal data, pp. 1-4; appointment
         to Naval Academy, p. 5-8; his philosophy on teaching
         younger men in the navy, p. 22-29; his employments
         in retirement, p. 33; advice given him in naval
         career, p. 34-5; selection for Captain (1945),
         p. 109; his views on speaking out, p. 122-123; how
         he came to be called 'Dave', p. 142-3; his illness,
         operation and recovery (1949), p. 146-8; value
         of his duty as aide to Secretary Kimball, p. 152;
         on school assignments in the navy, p. 154 ff;
         account of his heart abnormality, p. 252-257;
         ability with the French language, p. 260; p. 261-2;
         hernia operation, p. 287-8; circumstances surrounding
         his appointment as Chief of Naval Operations, p.
         316-326; his happiness over retirement, p. 396;
         a self portrait, p. 399.

McFALL, RADM. Andrew C.: Wing Commander V P-42 (1939), p.70-1
         takes over (1943) command of NAOTC, p. 97-98; p.
         119.

McNAMARA, Hon. Robert S.: his visit to London, p. 316-7;
         p. 322; p. 327; p. 350-1; p. 352-3; his role in
         naming Adm. Sharp as CincPac, p. 354-5; his views
         on budget, p. 359-60; his view on experience, p.
         361; p. 363-4; his refusal to say when President
         had overridden his plan of operation, p. 364-5;
         his espousal of the FDL, p. 365-7; p. 373; p. 382;
         his attitude on calling up reserves for Vietnam,
         a supplemental appropriation, etc. p. 282-3;
         asks McDonald to change the record on his testimony
         before the Senate, p. 386-7; p. 394-5; p. 409-410;
         McNamara and TFX, p. 427 ff.

U. S. MERCHANT MARINE: McDonald's views on U. S. Merchant
         Marine, p. 379-81;

MILLER, Vice Admiral Gerald: p. 363; p. 410; p. 421-23;

USS MINDORO: McDonald becomes her skipper, (1951), p. 168 ff;

USS MISSISSIPPI: McDonald's first fleet assignment, p. 31ff; p. 37.

MONTGOMERY, Vice Admiral A.E.: becomes N.A. Forces Pacific Commander (1946), p. 121.

MOUNTBATTEN, Admiral Lord Louis: p. 61-2; at SHAPE, p. 245-6; p. 291; his offer to assist the McDonalds to see London sights, p. 330-1;

MURRAY, Vice Admiral George: Commander, Naval Air, Pacific (1945) - orders McDonald as his Plans officer, p. 119-120.

NATIONAL WAR COLLEGE: McDonald attends (1950), p. 153-168 value of the course as seen by McDonald, p. 159 ff; spring travel limited to the U. S. - merit of that routine, p. 164-5; McDonald expresses himself on value of meeting foreign military, p. 230-3;

NATO: See entries under General Norstad: NATO country quotas p. 230-1; Spain and NATO, p. 239; NATO and use of atomic weapons, p. 246-7; Greek-Turkish fraternization, p. 306-7;

U. S. NAVAL ACADEMY: McDonald's appointment, p. 5 ff; McDonald's temptation to leave the Navy (1929), p. 9-11; as a plebe, p. 11; his resentment over dismissal of his roommate before graduation, p. 12-16; McDonald's comments on being a gentleman, p. 18-19; scholastic attainments, p. 20;

NAVAL AIR FORCES PACIFIC: p. 121; McDonald becomes Plans Officer for Adm. Murray, p. 119-120; for Adm. Montgomery, p. 121; demobilization problems, p. 125-6;

NAVAL AIR OPERATIONAL TRAINING COMMAND: Adm. Cook sets it up with headquarters in Jacksonville, p. 82; purpose of command, p. 82; p. 86-7; preparatory tour of similar Canadian bases, p. 87-88; list of air stations opened in south, p. 89; creation of core syllabus, p. 90-1; McDonald's role in the development of this command, p. 91-2; p. 93-4; use of flight instructors from combat zones, p. 95-6; McDonald recommended for Legion of Merit, p. 103 ff; p. 119.

NAVAL APPOINTMENTS: McDonald comments on secrecy surrounding appointments, p. 275-6; attempted interference on the part of the Secretariat, p. 277-8.

NAVAL AVIATION - PILOT TRAINING: McDonald's arguments on this subject with DOD, p. 362-3;

NAVAL RESERVES: McDonald comments on the contributions of the Reserves, p. 115-6.

NAVAL TRAINING COMMAND: p. 433-5.

NAVY RIFLE TEAM: McDonald is a member while at Academy, p. 28; p. 32.

NIETO, Admiral (Spanish): Spanish Secretary of the Navy, p. 198;

NITZE, Hon. Paul: SecNav, p. 139; accompanies McNamara to London, p. 316-7; his relationship with McDonald as CNO, p. 368; p. 371; p. 373; his interest in personnel matters, p. 373-5; p. 377-8; p. 389; p. 395; p. 398; p. 408; p. 410-11; p. 412-14; p. 427;

NORSTAD, General Lauris: (SacEur and Cinc Eur) head of SHAPE in Paris - McDonald goes to be on his staff, p. 285 ff; SAC EUR and the 6th Fleet, p. 233-4; p. 240; McDonald's picture of Norstad, p. 241-3; how he helped McDonald over the uncertainties of his heart abnormality, p. 254-6; his friendship with General Eisenhower, p. 259-60; his arrangements to transport Mrs. McDonald to Naples, p. 261-3; p. 284;

OBERAMMERGAU, Germany: SacEur establishes a course on atomic energy at Oberammergau - McDonald attends, p. 250-1.

OFFICER PROMOTIONS: McDonald's method of getting information on men considered for three and four stars, p. 374-5; p. 411-412;

OFSTIE, Vice Admiral Ralph A.: p. 190; p. 193.

Op - 05: the story of Op-05 and naval aviation, p. 423-4;

OPA (Office of Program Appraisal): p. 401-4;

ORLANDO - Naval Training Center: p. 372-3;

P-3: p. 206-9;

PENSACOLA: p. 10-11; p. 29-30; McDonald's aptitude tests preparatory to Pensacola, p. 36-7; McDonald's account of training course, p. 39 ff; back to Pensacola as flight instructor, p. 52; ff three years as flight instructor (1935-38), p. 55, inauguration of the Aviation Cadet Program, p. 56-7; program for training selected senior officers, p. 576-8; McDonald shepherds Lord Mountbatten around Pensacola, p. 60-61; p. 63;

POLARIS: p. 224.

HRH PRINCE DESTA: grandson of Emperor Haile Selassie of Ethopia, p. 332-3.

HRH PRINCESS GRACE: p. 296-7.

USS PUEBLO: p. 305;

PUGET, General Andre (French): French naval cooperation with NATO even after French withdrawal from NATO, p. 282-3;

RABORN, Vice Admiral Wm. F. Jr.: p. 224;

RADFORD, Adm. Arthur D.: p. 30-1; p. 35; p. 87; p. 100; p. 105; McDonald becomes operations officer on his CincPacFlt staff (1952), p. 170; his trip to the SE Asian area, p. 170-1; p. 173-5; goes to Washington as Chairman of JCS, p. 176-7;

RICKOVER, Adm. Hyman: p. 357-8;

RIVERO, Admiral Horatio Jr.: serves as Vice Chief of Naval Operations under McDonald, p. 397-8; p. 403; p. 406; his office of Program Planning, p. 406-7; p. 413; p. 417-419; p. 421-2; p. 423; p. 425;

RIVERS, The Hon. Mendel: Chairman of the House Armed Services Committee, p. 366;

RUSSELL, Senator Richard: the confirmation hearing on Adm. McDonald as CNO, p. 337-8; p. 351. kills the bill that provided for building FDL ship, p. 366-7.

RUSSELL, Adm. James S.: p. 425.

RUSSIAN INTELLIGENCE GATHERING: p. 304-5;

USS SARATOGA: McDonald in V-6 abroad, p. 45; 47; 49; new plane types, p. 50-1. fire in the fireroom, p. 265-9; p. 273;

SAUERS, RADM Sidney: frequent luncheon guest of Dan Kimball, p. 141-2;

SEAPLANES: p. 72-4; p. 212-3; p. 436-7;

SEATO: p. 186-8;

USS SEQUOIA: Presidential yacht - used by Dan Kimball, p. 144-5.

USS SHANGRI-LA: in CarDiv 6 - McDonald takes her as striking force to stand by in Dominican crisis, p. 273-4;

SHAPE: see entries under General Norstad:

McDonald's summary of his tour of duty, p. 240-
McDonald's travels in NATO countries, p. 248-251;

SHAPE - X: p. 244-5;

SHARP, Adm. U. S. Grant: (Oley) joins staff of Adm. Stump, p. 177-8; McDonald discusses struggle over his appointment as CincPac, p. 354-5, p. 391.

SITKA, Alaska: p. 65.

SIXTH FLEET: McDonald takes command - succeeds Adm. George Anderson, p. 274; p. 279; account of McDonald's visits and social engagements, p. 280-1; p. 294-5; the Sixth Fleet and the Cuban Missile crisis, p. 287-9; McDonald's comments on value of having transportation of his wife to various ports in Mediterranean during his command, p. 291-4; visit of Secretary Korth and the Missile exercise, p. 312-315;

SMITH, Adm. H. Page: p. 311; his appointment as Cinc Lant, p. 313-316;

SPRAGUE, Adm. Thos. L.: Superintendent of aviation training, p. 52-3; McDonald's tribute to him, p. 53-4; p. 58-9.

USS SPRINGFIELD: Flagship for Cinc 6th Fleet, p. 287-8;

STRAUSS, Rear Admiral Louis: frequent luncheon guest of Dan Kimball, p. 141-2.

STUMP, Admiral Felix B.: succeeds Radford as CincPac - CincPacFlt, p. 176-7; names Oley Sharp to his staff, p. 177-8; sends McDonald on mission to Far East to be with Gen. Van Fleet, p. 178 ff;

SULLIVAN, The Hon. John - SecNav: resigns, p. 138; p. 140.

SUNAY, General Cevdet: (President of Turkey) Chairman of

the Turkish Joint Chiefs (1963), p. 318-9; p. 323.

TFX: p. 426-7 ff; McDonald's view on the growth factor, p. 430-1;

TONKIN GULF: see entries on Vietnam.

TRUMAN, The Hon. Harry S.: p. 147

UNIFICATION: McDonald's comments as they pertain to the National War College, p. 161.

Van FLEET, Gen. James A.: President Eisenhower sends him as Ambassador at large to the Far East, p. 178 ff;

VF-6: the fighter bomber squadron to which McDonald was assigned after Pensacola, p. 40; p. 190.

VIETNAM: attitude of JCS over impending involvement, p. 382; the question of calling up the reserves (1965), p. 382-3; Tonkin Gulf, p. 384; a question of bomb supplies, p. 385-6; lessons from Vietnam, p. 387-8; McDonald reflects on administrative decisions on Vietnam, p. 390-6; p. 410; demands made upon the Navy, p. 415-6;

VILLA NICKI: p. 297-9;

VP-42: based at Sand Point, Seattle, Washington - McDonald assigned after Pensacola (1937), p. 60-63; the first Alaskan tour, p. 63 ff; p. 68; mission of Seattle based planes, p. 71-2.

WHIZ KIDS: p. 352-3; role in budgetary process of DOD, p. 359-60; the Whiz kids and experience, p. 360-1; p. 363; p. 405-6;

USS WILLIAMSBURG: Presidential yacht, p. 146-7;

ZUMWALT, Admiral Elmo: p. 348-9; aide to Secretary Nitze, p. 420-22.

www.ingramcontent.com/pod-product-compliance
Lightning Source LLC
Chambersburg PA
CBHW080624170426
43209CB00007B/1509